RESEARCH STRATEGIES

FINDING YOUR WAY THROUGH THE INFORMATION FOG

6TH EDITION

WILLIAM BADKE

RESEARCH STRATEGIES
FINDING YOUR WAY THROUGH THE INFORMATION FOG

iUniverse books may be ordered through booksellers or by contacting:

iUniverse
1663 Liberty Drive
Bloomington, IN 47403
www.iuniverse.com
1-800-Authors (1-800-288-4677)

Because of the dynamic nature of the Internet, any web addresses or links contained in this book may have changed since publication and may no longer be valid. The views expressed in this work are solely those of the author and do not necessarily reflect the views of the publisher, and the publisher hereby disclaims any responsibility for them.

Any people depicted in stock imagery provided by Thinkstock are models, and such images are being used for illustrative purposes only. Certain stock imagery © Thinkstock.

ISBN: 978-1-5320-1803-9 (sc)
ISBN: 978-1-5320-1804-6 (e)

Library of Congress Control Number: 2017904572

Print information available on the last page.

iUniverse rev. date: 04/03/2017

Acknowledgements and Additional Resources

Thanks to EBSCO Publishing for permission to use screenshots from their databases.

See the Research Strategies Website for:

- Updates: **http://williambadke.com/updates.htm**
- Live links: **http://williambadke.com/links.htm**
- Key to chapter study questions: **http://williambadke.com/RSKey.htm**
- Teaching resources: **http://williambadke.com/TeachingResources.htm**

See the Research Strategies Textbook site for more information about this book: **http://williambadke.com/textbook.htm**

Meet me on Facebook; search for: **Research Strategies**

Contents

Preface

Everyone does research. Some just do it better than others.

This book is definitely for you if you are:

❖ a university student whose research projects have been patented as a cure for insomnia

❖ a Dilbert of industry who's been told to do a feasibility study on the expansion potential of winter ice cream bar sales in Nome, Alaska

❖ a simple honest person trying to find the truth behind the advertising so that the next car you buy won't be like your last disaster-mobile, the car that made you *persona non grata* at the automobile association

Are you ready for your next research project? Really ready? Do you have the skills and strategies to get the job done efficiently and effectively without panic attacks and the need for a long vacation when you're done? Do you have confidence that you can start with a topic about which you know nothing and end with an understanding of it that is neither trite nor superficial? Are you prepared to enjoy the experience? (Yes, I did say, "Enjoy.")

If the previous paragraph has left you feeling somewhat queasy, this book is for you. Even if you think you have significant research skills, you can learn better ones if you take the time to read on. You have the privilege of living in the information age, with boundless opportunities all around you to find out anything about anything. But faced with a serious number of Internet sites, not to mention academic and commercial databases of increasing size and complexity, knowing how to navigate through the information fog isn't something you can pick up easily on your own. Truth to tell, there is a ton of studies telling us that most people have vastly higher opinions about their research ability than actual tests of that ability can demonstrate.

Yet you can hardly call yourself educated if you don't have really good skills to handle complex information systems and do research effectively, not in a world in which most careers are built more on what you can find out than what you already know.

Who am I to try to teach you about research? Just someone who has taught the strategies in this book to thousands of anxious university students, both undergraduate and graduate, for over 30 years (making me a dinosaur?), and who likes nothing better than to walk people through the information fog. I am Associate Librarian for Associated Canadian Theological Schools and Information Literacy at Trinity Western University. Being the author of a number of books and scholarly articles myself (see my bio at **http://williambadke.com/badke.htm**), you can rest assured that I've devoted a lot of my life to doing research and not just teaching it. So I understand what you're going through.

One caution: This book is about *informational* research. It won't teach you how to do a science experiment or determine the best way to train a rat how to ride a tiny bicycle (though it will help you do a literature review). But if you need to identify a problem, and then acquire and use information to address the problem, this book is for you.

Learning how to do research does not have to be painful. It can be fun. Honestly. Personally, research gives me so much pleasure that my family has to kidnap me out of the library whenever they want to go on an outing or buy groceries. You can have the same joy that I have. Read on.

Updates to the textbook will be posted at:
http://williambadke.com/Updates.htm

For live links to each of the URLs in Research Strategies: **http://williambadke.com/links.htm**

See my website for courses, syllabi, presentations etc.: **http://williambadke.com/TeachingResources.htm**

Meet me on Facebook. Search for: **Research Strategies**

1

Welcome to the Information Fog

We have been living in the middle of a revolution since the 1990s. Not since the creation of the printing press (and maybe not ever) has our concept of information been so disrupted. The driving force of the information revolution is the World Wide Web, which has given us access to more knowledge than ever before in human history.

Information used to be scarce, thus creating a demand for experts who knew things and could share those things with the rest of us. Now we have Google, the information candy store, which makes information abundant and challenges the role of the expert. "Information candy store?" Yes. Google serves up lots of enticing stuff right there at our finger-tips, most of it looking good enough to devour. The down side of a candy store, if there ever could be a down side, is that candy tends to be loaded with empty calories.

No, I'm not down on Google or Bing or whatever search engine suits your fancy. We won't be Google-bashing here. But there is so much more than Google. The revolution in information has led many of us to believe that Google is god, or at least the ultimate information source. But nothing is that simple. Fact is, we live in an era in which there is untold opportunity to go beyond Google. And we also live in an era that is much more complicated than it used to be.

At one time we thought we knew what information was. Now we're not so sure. These days we're buried in data, and defining what is and what is not genuine information is getting to be more of a challenge all the time. (For a related graphical presentation, see my Prezi, "No One Knows for Sure what Information is Anymore," **http://bit.ly/1S6m4pb**).

Information is supposed to inform. That means it has to be reliable, relevant, current, and so on. There was a time when people believed that, given the right information, we could solve any problem the human race encountered. They thought that the power of reason could be used in a totally objective way to wade through all the data and come up with the right answers, even arrive at the truth. Now we're no longer even sure what the questions are (and we can't remember last Tuesday).

To be sure, we've always known that some of what passes for information can't be trusted. That's why we have law courts to determine the facts of a matter, though the best liar often wins.

We've come to understand over the past hundred years that information is colored with subjectivity: What we know depends on how we interpret our information base. Even the best authors of information bring their own biases into the mix. Thus, for good or ill, we are no longer as trusting when it comes to interacting with information. It's like buying a Rolex from a man in an alley: It might be a real Rolex coming from somebody down on his luck, but, unless you know Rolexes, you could well be getting a knock-off.

I'd like to take a bit of time to trace the events that have led us to this place. Textbooks, after all, are supposed to lead you on a journey through history and philosophy-of-whatever before they get to the good stuff. But in the case of information, the next few pages really are essential to doing good research. Believe it or not, you need to understand our world of information if you want to do intelligent research within its often foggy terrain.

So how did we get here, to an age dominated by the World Wide Web?

1.1 Before there was print

Throughout the entire history of humanity, knowledge has been passed down from one generation to another. Before this was done in written form (and in non-literate societies today), ***speech and demonstration*** were the source of humanity's information - historical tales told around campfires, children learning about agriculture by doing it with their parents, and so on. These were "traditional societies." I use the word "traditional" not in the sense of 1920s country music and picket fences, but in the sense of knowledge viewed as a *tradition* to pass down from generation to generation, often for the very survival of the society.

Here's an example of why these kinds of societies need traditional information: When I lived for a couple of years in Nigeria, West Africa, people would point to this plant or that one and tell me, "You could eat this." It happened often enough that I finally asked someone why it was so important for me to know what plants I could eat. He explained that during the recently ended civil war, the people had been forced from their city homes into the jungle. They began starving, because no one knew what was edible and what was deadly. Their ancestors had once carried this knowledge with them, but these city dwellers had stopped passing it on to their children, and the knowledge had died.

So the former urbanites, now living in the bush, cooked various plants and fed them to their chickens to see if the chickens would cluck or croak. And gradually they rebuilt their knowledge base. "We have decided," my friend told me, "that we must never again forget what we can eat, so that's why we tell one another what is

3

edible." Their traditions had meant the survival of their society. If you forgot what you could eat in the jungle, you might have to choose between potentially poisoning yourself and starving.

Clearly, though, traditional information has to be reliable. Thus, in societies that depend on their traditions, knowledge is passed down only by people qualified to do so. Unregulated production of new information is not encouraged. And there is an emphasis within traditional societies on memorizing the existing information rather than using existing information to create new knowledge. The development of new knowledge in such cultures is a deliberate and slow process performed with care and authorized only by experts in the existing tradition. Otherwise, the next plant you eat could well be your last.

1.2 Reading and inscription

The development of *written* language in the ancient world brought a number of changes to the world:

❖ Knowledge could be preserved in print. Thus there was less of a need to pass it on orally (though the oral element remained important in daily life), let alone a need to memorize huge amounts of information. Memorization continued, to be sure, but you didn't need to know everything, because it was possible to look it up if you had access to written documents.

❖ Since the knowledge base was more secure, people could pay more attention to discovery, thus hopefully adding to the knowledge base.

❖ The keepers of knowledge (i.e., the tradition experts who actually had the books = the librarians) were more elite than they had been in an oral society. And only the people who could read had direct access to the written tradition. What is more, there were few copies, because everything had to be transcribed by hand. Thus a small group of people in society controlled the knowledge base, and these people (recognizing that knowledge is power) generally worked against the forces of discovery (who tend to take the power away from the people who control the knowledge base). As long as access to documents was controlled, most people continued to rely more on oral tradition. The full transition from oral to written cultures took many centuries.

1.3 The printing press

The Chinese actually invented the printing press centuries before the Europeans did (as was the case for many things, including gunpowder), but it was the Europeans who used it to revolutionize the use of information in society. In 1447, Johannes Gensfleisch zur Laden zum Gutenberg (Gutenberg for short) created a moveable type press, a development so revolutionary that the A & E Television Network in 1999 named him #1 in its list of "People of the Millennium." The printing press was such a big deal because:

- ❖ From a "preservation of the tradition" standpoint, it meant that multiple copies could be produced, thus making the tradition more secure (previously, it would have taken only one match lit by a careless monk to burn up the single manuscript that had everything you needed to know: Sort of a medieval server crash, only more permanent).
- ❖ More people could actually get their hands on the knowledge base, thus creating a better-informed society that was not as dependent on oral tradition. The elitism of knowledge was undermined as "holders of the tradition" found they no longer had an exclusive right to control who saw the knowledge base and who added to it.
- ❖ The possibilities of discovery were greatly increased, because so many more people had access to existing knowledge. It was

thus much more likely that new knowledge would be built on the foundation of the old.

Knowledge multiplied in the centuries that followed. In fact, the major discoveries and inventions that make our lives what they are owe most of their existence to the printing press. Yet there were pros and cons to this invention. The pros are obvious, the cons not as much.

The Cons:

- ❖ The printing press was only as useful as the population was literate. We are still working on that problem.
- ❖ A new form of elitism developed, and whether it was good or bad remains a matter of debate. It came from the fact that production of new information depended on two things: bright people to make the discoveries and money to publish their words. The bright people created the elitism of universities and the money people determined what would be published and what would not.
- ❖ The money issue put a limit on who could get his or her ideas into print. Publishers, wanting to be sure they didn't lose their shirts, added "gatekeeping" processes to their requirements. Gatekeepers ask two key questions: First, is the information worthy to be published? This is a value judgment, usually based on level of scholarship or reliability or entertainment value, but sometimes focused on the aims of the publisher or the desires of the marketplace (thus the existence of romance novels). Second, will it sell? Many a worthy manuscript goes into the trash simply because the publisher doesn't think there's an audience to sell it to. Alternately, there might be a small audience that has to pay a large amount for each copy published (as with most scholarly books).

Gatekeeping is a good thing when it helps to preserve quality. No one wants our knowledge base to be filled with shoddy stuff that no one can trust (or so the wisdom of commercial academic publishing would tell us). On the other hand, gatekeeping has been used to censor valuable information, keeping it away from the very people who need it most. This has prevented perfectly good ideas from seeing the light of day, simply because someone viewed those ideas as unacceptable or there wasn't a good market for them. Thus gatekeeping has tended to maintain the status quo or promote certain biases, because new, radical concepts (or concepts the publisher doesn't like) are not as sure to sell as the tried and true. On this, see Brian Martin, *The Politics of Research,* **www.uow.edu.au/~bmartin/pubs/98il/il07.pdf**.

Certainly, people have always been able to self-publish material that the gatekeepers rejected, but distributing self-published books can be a tough game. Would-be buyers often ask, "If this is such a good book, why didn't the commercial publishers want it?" Thus self-published material tends to stay more or less underground, though much of it is of high quality.

More recently, several very entrepreneurial self-publishing companies have made it possible to produce your own book at minimal or no cost and without the need to stock thousands of copies in your basement. You even have the opportunity to publish it in multiple e-formats as well as print. Thus the self-publishing of books has come into its own, so much so that we now find that there are more self-published books on the market than there are commercially produced titles. Still, getting a self-published book into the hands of eager buyers remains an uphill battle, even if you can upload your own book to Amazon Kindle for free.

Along with the rise of the printing press came the development of the "subject discipline" (think biology, history, psychology, and so on), allowing people to specialize in particular fields of discovery. The idea of a "discipline," a defined subject area within which discovery is made, has its good points (the main one being the ability to focus narrowly to provide more depth of research) and its bad points (the main one being the separation of knowledge into categories that don't talk much with each other). But the fact is that most advancement of knowledge these days is done within disciplines.

What does that mean for people doing research?

❖ Each discipline has its own "language" which is more than just its technical words but also involves the ways in which that discipline communicates information. A historian has a different mode of expression than that of a physicist (or an expert in the sex life of nematodes).

❖ Each discipline has its own method of doing research. While method, even in the humanities, has some connection with the scientific research process, there are distinct features that make research in English literature different from research in Korean history or in the biology of nematodes.

❖ Each discipline has its in-crowd, its elite group of highly regarded scholars. Knowing which writers and which works are the most highly regarded is very important to doing research without looking like an outsider.

1.4 Enter the World Wide Web

A revolution even more revolutionary than Gutenberg's has happened within our own generation: the creation of the World Wide Web, a popular subset of the larger Internet. In the short span of time since the early 1990s, the WWW has blown the lid off much that we've known about information since the beginning of time. Why? Because it has pushed aside most of the boundaries that once prevented us from having all the information our knowledge-greedy little eyes could want.

It comes down to one basic fact: **On the WWW, anyone can publish almost anything he or she wants to say, without impediment**. Let me unpack this a bit:

❖ On the WWW, gatekeepers are no longer required. They still exist, and they still have great value, but we can publish without them. Whether or not it's always advisable to do so is another issue, but for the first time in human history we can have our say without anybody editing our words or stopping us outright. The Internet, for good or ill, is the greatest vehicle for free speech the world has ever known. Add to that all our social media tools (Facebook, Twitter, YouTube, Snapchat, and whatever new thing pops up between my publication date and your reading this), and we have an almost limitless way to get our ideas, news, media, etc. out to the world without censorship.

❖ We can publish and acquire information at a level never before possible. The Web enables us to have access to so much, in fact, that we can easily become overwhelmed by it. As far as getting our own message out, we have a potential audience that can number in the millions. This means that information is no longer scarce but cheap and plentiful.

❖ What we lose (perhaps) is certainty. If anyone can publish on the WWW, we no longer have many of the normal checks and balances that once kept the world from being inundated by nonsense. This isn't a new problem, because even with gatekept print material, readers should always be exercising discernment. But we now have the challenge that, for a large portion of Web-based information, no one except the author has done any gatekeeping at all. This is a classic two-edged sword - if anyone can publish on the Net, then we have an amazing resource for freedom of speech and the democratic way of life. The old elitism is gone. But it also means that *we, the readers, have to become the gatekeepers to an extent never before seen, due to the lack of external quality control.* This demands that we enhance our evaluation skills.

❖ One more concern: If we are not careful in our gatekeeping, the whole concept of authority can disappear. What do I mean by "authority?" Simply the fact that every field of knowledge has its experts, its wise voices, its people who understand that field better than the rest of us, because they have immersed themselves in it. We might want to resist authority, but the people who really know a subject area are assets who we can't afford to ignore.

The WWW tends to level out authority. A Google search can bring you the work of an expert in the field as well as a website produced by Ms. Jackson's third grade science class. To fail to discern the difference is to miss the power of getting our information from people who really know what they are writing about. This is not to say that every great scholar is right all the time. But ignoring that scholar in favor of a website on the same topic from your uncle Frank is going to put you at a disadvantage. Right now, the average person selects the first five results from a Google search and does very little evaluation of their relative quality. For more on this, see the excellent article by MaryBeth Meszaros, "Who's in Charge Here? Authority, Authoritativeness, and the Undergraduate Researcher," *Communications in Information Literacy* 4.1 (2010): 5-11. **http://tinyurl.com/ln6r49m**. She has a bit of fun at my personal expense, but I forgive her.

My own contribution to the field comes in my article: Badke, William. (2015). "Expertise and Authority in an Age of Crowdsourcing," in *Not Just Where to Click: Teaching Students How to Think about Information* (pp.191-215). Ed. Troy Swanson; Heather Jagman. Chicago: Association of College and Research Libraries. You can find it at **http://williambadke.com/BadkeExpertiseAuthority.pdf**

You might also want to look at the white paper produced by the anti-plagiarism service, Turnitin, which compiled data from millions of student papers to show that most of you are not really using high quality resources (don't you just hate it when data reveals the real you and it's something unflattering?): **http://pages.turnitin.com/sources_in_writing_sec_2012.html**

Before you accuse me of being overly simple-minded (something

I've heard a lot), let me point out that it's not as "either-or" as I may have implied, so that you either have to love the Net or hate it. You see, the WWW is really less a content-provider than a *vehicle* for information. Thus it is also used by publishers who still demand rigorous gatekeeping procedures. Commercial e-books and scholarly articles are carried for a fee by the same system that provides us with a free copy of Aunt Bertha's remedy for lumbago. Many of these resources are part of the "hidden" or "invisible" Internet (found behind password gates so that only authorized users can see them), but they have as much of a home on the WWW as your cousin's jumpy YouTube video of river-rafting last summer.

1.5 Information today: The state of the art

Let's look at the status of some of the main sources of information today:

1.5.1 Books

Book publishing is continuing, with no hint of a slowdown. The big story in recent years has been the rise of the e-book. To say that the move to the e-book has been confusing/frustrating for both publishers and readers alike would be an understatement. In a short period of time, traditional hardcopy book publishing has been challenged like never before, starting with the creation of Amazon Kindle, followed shortly after by Nook, Kobo, Kindle, the iPad, numerous Android devices, and so on. Now the dedicated e-book reader is steadily becoming pretty much a dinosaur, and people are reading e-books on whatever device they have at hand.

E-book interfaces will change over time as books move from static text to interactive experiences. From pages that will allow flipping similar to print books, but with additional options to make the flip even better (**http://www.youtube.com/watch?v=rVyBwz1-AiE&feature=youtu.be**) to amazingly interactive adventures in reading and viewing (**http://www.youtube.com/watch?v=LV-RvzXGH2Y**), the e-book is due for a format revolution. Right now, a lot of academic e-books you read are accessed via software more intended to prevent you from getting decent downloads than to make it easy to use the content.

Meanwhile there are many projects working at digitizing the information universe. Beyond Google Books (**https://books.google.com**), the Internet Archive (**http://archive.org/details/texts/**), the HathiTrust Digital Library (**https://www.hathitrust.org/**) and the Open Library (**http://openlibrary.org/**) offer millions of books available for online viewing. The Open Content Alliance (**https://archive.org/details/opencontentalliance/**) is quietly snagging key contracts to supply out-of-copyright and open access e-books to major libraries and library systems that are uncomfortable with Google's growing control in the e-book market. The Digital Public Library of America (**http://www.dp.la/**) is developing a book collection (**https://dp.la/info/get-involved/dpla-ebooks/open-ebooks/**). In 2016, the Library of Congress became a major content provider to DPLA.

We also have the Universal Digital Library Million Book Project (**https://archive.org/details/millionbooks**), another non-commercial enterprise, with backing from Carnegie Mellon University and other groups, which has had over 1.5 million book titles digitized. Items not in copyright are available in HTML, TIFF and a type of PDF format. Those under copyright offer only an abstract. A significant feature of this collection is the number of Chinese, Arabic and Indian language titles in it. The project has now been taken over by the Internet Archive.

The Online Books Page (**http://digital.library.upenn.edu/books/**) offers over a million books for free, though most are out of copyright and thus old. The Oxford Text Archive (**http://ota.ahds.ac.uk/**) offers several thousand carefully chosen books important to academic study. One of the longest standing enterprises offering free e-books is Project Gutenberg (**http://www.gutenberg.org/wiki/Main_Page**) which has over 40,000 titles of its own and offers a further 100,000 free titles through its affiliates. OAPEN is a European platform for over 2500 peer reviewed open access academic books, mainly in the humanities and social sciences: (**http://www.oapen.org/home**). Finally, Directory of Open Access Books (**http://www.doabooks.org/**) opened in 2012 and offers peer reviewed academic books for free from close to 40 publishers.

What about the grand dream that every book will one day be online for anyone to read? Well, I think you can put that one to rest alongside the story of the baby alligators, long ago dumped into the sewers of New York, that have become twenty foot student-eating monsters. Even if all the books in the world were digitized, the full text of anything in copyright would only come to you at a cost. Authors like to get paid, and well they should, because they are all wonderful people who deserve it.

Thus it is futile to believe that any book you want to have can be accessed electronically for free. Publishers won't give away their books any more than music producers want to give away their songs, though pirates made it happen anyway (and book piracy is growing and now making a liar out of me). As well, many older books are not commercially viable for digitization unless they end up in a project like Google Books.

Even with all these efforts, though, the e-book is still struggling to find its way. Sales have actually been dropping. Students, for example, still generally prefer a print textbook to digital one (though having no textbook at all is their first choice, sigh...). Don't expect that everything you need will soon be available to you electronically at home in the middle of the night while you're munching on a pickle and desperately trying to finish that research project before the doom of morning strikes.

There is another growing movement, fed by newer "print on demand" technology, which supports self-publication without the enormous cost and distribution problems that once existed. You can now, for $2000 or less, publish your own book (even having it editorially reviewed) and have it distributed through normal book distribution channels without the need to have 5,000 copies in your basement. You can also publish e-books yourself for free through Amazon (Kindle), Scribd, and so on. Other than offering some editorial help, most such options have little if any real gatekeeping to them. Does quality suffer in the process? Possibly, though even without gatekeepers a lot of self-published authors are putting out high quality material that traditional publishers did not consider marketable.

1.5.2 Journals and magazines

The end has arrived for most paper versions of scholarly journals, magazines and newspapers. Virtually all scholarly journals now have an electronic presence. As the popularity of electronic versions grows (and it definitely is growing), more and more journals are appearing electronically only.

Does all of this electronic publishing of articles diminish quality? No. Most scholarly journals continue to use the gatekeeping process of *peer review*, by which submitted manuscripts are evaluated by scholars in the subject discipline in order to determine whether they are worthy to be published. This is a key distinction between a scholarly journal article and what you might find through the average Google search. A website on a topic may be as electronic as the journal article on the same topic, but the journal article has been evaluated by experts before it ever sees the light of day. Maybe those experts were biased or missed something important (like faked lab results), but on average the peer review process does provide more confidence that the article is reliable than you would have from a website on the same topic written by your Aunt Kate.

Before we get too far into this, though, we need to answer the more foundational question: *What is a scholarly journal?* The answer is not as simple as it once might have been. In general scholarly journals are publications from universities, academic societies and academic publishers. The articles in them tend to be short on pictures and long on citations and reference lists (or bibliographies). In general, they are not accessible through a Google search and require you to search specialized academic databases available through academic libraries.

A serious challenge to the availability of scholarly journals has been price. The average annual journal subscription can range from fifty dollars to the cost of a new Toyota Corolla or more. In fact, the most expensive journals top $30,000 per year. Only the major universities can afford this kind of thing, thus limiting who can get access. A number of public bodies that fund research have done a double take and said, "Wait a minute. If we fund the research out of public money so that scholars can publish articles (getting paid nothing for doing so), and then publicly funded universities have to pay through the nose to acquire the journals that present the research we've already paid for once, where is the justice in it all?" Thus, increasingly, funding bodies are demanding that articles based on the research they have paid for must be made available online at no cost a set number of months after being published in a journal.

This open-access journal movement is growing in opposition to the outrageous costs of scholarly journals. Many new journals are being published directly online (after proper peer review) and are available for free to anyone who wants to read them. In this we have the best of the gatekeeping approach of traditional publishing and the free dissemination of information provided by the Internet.

For searchable databases of open access journals, go to Directory of Open-Access Journals (over 9000 journals covered: **http://www.doaj.org/**), or Electronic Journals Library (**http://rzblx1.uni-regensburg.de/ezeit/index.phtml?bibid=AAAAA&colors=7&lang=en**). Paperity (**http://paperity.org/**) is an online database offering searches of open access journals at the article level. JURN (**http://www.jurn.org/**) offers searches for millions of open access articles, chapters, and theses.

A really good open access journal directory is ROAD Directory of Open Access Scholarly Resources: **http://road.issn.org/**. While it won't do keyword/subject searches within articles, it does a good job of identifying specific journals as open access and linking to their home pages.

Cornell University has **http://arxiv.org/**, a collection of hundreds of thousands of papers in the sciences, computer science, and finance. A newer player is SocArXiv (**https://osf. io/search/?q=%22socarxiv%22**), an open archive of the social sciences. The Social Science Research Network (**http://www.ssrn. com/en/**) provides access to abstracts of over 500,000 resources in the Social Sciences and open access full text to nearly as many scholarly social science journal articles. Two highly touted public open access sites for academic resources are Public Library of Science (PLOS: **http://www.plos.org/**), which has created its own super journals, and the similar Open Library of Humanities (**http://www. openlibhums.org/**).

There are, of course, fakes and charlatans out there who produce supposedly "academic" online journals that are anything but. Several scholars have published lists of such predatory enterprises to help you be aware of them, for example, **https://web.archive.org/ web/20170112125427/https://scholarlyoa.com/publishers/** and **https://web.archive.org/web/20170111172309/https:// scholarlyoa.com/individual-journals/.** At the time of publication, these sites are no longer being updated. We can only hope that others will step up to continue the work of calling out predatory publishers.

The pay vs. open access distinction may not mean much to you if you are a student in higher education, because your institution provides journals as part of those incredibly high tuition fees you pay. Once you have graduated, however, and no longer have access to the same databases, open access journals may well be a lifeline. Unrestricted availability of journals will increase over the next couple of decades due to open access initiatives. The Compact for Open Access Publishing Equity (COPE: **http://www.oacompact.org/**) represents a movement within universities to provide scholars with funds to publish own their journal articles within open access venues, thus taking funds from expensive journal subscriptions and using the money to support open access.

I am noticing, as well, that an increasing number of scholars are self-archiving their published articles, putting them up on their own websites. A good tool to find such self-archived material is Google Scholar (**http://scholar.google.com**).

Despite this growing trend toward open access (available for free) journals, the majority of journals and magazines are not accessible full text through a Google search. Using a search engine on the Net generally gets you a very different class of information than does using a journal database through an academic library. That is why using a search engine like Google or Bing for a large portion of your academic research will greatly limit your ability to do good work.

While not quite in the category of "journal articles," there is a growing interest in materials put into institutional repositories (think of electronic filing cabinets full of all kinds of academic information from in-house studies to dissertations). A great tool for finding such stuff is *OpenDOAR: The Directory of Open Access Repositories* (**http://www.opendoar.org/**).

Publishers are beginning to think through the very nature of the "journal article" to make it much more interactive, using video and animated features to bring it to life and help readers to see data in new ways. See, for example, **https://www.youtube.com/watch?v=1dXkmgkYuEg** from Elsevier, an academic publisher.

1.5.3 Government and corporate documents

Governments and other corporate groups continue to publish vast amounts of information. Due to the convenience of the WWW as a vehicle, more and more government information is moving to an online environment, where it is usually freely available. For directories to such resources, go to the International Government Information site at **http://www.lib.utexas.edu/government/world.html.**

1.5.4 The World Wide Web

We have already looked at advantages and challenges of the Web. Ongoing issues include use of the Web for highly negative purposes (terrorism, child pornography, etc.), quality challenges which become evaluation skill problems, the need to catalog the more important websites in order to provide better searchability, a demand for search engines that are better able to identify the information we most need, and a requirement for increased instruction for users so that they can optimize the Web experience.

1.5.5 Web 2.0

Web 2.0 is really a concept rather than a defined area of the Internet. If you imagine the average web page to be a publication, a one-way communication from the author to the reader, Web 2.0 forms those parts of the WWW that are interactive. We can include here social networking sites, blogs, wikis, online office tools like Google Docs, RSS feeds, forums, chat, messaging, e-mail, and so on. As a concept, Web 2.0 doesn't mean too much unless we look at what it does for information.

Take the wiki, software that enables you to create web pages that others can edit. One scholarly use for a wiki is in collaborative research projects where several people contribute to an article or some other piece of writing. Another is embodied in Wikipedia, an online encyclopedia that is shaped and revised by its users (and its smaller but more upscale cousin, Citizendium). More recently, sites like Draft (**https://draftin.com/**) and Authorea (**https://www. authorea.com**) are bringing a level of sophistication to collaborative writing, enabling each partner to save his/her own drafts of work done together.

Blogs offer opportunity for one person to post ideas and others to comment on those posts. Forums and chat enable two or more people to share information that can then be revised as the discussion proceeds. Social networking websites like Facebook, LinkedIn and Twitter are enhancing opportunities for people to group-think about information that is of interest to them.

Web 2.0 assumes that connectivity and collaboration create better ideas and make a better world than did one-way communication. This, of course, is not a new insight. Those pre-literate people who recounted and discussed their history around the campfire so many centuries ago were doing the same thing, but without our technology.

We need to be careful, however, not to put Web 2.0 above Web 1.0 and traditional publishing as if collaboration gives our information an edge or credibility that one-way publication could not do. Certainly, a meeting of minds can often result in something better, but that is only the case if the collaborators actually know what they are talking about in the first place.

Truth to tell, much of what you find on Web 2.0 is simply the same old shallow thinking you find in a lot of person to person conversations. Information is no more valuable than the ability of its authors to know something about their subject and express it well. One thing a researcher must guard against is the assumption that because a number of people believe something, it is actually to be believed. Shared opinion is not fact. To move to a level of certainty you can live with, you need to evaluate information by acceptable standards.

[Some people are now discussing Web 3.0, which is essentially artificial intelligence, the ability of our technology to learn our preferences and anticipate our needs. While not yet a reality in most situations, 3.0, also sometimes called "The Semantic Web," will be a growing interest in the information world].

1.6 Primary and secondary information sources

Books and articles that come right from the context of a subject, straight out of the horse's mouth, so to speak, are *primary sources*. Books or articles that comment on the work of pioneers in a subject are called *secondary sources*.

Here are some examples:

Primary	Secondary
Text of Homer's *Iliad*	A scholarly study of Homer's *Iliad*
A scientific report written by the researcher	Someone else's analysis of that report
Firsthand account by a witness of 9/11	Book on 9/11 by someone not there
Street person's account of street life	Research about street people
Text of the Trials of Galileo	Commentary on the Trials of Galileo

Your professor may well want you to consult primary sources on your topic. The key to figuring out what is primary and what is secondary is to ask whether it is an eyewitness account, comes from the subject's time period, is written by a key scholar who actually developed the subject area, is a direct report by a researcher of an experiment done, and so on. If so, you have a primary source. It's "right from the horse's mouth." If not, you likely have a secondary source. Secondary sources, in general, comment on, analyze or explain the material you would find in a primary source.

— • — ◖▬◗ — • —

Clearing the Fog: What's all this talk about academic information?

[This is the first of a number of vignettes in this book that will answer specific issues in the research process. Each will come under the moniker of "Clearing the Fog." I hope you find them helpful.]

When Dorothy from *The Wizard of Oz* discovered she was now in the Land of Oz, she told her dog Toto, "We're not in Kansas anymore." If you've recently come into (or come back to) higher education, one of the first things to recognize is that this isn't Kansas, this is Academia. It has new rules, new players, new sources of information and new ways of doing research.

Some students believe that, if Google and Wikipedia were good enough for Kansas, they're good enough for Academia. But most soon discover that these tools just don't work very well for academic information. Why do I mean by "academic" in this sense? I could tell you that it's written by people with higher degrees (Ph.D.) or that it's peer reviewed (checked out by other scholars in the field before it can be published) or that it has to have notes and bibliographies.

But let's get the inside story: A piece of information is academic if it is accepted as academic by those in the field (like your professor). Each scholarly discipline has its favored sources of information, favored scholars, favored rules for doing research, favored patterns of evidence, and so on. So your professor will tell you to make use of academic or scholarly or peer reviewed literature, and anything else will probably give you problems. In this environment, Google and Wikipedia are far less helpful than the sophisticated academic search engines you'll be learning about in this book.

A social media wrinkle on the traditional review process is open peer review, which facilitates comment on articles that have already gone through the traditional review and publication process or which are hoping to do so. It provides an additional means for scholars to tell other scholars what they think of their scholarly work. PubPeer: The Online Journal Club (**https://pubpeer.com/**) is an example of an open peer review website. This is one additional tool that shows promise to improve our ability to assess academic literature, particularly in the sciences.

Many of us see a piece of information as acceptable if it "sounds right" or "looks right" or "makes sense." That's the essence of what we do with Google results, many of which don't give us a clear indication of whether or not they are academic. But in the land of Academia, our gut feeling about information doesn't come near to helping us determine whether or not a professor will accept it. Google citations are often at a lay level, far below academic requirements.

While academic library catalogs and databases are not perfect, they are much more likely to take us to genuine Academic Information.

So we need a change in mindset. Google and Wikipedia can be helpful, but they need to take third or fourth stage when we are in Academia. There are better tools for Academic Information, tools that will much more reliably get us the resources that a professor thinks are worthy. (More on concepts like "academic" and "scholarly" in the next chapter.)

1.7 Warning: Not all information is informative

We live in a world of many words. The sheer number of words we encounter every day is far greater than it ever has been in all human history. Some of those words come together into information that we can use. Others come together into nonsense. **Not all information is equal.** As you enter the information fog, there are signposts that can help you to discern genuine information from everything else that passes for the real thing. Ask yourself:

- ❖ What are the qualifications of the author of this information? (usually your best measure of quality, though it entails not only objective things like educational level, but also things like bias, fit between author qualifications and the topic being written about, etc.)
- ❖ Who else believes this?
- ❖ Has this information been subjected to some kind of peer review or other form of gatekeeping?
- ❖ Are there vested interests at stake? For example, is that glowing description of the latest gadget actually authored by the company that wants to sell it to you and knows that you have money?
- ❖ What are some good reasons for *not* believing it?

Get ready. You are about to step into the information fog. I hope you enjoy the journey.

1.8 For further study

Study guide
1. How do traditional societies handle information?
2. How did the invention of writing change the pre-writing methods by which a society handled information?
3. Name several significant changes to the world of information brought about by the printing press.
4. In the process of publishing information, what is "gatekeeping" and why is it significant?
5. In what ways is the creation of the World Wide Web a "revolution" for information?
6. Name some advantages of e-books. Can you think of drawbacks?
7. What is peer review in journal article publishing?
8. What is the open access movement, and why was it seen as necessary?
9. Where is the best place to find government documents?
10. What are the advantages and limitations of Web 2.0 for information?
11. Why is not all "information" actually informative?

2

What is this Thing Called "Scholarship" and Why Does it Matter?

In early 2015, the Association of College and Research Libraries tabled a new document: "Framework for Information Literacy in Higher Education" (**http://www.ala.org/acrl/standards/ ilframework**), which it has now fully endorsed. Essentially, it's a doorway for student researchers into the mysterious world of scholarship.

I know the questions you are asking: Why would I want to enter anything called "scholarship," since I'm not a scholar? Aren't scholars those stuffy, out of touch white guys who make pronouncements that only other scholars can understand? Doesn't being a scholar mean you have to give up your humanity and spend hours lecturing or sitting in dusty offices reading obscure books?

And the answer to all questions is "No, no, a thousand times no." Fact is, you're already a scholar if you are studying anything in higher education. Scholarship is not stuffy, not boring, not out of touch, and certainly not so blindingly intellectual that only the smartest 1% can engage in it.

Scholarship is as adventurous as an action movie (well, maybe not that adventurous, but pretty close). Scholarship is a quest, a solving of mysteries, and the ultimate answer to many of the ills of this world. It is done by active, engaged people who care less about big words and lofty ideas than about leaping into problem-solving on an enormous scale. And it has a lot to do with the kinds of research strategies you need to develop.

2.1 Defining Scholarship

In the broadest sense, scholarship is a method of discovery and problem-solving that uses well-defined methods. A scholar is someone who employs these methods to advance knowledge by meeting challenges and working toward solutions. But that's all pretty generic. When you find scholars and scholarship in the real world, there is a lot more variety and a ton of complexity.

Any student who has stumbled into a course on a new subject is at first overwhelmed by the strangeness of it all. Not only are there new terminology and new concepts, but there seems to be a foreign culture surrounding whatever you are studying. It's as if the professor is part of some strange in-group and the student is an intruder who doesn't (and might never) belong. The fact that the professor is the expert and the student is not makes this sense of alienation even stronger.

Scholarship, in fact, is all about in-groups. Scholars belong to exclusive clubs, and entry is won only by paying your dues in scholarly activity until you are recognized as an insider. This might seem like a harsh and uninviting environment, but it's actually essential to keeping scholarship going at a high level.

Do you want to belong to the discipline you are studying? Do you want to be part of the scholarly club? Maybe not, but you do want, as an aspiring student, to be able to navigate within scholarship without looking like a political candidate who wasn't properly briefed before the big debate. Knowing how to do research projects that look even somewhat like similar projects done by real scholars is a key to succeeding in higher education. So let's see what I can do to give you the inside story on scholarship. It starts with three big words: epistemology, metanarrative, and methodology.

2.1.1 Epistemology.

This is not all that complicated. Epistemology deals with the knowledge base within which a scholar in a certain discipline works. Every area of study has foundational knowledge upon which it relies. Epistemology deals with the whys of the knowledge base: Why this knowledge and not some other types of knowledge? Why do you trust it? Why do some scholars successfully add to the knowledge base while others fail to have their work accepted?

For scholars, what they know is like a sacred trust to be honored and protected. Sure, scholars understand that the knowledge base will change over time and that some knowledge may even be suddenly disrupted by a radical new idea. But being a scholar means being confident for the most part in the discipline's best understanding of itself to this point.

As a student, all those textbooks and lectures you have to endure actually embody the treasure of the discipline, the content that its scholars rely on. That's why asking, "Why do we have to learn this?" is such a slap in the face to the professor teaching you. Word of advice: Never ask a question like that unless you want your prof mentally to exile you to the darkest corner of academic oblivion.

2.1.2 Metanarrative.

Who are you? How do you explain your place in the world? What do you value? What do you want to accomplish? Who are your friends, and how do they define you as a person? All these questions have to do with your culture, your existence in the particular environment in which you live. That's your metanarrative, your overarching story that explains who you are while you live out your life. The term "metanarrative" comes from root words meaning "that which accompanies the narrative, the story." All of us live a narrative day by day that forms all the things we think, say and do. Your metanarrative is the overall explanation of *why* you think and act the way you do. Your metanarrative defines both you and the culture you live in.

Scholars live within a metanarrative that makes sense of their disciplines: What is important to them? How do scholars in this field conduct themselves? What do they value and what do they reject? How do they converse with one another? How do they explain their importance to the world? A scholar's metanarrative is essentially the culture that defines that scholar and his/her work.

Metanarrative is very significant to scholarship. For example, the metanarrative of a scientific discipline says it is not OK to falsify data in order to make it look like your hypothesis was correct. Not only is it not OK, but it is an outrage that puts the whole discipline at risk. A historian will insist on seeing primary sources, because merely relying on what people after the fact have to say about historical events is not nearly as useful as studying the personal journal of a key person bound up in those events.

Metanarrative describes what a scholar values and determines the identity of individual scholars as "our kind of people." It provides the motivation to believe that the work that the discipline's scholars do is important and worthy.

Here's the key: You need to learn to read the discipline culture (metanarrative) your professor lives in. What drives him/her? What are the values? What are the motives? Listen to how your professor talks about the subject, what your prof finds important in the work of other scholars, and so on. Enter your professor's world to discover the culture of the discipline.

Why should you care? For the same reason that a new refugee to your country does his or her utmost to figure out the new culture in order to "fit it." If you want to function as a student, you need to grasp how the academic culture of your professor works. Not only does this give you a greater sense of belonging in your classes, but it helps you do better work in research projects.

Here's an example. One of our master's degree students was defending his thesis before a body of examiners. As I watched the process, I quickly realized that something strange was going on. The examiners weren't quizzing him in the normal way to ensure that he actually knew what he was talking about (sort of a mild version of the Great Inquisition). They were trying to figure out how his amazing new method of analysis would work with their own research. It wasn't examiners and student. It was a meeting of equals, of colleagues. This student had so understood the metanarrative of his discipline that he could discourse with the examiners like an equal. He'd joined their club. He got an A.

You may not become an equal with your professor, but understanding your professor's metanarrative is the key to succeeding in your program and doing good research.

2.1.3 Methodology.

While there are some common elements, every discipline has a special set of prescribed procedures for doing research. This book will teach you the basics that are found in most disciplines, but it will be up to you to understand how research is done in the subject area you are studying.

What is the best way to learn methodology?

❖ Figure out the basics of research itself, i.e. that research is problem-based, that there are specific tools for finding information, that you have to use good methods for evaluating information, and that writing in your subject field has to follow that subject's rules, from the way you present information to the way you cite your sources.

❖ Read books and scholarly articles in your field, studying them, not just for content, but for method. How does the author present the problem to the reader? How does the author present arguments and evidence? And so on.

❖ Pay attention to what your professor asks you to do in research projects. Those elements that don't seem important to you are important to your professor. Do your research the way your professor asks you to do it, and don't cut corners. You'll be happy you followed directions.

Since we'll be devoting so much effort to methodology in the chapters that follow, I'll spare you any more right now. Just understand that I've given you a lot of insider stuff that can really help you succeed in the information fog.

2.1.4 What about not fitting in?

All of this talk of epistemology, metanarrative and methodology may have made you feel uneasy. So much of academia seems devoted to fitting in, acculturating, being part of the in-crowd, sharing a kind of groupthink that reeks of the establishment. Am I, indeed, suggesting that you become an academic sheep, a yes-person, an uncritical acceptor of whatever the discipline tells you that you should be or think?

Not necessarily. But before you assume that I plan to say, "No, be your own person and think for yourself," you should recognize that you do also need to survive academia. Being known as a radical and a free-thinker is fine, but it works better if you first understand well the academic culture you are working in. Thus choosing between being a critic and a joiner is not an either/or. There is a possibility to do both.

Any culture, including that of an academic discipline, is prone to old-boy networks, uncritically accepted premises, and resistance to change. That does not disqualify the discipline, which most likely still produces innovative and valuable work. It does mean, however, that your approach to higher education needs to be critical (not in the sense of criticizing everything, but in the sense that you are always aware of the need to look for flaws and biases that can slow or divert academic work).

In learning how to do research, there is actually a method of "critical information literacy" by which nothing that you search for, read, or evaluate is above critical investigation. Rather, all research requires "ongoing questioning and struggling for meaning." [Elmborg, J. (2012). "Critical information literacy: Definitions and challenges." In C. Wilkinson & C. Bruch (Eds.), *Transforming information literacy programs: Intersecting frontiers of self, library culture, and campus community* (pp. 75–80). Chicago: American Library Association. **http://ir.uiowa.edu/cgi/viewcontent. cgi?article=1013&context=slis_pubs**]

Some advice: Get to know the discipline you are studying, as well as its epistemology, metanarrative, and methodologies that define it. Get to know all of this before you move in (guns a-blazing) to tell everyone what's wrong with the way the discipline does things. This doesn't mean you have to be uncritical and accepting of everything. Rather, you should navigate the territory carefully, spotting the flaws and choosing which hills you would rather die on (i.e. what causes you want to pursue to the end, with some risk that your progress as a student may be hampered). There's plenty of room for critical information literacy if you exercise it wisely.

2.2 Scholarship in Practice

One of the best ways to get into the details of what scholars do (and what you will need to start doing in order to succeed in the scholarly world of higher education) is to follow the outline of the "Framework for Information Literacy in Higher Education" from the Association of College and Research Libraries (**http://www. ala.org/acrl/standards/ilframework**). If you want to see my own take on the Framework in graphic form, have a look at my Prezi, "What is Scholarship?" at **https://prezi.com/sq7xqbxurr9p/**

what-is-scholarship/ (it's somewhat animated, so it might keep you awake better than what follows).

So, here we go:

2.2.1 Authority is constructed and contextual.

By "authority" we mean the ability of a scholar to have a reader/hearer trust what that scholar is saying. There was a time when the mere fact that a scholar was an expert meant that the words of the scholar could be trusted. Several factors have changed the easy acceptance of the pronouncements of scholars:

❖ We recognize that the knowledge base is always under revision, so that what a scholar claims today may not be true tomorrow (even though scholarly knowledge tends to be pretty stable overall);

❖ There are many factors that can limit the absolute authority of a scholarly statement: the culture of the reader/hearer, the extent to which the statement is believable in all situations, the amount of evidence (or lack of it) behind the statement, the biases of the scholar that may skew the trustworthiness of the statement, and so on.

❖ It is a fact that scholarship is very often a matter of competing claims to truth, as in, "You say this, but I say that." A lot of scholarship is in flux, and the number of absolutes is smaller than you might think.

These days, we tend to be less trusting of experts than we once were. That is not to say that experts have no authority, just that their authority is "constructed" (recognized at different levels of trust and value by various reader/hearers and their communities) and "contextual" (so that the trustworthiness of a piece of information may well depend on how or where the information is used, not just on the qualifications of its creator).

If authority is constructed, we need to find ways to determine why we should trust the information we are encountering. This means that authors have to prove themselves to us. We should be asking them: What are your qualifications? How good is your evidence? How have your biases influenced what you are saying? How well are your work and your views accepted by your peers? And so on.

If information is contextual, we need to evaluate the information we receive to determine if it meets our need, is credible, and so on. Not all information is created equally, and not all information is relevant for whatever problem we are trying to address. It must suit our own context.

If we are the ones doing a research project, our professor or other reader becomes our context, our audience. The reader of our work calls the shots when it comes to evaluating what we are producing. So we must determine how much authority we need to enlist for ourselves to back up what we are saying in our own research projects. Do we need to find scientific evidence or primary sources in order to support our statements, or does the nature of our research call for pulling up secondary evidence and clear arguments to support our interpretation of an issue? Do we have to use academic articles or will a blog post by a noted scholar do just as well? Does everything we say in a research project need to be backed up with scholarly citations or are some things just common sense/knowledge without the need for expert authority to support them?

2.2.2 Information creation as a process.

It might be your greatest wish that your next research project would just fall from the skies in final form so all you needed to do was turn it in to your professor. Maybe you could accomplish something like that if you bought your paper online, but that is a bad, bad thing that no self-respecting student should even contemplate.

No, most of our research is a matter of long and sometimes agonizing development (or panicky keyboarding through a long night filled with coffee, energy shots, and sheer terror). In any case, creating a piece of information is a process. It takes time, it has stages, and it often requires several versions to get it right. That's normal.

For a scholar, how a piece of work has been assembled is often as important as what appears in the final form. You as a researcher want to know the amount and kinds of research that went into someone's book or article, as well as the amount of gatekeeping required before it was published. All this determines its level of authority.

The kind of venue an author chooses for publication – scholarly article in a journal, popular article in a magazine or blog – also speaks to how it was developed. For example, a scholarly article requires data gathered through experimentation or other forms of rigorous evidence-gathering, while a popular article doesn't do the groundbreaking research but bases itself on what other scholars have already found or on the opinions of the writer. A blog often looks at existing scholarship and provides a perspective on it. In each case, what the reader finally sees has gone through its own unique creation process, and that process says a lot about a work's authority and usefulness.

This is where you, as a developing scholar, need to evaluate the processes by which the things you are reading came into being. It's not as difficult as you might think. What you require is the ability to tell the difference between a scholarly article (think citations, reference lists) and a popular one (few or no citations). You should be able to find out if a piece of work was peer reviewed (the home page of a journal will tell you that) or if it comes from a scholarly publisher, like a university press. If you are reading a blog, look up the background of the author to determine whether or not s/he is used to doing solid scholarship or just likes to share opinions willy-nilly ("willy-nilly" is not a good thing, usually).

Similarly, you need to think about the processes required in your own creating of information to ensure that it meets the needs of your readership. If that readership is a professor, you need to understand and follow the requirements of the professor's assignment handout. If you are writing for another audience, be sure you are working up to the standards that this audience expects to see.

2.2.3 Information has value.

Did you ever spend $150 on a textbook and then rue the day you signed up for that particular course? Information can really cost you. But there's more to the concept, "Information has value," than mere money.

Websites are free to read, right? Massive amounts of information available without any cost to you. That's what makes Google such a treasure. But think for a minute: Why are websites free to read and your psych textbook costs 149.95? In scholarship, questions like that matter. And none of the answers, as you might expect, are simple.

Let's consider money as one measure of value. Large quantities of academic literature (the products of scholarship) are very, very expensive. Books can go for $300 or more, and individual journal articles for $40. The journal subscriptions that libraries pay for can cost in the tens of thousands of dollars for one journal over the space of one year. Does this mean that academic literature is more valuable than other kinds of literature (such as a latest bestselling novel on Kindle?). This is where it gets complicated.

We can measure value in lots of ways: what something costs, how important something is to its owner, what contribution something can make to society, and so on. If we look just at price, we miss the importance of the value of information to ourselves and our society. Information doesn't need to be expensive to be valuable.

At the same time, price may determine whether or not you personally will have access to the information you need. In today's greatly overpriced academic information market, all sorts of resources are out of reach financially for many people. That is why the open access movement is so important. The information we value needs to be information we can also access. At the same time, we need to understand that copyright protects authors from other people simply stealing their work. Thus information is never utterly "free." Access to it is governed by rules that ensure that authors get reasonably paid and recognized, if that is what they need to continue writing.

The Open Access Network (**http://openaccessnetwork.org**) is the latest attempt to pull together all the players in scholarly publishing to fund publications that will be made free to everyone. Essentially, it calls for universities to pay a fee so that open access can become a reality in a big way. Thus "information has value" can mean that you still need someone to front the cash to get the information to the rest of us, even though the public may not pay directly.

Knowing the various parameters of value (price, importance, significance for society, restrictions of copyright) is very significant to being able to do research with your eyes open.

2.2.4 Research as inquiry.

This is a big one. People who do research are not merely trying to summarize what other people have said (which is boring and makes little sense when you can get the same thing from a Wikipedia article). Research is about discovery. As I once put it in an article I wrote:

> Scholarship is all about a profound discontent, about
> a quest to discover more, about a burning desire to
> solve society's problems, and make a better world.

Pretty high-blown stuff, but I believe it. You may be used to "research projects" that are little more than compilation exercises, as in, "Everything that I could find out about climate change and boil down to five pages." Those sorts of submissions are doomed before they ever arrive in a professor's in-box. And they must end now, because I am going to show you a better way.

Research is really a problem-addressing exercise, an inquiry that takes you from an issue to a potential resolution. In this book, starting with the next chapter, you will learn how to:

- ❖ Formulate problem statements in the form of research questions or thesis statements;
- ❖ Figure out how to find the best information to address your problem;
- ❖ Evaluate and use the found information, along with your own critical thinking, in order to grapple with your problem and wrestle it into submission (sorry for the aggressive imagery).

So be prepared to have your cherished notions of research be tossed on their heads. But that's not much of a loss, because you always hated research anyway, didn't you? The reason you hate it so much because you've never experienced the fierce joy of engaging in genuine research, which is inherently exciting, fulfilling, and the best way to occupy your time. Research as inquiry is a whole different thing from what most people do, and it is going to change your life as student. Really.

More on this in the next chapter.

2.2.5 Scholarship as conversation.

This is a fun concept. We can tend to think of knowledge as a static body of all that we know. But it's far from that. Let me ask you: How does knowledge develop? Is it a matter of someone making a discovery and then everyone in the whole world, like a flock of sheep, simply echoing, "Oh, that's a terrific discovery. Yes, let's add that to our knowledge base, and then we'll all believe it, use it, and forever express our gratitude to the researcher who found it"?

Maybe that happens in the world of Mickey Mouse, but the following is closer to the way things work:

- ❖ Most ideas come up through a history of earlier versions of those ideas, so that there is little that is absolutely unique (though there are occasional "scientific revolutions" that emerge without warning).

❖ When someone comes up with something fresh, a process of interaction with others also working in the field begins. It's a conversation, with some people agreeing, some possibly disagreeing and others suggesting modifications.

❖ All of this forms into a history of "conversations" in which ideas are batted back and forth, hopefully making progress, as time passes.

As the Framework for Information Literacy in Higher Education puts it, "Research in scholarly and professional fields is a discursive practice in which ideas are formulated, debated, and weighed against one another over extended periods of time."

This is where it gets exciting. Person A comes up with a new take on something, only to be opposed by her archenemy, Person B. Person C comes alongside Person A, while Person D thinks A is on to something but some of the things B suggested could be used modify A's view and make it more reasonable. All this activity means that knowledge is not one static thing but is constantly in flux, more like a flowing river than a very still lake. Scholarship is always changing. There's always an aura of anticipation about the next big thing.

For scholars, the active give and take of knowledge as it develops is the very essence of how it all works. It's a conversation among participants who are all on a quest. They may not agree with one another, but that's part of the process. Scholarship is not static. It's a conversation.

You as a researcher need to find the conversation around your topic and make sure you include that conversation in your project. That's why you need more than a couple of sources. Your sources capture the major voices into the conversation that is going on.

2.2.6 Searching as strategic exploration.

Google is great, right? Throw some words in the box and up comes everything you need. On the other hand, if you've ever tried one of those academic databases from your library, they seem kind of nasty.

So much needless complication obviously created by sadistic and out of touch people who just want to make life harder for suffering students.

The fact is, however, that Google has lulled a lot of people into the false, wrong, mistaken, and hopelessly in error notion that searching for information is easy. Sure it's easy to throw words in a search box. But actually finding the information you really need is hard. That is why searching has to be strategic and why library-based academic databases are often the most effective, efficient means to find the best information.

Good searches are based on a clearly stated research problem which is often in the form of a question. That question tells you why you need the information you are seeking and helps define the kind of information you need. With a solid question in hand, you can effectively plan how you are going to find the resources you require to address that question. When you know what finding tools are available to you, and you understand how to use those tools effectively, the strategies of searching become clearer.

One large task of this book is to help you learn how to find the best resources for the problem you are dealing with. Finding those resources is not easy. It takes strategy. But, as your skills develop, the path forward will be clearer.

2.3 Who Determines What Is Academic/Scholarly?

Your professor says, "Class, for your research papers I want only peer reviewed, scholarly (or academic) sources. No websites, no blogs." And then it's up to you to figure out what is academic/scholarly information and what is not. Sure, some search tools like Google Scholar or those individual databases offered by your library allow you to limit only to scholarly resources, but how can you be sure they are doing it right?

If you want to step back and look at the big picture, scholarship is governed by a series of exclusive clubs. Each discipline and sub-discipline has its contingent of scholars who set the rules for how their club works. They also establish methods for recognizing scholarly work as scholarly. The predominant method is some form of "peer review," by which a manuscript submitted for publication is scrutinized by other scholars before it is published. Other kinds of recognition come from one scholar citing another scholar's work, from invitations for scholars to speak at academic conferences, and from acceptance of the views and ideas of scholars by other scholars in their field.

Ultimately, a piece of writing is scholarly if other scholars see it as scholarly. This might sound very circular, but that's how things work. Scholars in each discipline set the rules for what they consider acceptable, and they determine whether or not any piece of writing meets the requirements of those rules. That may all look elitist (and sometimes it is), but it also helps maintain the level of scholarship coming out of the discipline. Scholars, like movie censors looking for naughty stuff, "know it when they see it."

For you, look for signs. Has the article you are reading been published in an academic journal? Has it been peer reviewed (you can Google a journal's home page to find out if its articles are normally peer reviewed)? If it is a book, does it come from a recognized publisher of scholarship? Above all, what are the qualifications of the author(s) to write what has been written? When in doubt, ask your friendly professor, or (if the professor is not as friendly as you'd like) ask your undoubtedly friendly librarian.

2.4 For further study

Study Guide
1. Give a brief definition of "scholarship."
2. As a means to describe the inside world of scholarship explain these words: epistemology, metanarrative, and methodology.

3. Briefly describe what is meant by each of the following:
    a. Authority Is Constructed and Contextual.
    b. Information Creation as a Process.
    c. Information Has Value.
    d. Research as Inquiry.
    e. Scholarship as Conversation.
    f. Searching as Strategic Exploration.

3

Taking Charge

You may be saying to yourself, "I've never been good at this research thing. In fact, I don't think I have a good research project in me."

My response is, "Of course you don't. A good research project is *out there*, not inside you. What you have to do is get out there, find the data, work with it, and use it to make a difference."

At this point, be aware that we are talking about a certain kind of research here, not the social scientific or scientific research that involves experiments, but informational research such as you will find in the humanities or in literature reviews in the social sciences and sciences. This kind of research is all about verbal data and information, its discovery and use.

Now, before you run off to a dark alley frequented by black market sellers of data, let me offer you a safer alternative. What follows is a list of basic things that you need to have working for you in order to turn your anxiety into a brilliant project, leading to an excellent product.

1. You need an intense desire to do a brilliant project, not just an average one. By definition, most people can do an average project.

2. You need to take your time and plan your research as a *strategy* rather than as a mad dash through libraries and databases. Google can provide you with a lot of resources, but Google results have a nasty tendency to be academically uneven. Even libraries know when you have reached the panic stage. The books close ranks and refuse to be found. Titles in the catalog trade places so that you can't locate them. The smell of musty books renders you numb and silly. Databases can do even worse things to you (don't ask).

   Don't panic. Take it easy. Work out a plan and show that data who's in charge here.

3. You need to become a friend to structure. If you're the kind of person who might follow your schedule if you could remember where you put it, or someone who views a library fine as a reasonable price to pay for never having to think about a due date, research is going to be a battle for you. Structure and organization, from the beginning of the process all the way to its triumphant end, is crucial, no matter how much pain it will cost you to adapt.

4. You need to develop *lateral thinking*. Lateral thinking is akin to what happens in a football game: The quarterback has no openings at all. If he runs with the ball, he'll be flattened. So, instead of moving forward, he launches the ball sideways to another player who can move it forward. These are the steps:

   ❖ Recognize that your advance along one line is blocked.
   ❖ Abandon your approach and look for another.
   ❖ Run with your new approach and make it work (or try yet another).

It's like the old story of the truck that got stuck in a highway underpass. No towing vehicle of any kind could get it out, and so the workers were left with the option of dismantling an expensive truck or tearing down an even more expensive underpass until...

...until the light bulb went on and some bright lateral thinker suggested letting the air out of the truck's tires to *lower* it. Lateral thinking works beyond the obvious, in the realm of the creative.

Nurture this gift of lateral thinking within you. It will help greatly in that moment when all your cherished strategies have failed you and you still don't have the information you need.

Here's an example: Suppose you are doing research on the legal trial of Galileo and discover that every book with the texts of the verdicts against him is already signed out (something that actually happened to one of our students). Rather than thinking that the library has let you down, and you are doomed to wander the streets as a pathetic warning to others, think beyond the library (a lateral) and check to see if someone has posted the verdict transcripts on the Internet (they have: **http://www.law.umkc.edu/faculty/ projects/ftrials/galileo/galileo.html**). That sort of thinking can save you from the disaster which often lurks, ready to bite the unsuspecting. (The student got a B+ on his project).

3.1 Wrestling with a topic

"I have to write a research paper on Climate Change. Right now I don't know much about it, so I better get into Wikipedia, then find two or three books. I'm hoping it's not a lot of work to pull everything together, but do I have enough for ten pages? Seems to me that it shouldn't take that many words to explain that the climate is messed up because of greedy human beings."

My response? *Oh, if I could only help the speaker of these words see how absolutely off course s/he is...*

Do you know how many glaring problems I found in that one brief rant? The most serious one is that our Climate Change, research-paper-writin' student is not going to end up with a research paper, because reading up on a topic and explaining it is not research.

"What?" you say. "Not research? The student has a topic – Climate Change – finds some stuff on it, and writes it up. If that's not a research paper, what is? Don't tell me it's not research."

All right, I won't. If I were a member of the tough-love school of thought, I would say something like this to you: "Go ahead and write your paper explaining everything you can find out about Climate Change (something your prof has read a thousand times in a thousand papers just like yours). Turn it in and wait for your professor to read the thing and give you the usual dreary mark. Obviously, you don't like your prof anyway, and that's why you keep doing this to him/her. Professors are no strangers to the kinds of boredom you inflict on them. In fact they're quite used to the tedious task of marking your essays. You bore the professor, and the professor pays you back by giving you a C. Any illusion that you actually did research will be dead by the time you get the essay back."

Not *ever* wanting to be as harsh as that, at least without providing some help, let me ask instead: "What is good and useful research if it's not what you've been doing?" To answer, let's begin by looking at what it is not.

3.2 Elements of inadequate research

❖ Inadequate research assumes that the task is merely to gather data and synthesize it (the data-as-goal philosophy). Thus the typical student "research" project involves amassing information from a few sources, reading and absorbing it, then regurgitating it back onto a fresh piece of paper (sorry for the disgusting image). The purpose of the project is simply to study up on something and then explain it, using other people's writings as a guide.

❖ Inadequate research deals in generalities and surveys. It loves a superficial look at a big topic, and it abhors depth and analysis.

❖ Inadequate research asks no important questions and makes no pretense of advancing knowledge. It's happy just to report on what has already been done, to summarize the past.

❖ Inadequate research is so boring that you should be surprised that it ever gets completed, let alone foisted on your poor longsuffering professor.

3.3 The key to great research

What's the point of doing research, then? A flip response might be that a professor or employer told you to do a research project, and you're just following orders. But that's not the answer I'm looking for.

You should recognize first that there is a big difference between seeing data as a goal and data as a tool. What do I mean? Consider these two models:

Data as goal: Find out everything you can about a topic → Explain what you've learned.

Data as tool: Gather basic information about your topic→ Identify a problem or issue related to that topic → Use the data you collect as a *tool* (a means) to try to solve that problem or issue.

Let's consider Climate Change (CC) as an example:

Data as goal: Find out what you can about CC and its causes → Explain all this in a paper.

Data as tool: Read some basic data on CC → Discover an issue (e.g. the persistent counter-argument that current climate change is a natural phenomenon rather than something caused by greedy human beings) → Ask a question like this one, "How convincing is the scientific support for climate change as a natural phenomenon as opposed to being primarily the result of human activity?"

You may find this approach a bit strange. Not only does "data as tool" ask you not to cover the whole topic (aren't you supposed to cover the whole topic?) but it focuses on an issue or controversy rather than merely explaining what you can find out about the topic in general. Its purpose is analysis and problem–solving.

Consider the alternative: You set a goal of retelling the CC story, then go through the tedium of finding a bunch of sources, reading them, deciding what details to synthesize, snagging some good quotes, and making sure you cite your sources properly. After all that, you know you'll only get a mediocre grade unless you do something brilliant. But you don't have the time, and what is "brilliant" in a research paper anyway? There seems to be no clear path to go from mediocre to an A when you are only reporting on what you read. No wonder students seem to hate research papers so much.

Have you ever had a professor tell you that s/he expects critical thinking in your paper? If so, you have probably wondered how critical thinking works in research. So here is the answer: It involves grappling with a problem, issue or controversy. The approach I'm suggesting in this book should take you a long way in the direction of genuine critical thinking, but first we need to address a couple of questions:

1. Does the professor actually expect you to write on the *whole* topic? There won't be many cases at all when the answer is "yes." In most situations, professors expect you to narrow down by choosing only one aspect of the larger topic.
2. Does the professor want description (data as goal) or analysis (data as tool)? Once again, a few profs may merely want a summary of what you read, but most (especially those who refer to "critical thinking") want you to address a problem, using data as a means to analyze the issues and come up with some kind of solution.

If you are at all in doubt, contact your professor and explain to him/her what you want to do. Get advice. Not checking in advance may have you getting one of those fateful comments: "This fails to meet the goals of the assignment," along with a low grade. If you check before you start your research, chances are the professor will give you a green light and maybe even a "well done" at the end.

The key to genuine research is a *good question* that addresses a problem calling for analysis. Without posing a question, nothing you are doing can be called research.

What, then, constitutes a good question? Here the situation becomes more challenging, because you need to begin rethinking the whole research process. Later in this chapter, we will consider the actual strategies involved in getting a topic ready for research, but for now let's interface with some basic principles.

The first of these is that most any research topic presented to you needs some work before it is viable enough to use. Assume, unless you know otherwise, that the topic is too broad to be workable short of writing a book on it. A topic like the Climate Change, or Theology of Suffering, or Economic Conditions in Russia today is not likely to inspire depth of analysis because you don't have space in ten or twenty pages to be anything but superficial. You are going to have to focus on a more narrow aspect of the topic so that you can deal with it in depth.

Consider a bathtub with a gallon of water in it as opposed to a bathroom sink with a gallon of water in it. Which is deeper? The sink, because its borders are narrower. The same principle works in a research project—the narrower your focus, the more chance you have of getting some depth into your project.

Assume, second, that you are going to have to develop a sound working knowledge of the topic before you're going to know what to do with it. I see a lot of students floundering for hours at the beginning of a project because they really don't understand the basics of the subject matter they are dealing with.

Third, and I repeat this for a reason, assume that you may have to negotiate with the professor who gave you the project. You need to know that what you propose is actually going to fly with the person ultimately responsible for your fate. But cheer up—professors are generally thrilled by any tiny evidence of creativity in their students.

Go to your professor and ask politely, "Would you mind if I pursued *this* issue raised by Climate Change? It looks really interesting." Your professor's heart will turn to mush and he or she will say quietly, "Yes, all right," while inside he or she is shouting, "A new approach! I'm getting a new approach!"

Caution: Don't ever say, "May I write on Water Pollution instead?" This signals to the professor that you don't like the topic you were offered, and you most certainly will end up having to write on it anyway.

3.4 A model for research

What, then, is research all about? Here's a model:

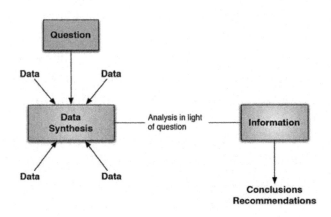

Explanation?

- ❖ You begin with a question.
- ❖ You collect data.
- ❖ You synthesize it (put it together in some coherent form).
- ❖ You analyze the data in light of the question (figuring out how each piece of data could be used to answer the question). This analysis turns data into information (processed data that is ready to be used to answer the question).
- ❖ You come up with conclusions and recommendations.

The key to the whole thing is that *you need to move beyond merely gathering data, reorganizing it (data synthesis) and reporting on what you read.* When a question is injected into the mix, the data becomes more than an end in itself and turns into the raw material needed to answer the question. The result is analysis that turns data into information that can then be used to reach an answer. Remember that research is all about "inquiry," not simply rehashing information that is already out there. This may still seem a bit foggy to you, but we are about to embark on a journey that will make things much clearer.

For a tutorial on the research process, go to: **https://www. youtube.com/watch?v=p-qLraS3sGk&feature=youtu.be**

3.5 Getting started in research

3.5.1 Getting a working knowledge through reference sources

Before you go off in all directions at once (like a draw-and-quarter execution in merry old England), get a grip on yourself. As a librarian, I see the same awkward experience repeated day after day—students walking uneasily through the front door of the library, then stopping, frozen to the ground.

I know what's buzzing through their battered minds: "I'm here, I'm actually here in the library, about to start researching my topic, and I don't have a *clue* what to do. Time has stopped, and people are staring at me. Why can't I move my limbs? Why is my head so numb? Maybe I'll die here, rooted to the floor, and they'll bronze me as a monument to the unknown student."

Take heart: it doesn't have to be like this. Let me give you the first step you need to take so that you break free from bondage. It's simple. *Get a working knowledge of your topic.*

Right, so what's a working knowledge? Here's a basic definition:

You have a working knowledge of a topic when you can talk about it for one minute without repeating yourself.

To start your research, all you need to do is acquire one minute's knowledge.

"One minute?" you say. "I've been told I have to present a fifteen page research paper with a dozen footnotes including appropriate journal references (whatever they are). Why talk to me about one minute of working knowledge?" I do so for the same reason that you take a flashlight with you to avoid stumbling around in the dark. A working knowledge gives you the basics of a topic and enough light so that you won't hurt yourself as you move on into more complicated territory. It isn't complete knowledge, but it's enough to tell you what the topic entails, what its boundaries are, even what some of its controversies, mysteries and dangers might be.

So where do you get a working knowledge? You could simply go on the Internet, where virtually anything is explained by some site or other. But, if you don't know much about the topic to begin with, the Net may not be the best source, because it's not easy to judge the reliability of information on a new topic. (We'll deal with that issue more fully in Chapter Seven).

You would do better to investigate authoritative ***reference sources*** first. All academic libraries have recognized reference tools that provide concise and authoritative information on virtually any topic you might think of. Reference books will generally appear in the form of dictionaries or encyclopedias on general or specific topics. As well, handbooks, atlases—in fact, any tool that involves looking up brief information—may be found in a reference collection. You would be amazed at how many topic areas have dictionaries or encyclopedias devoted to them. From broader disciplines like psychology or chemistry to narrower ones (as, for example, *Encyclopedia of Christmas*) you will find good, brief information on virtually anything you want, unless it is a very recent topic.

Many references sources are available in electronic form, but you (or your library) need to subscribe with real money to the best of these. The higher quality reference sources are not available without cost on the Internet, though some older or lite versions of reference tools are appearing there for free. Your most useful venue for good reference information is still a library, either in print form or electronically through the library catalog or some other database.

So you're working in a library context and wondering how to find a reference book that will give you information on marriage customs of the Kurdish people. You could do some sort of keyword search or wander the physical shelves of the reference collection, but there's an easier way to find what you want. *Think of the broad subject within which your topic lies.* In this case, you are looking at customs of a particular culture. Thus you could look up a subject heading in your library's catalog like **Manners and Customs - Encyclopedias** to find a reference source like *Worldmark Encyclopedia of Cultures and Daily Life.* Then just look up "Kurds." Alternatively, you might find this reference source with a keyword search on **cultures AND (encyclopedia or dictionary)**.

Let's try another example of the sort of material you're looking for in a working knowledge. Suppose you were taking a History of the Middle Ages course and one of the topics was the Lollards. The *what?* Let me give you a clue: They were a group of religious people who flourished in the late Medieval and early Reformation period. What sort of a reference source would you use for Lollards? How about a dictionary of medieval history or of church history? If you check into a reference source or two, following the famous Five Ws of inquiry, you might discover the following:

Who?

The Lollards were followers of John Wycliffe; more generally, the term was used of any serious critic of the English church in the late Middle Ages. Key figures in the movement were Nicholas of Hereford, William Swinderby, and John Purvey.

What?

Their teachings, summed up by the Twelve Conclusions of 1395, included personal faith, divine election, and the Bible as the sole authority in religion. They asserted that every person had the individual right to read and interpret the Bible.

Where?

The movement existed primarily in England and Scotland.

When?

It began in the 1380s (AD) and went underground after 1431, due to persecution. The movement declined in the mid–1400s but revived about 1490. It figured prominently in the congregational dissent of the seventeenth century and in the rise of the Hussites in Bohemia.

Why?

The Lollards claimed to be a reaction to the control over human life and spirituality that was exercised by the Church of the time.

My two reference sources were: *Dictionary of the Middle Ages* and *Oxford Dictionary of the Christian Church*.

Now we have basic data to work with. Have I convinced you of the need for a working knowledge? If not, you're going to end up spinning your wheels and wasting time. Unless you start with a working knowledge you will inevitably find yourself sinking the moment you reach deeper waters.

3.5.2 Excursus: Wikipedia, the professor's dilemma

A lot of students use Wikipedia, the free online encyclopedia with an awesome range of articles on every conceivable topic (**http:// en.wikipedia.org/wiki/Main_Page**).

Technically speaking, the Wikipedia phenomenon should have been a disaster from the beginning. Normally encyclopedias are created by an editor who contracts known experts in their fields to write articles that are then then carefully studied for accuracy and clarity before publication. Wikipedia's articles are written by the "hoi polloi:" the public, you and me, any Jane or Joe Blow who wants to add an entry. Sure, there are safeguards to help maintain a measure of objectivity and preserve a structure for what is included in a good article. But not only can anyone write most kinds of articles, almost anyone can edit an article too, though changes to certain entries may need to be verified by other users. In fact, the edits that actually stick (without being changed back by one of the volunteer watchdogs who guard articles from being vandalized) are those for which a large number of people agree that the change is needed.

Stephen Colbert, the TV satirist, coined the term "wikiality." According to Wikipedia: "Colbert defined wikiality as 'truth by consensus' (rather than fact), modeled after the approval-by-consensus format of Wikipedia." (For more fun criticism see the Wikipedia article "Wikipedia in culture.") Colbert, on one of his shows, told his viewers to test his "truth by consensus" theory by changing the Wikipedia entry on "African Elephant" to say that the population of elephants had tripled in the past six months (it hadn't). Wikipedia ended up having to restrict editing on African elephant material due to the large numbers of changes that were made.

All kidding aside, is Wikipedia good or bad? That's a tough question to answer. The information in it is often amazingly reliable, but there can be errors. Some professors have simply opted for the safest road and told their students not to use it. Wikipedia itself tells its readers not to include its articles in research bibliographies. On the other hand, the journal *Nature* did a study that found the mistakes in Wikipedia to be only a few more in number than those in *Encyclopedia Britannica*. *Britannica* answered with an angry rebuttal claiming poor methodology, but *Nature* has stuck to its original findings. [*Nature* 438, no. 7070 (December 15, 2005): 900-901; **http://corporate.britannica.com/**

britannica_nature_response.pdf; http://www.nature.com/ press_releases/Britannica_response.pdf].

So, should you use or not to use Wikipedia? I'm more on the side of "use with reasonable discernment." Since it is an encyclopedia, you would not in most cases include it in a research bibliography. Research papers normally don't contain reference book information, which is just background for your own development of a topic, unless the reference article is several pages long. You likely will use the Great W to develop your working knowledge or to plunder the often useful notes and bibliographies at the ends of articles. But be careful. Don't rely *just* on Wikipedia. What you read there at any one moment might be a sabotage of an article (to be corrected in a couple of hours) or something that is just wrong and hasn't yet been noticed. Wikipedia has even been known occasionally to have articles on completely made up topics that don't exist. Compare what you read in Wikipedia with other, traditionally published, reference sources.

[For further discussion, see Badke, W. (2008). What to do with Wikipedia. *Online*, *32(2)*, 48-50. Available: **http://www. infotoday.com/online/mar08/Badke.shtml**].

3.5.3 Full text reference tools

There is a growing number of reference works that are available in either print or online format. Each academic library will have its own collection of such tools, often available through your library home page or catalog. These resources are different from Google search results or Wikipedia in that they have come through the more traditional publishing process of editors and expert writers (gatekeeping). Your profs will thus find them reliable, even in electronic form. Remember, though, that reference tool entries don't normally appear in your research bibliographies unless they are of substantial size.

On the World Wide Web, the availability of reference sources that use traditional production and editing procedures is pretty limited.

Here's a wildly eclectic list of high quality openly available online reference sources chosen at a whim for reasons I no longer recall except that I liked them:

- ❖ *Cambridge History of English and American Literature* (searchable by keyword and thesaurus):
  http://www.bartleby.com/cambridge/
- ❖ *Encyclopedia Smithsonian*:
  http://www.si.edu/Encyclopedia_SI/
- ❖ *Stanford Encyclopedia of Philosophy*:
  http://plato.stanford.edu/
- ❖ *The Canadian Encyclopedia (Historica Canada)*:
  http://www.thecanadianencyclopedia.com
- ❖ *Baker's Evangelical Dictionary of Biblical Theology*:
  **http://www.biblestudytools.com/dictionaries/
  bakers-evangelical-dictionary/**
- ❖ *Global Edge* (international business information):
  http://globaledge.msu.edu
- ❖ *WolframMathWorld* (a mathematics encyclopedia):
  http://matworld.wolfram.com/
- ❖ *Computer Desktop Encyclopedia* (definitions of terms in technology and computing):
  http://www.computerlanguage.com/

3.6 Finding a good question

An investigation of a topic is not research until you have focused it around a solid question that addresses a problem or issue. But how do you come up with a research question that is going to work?

3.6.1 Narrowing the topic

Narrow your topic to one aspect. One big reason why research can fail is that the researcher is trying to conquer the world with one project. You simply cannot cover everything about teen anxiety or abortion or the causes of World War One or why the moon *isn't* made of green cheese. You have to choose an aspect that is distinct enough that you can really work with it. Otherwise you end up with a superficial survey, because you are trying to cover too much.

The broader your focus, the more shallow your paper. You want depth. Avoid questions that survey and then compile large amounts of data. The resulting projects will never dwell on any one thing for more than a few lines, and they will have bibliographies that cover a wide variety of issues. Instead of looking at the life of Napoleon, analyze why he lost the Battle of Waterloo. Narrow is good; big sweeping topics breed ugliness and despair (or at least boredom).

3.6.2 Identifying Issues

Identify controversies or questions related to your narrowed approach. There's no point in re-describing what has already been described, since research is not merely the gathering of information but the use of information to solve a problem. Information is not an end in itself, but a means for inquiry. To tell me the life story of Napoleon or explain the problem of teenage drinking is to do what every reference source on the subject has already done. You are simply re-packaging existing information into a summary of the topic. This is where those excruciatingly boring and superficial "research" papers come from. You must vow never to write another one. Find something worth investigating and investigate it.

In the case of teenage drinking you might want to evaluate various kinds of social media advertising to determine which is most effective in reaching problem drinkers. (This could lead to the research question: Which form of social media advertising is best able to reach teenage problem drinkers?)

3.6.3 Thesis statements

What if, instead of a research question, you have been asked to provide a *thesis statement?* Is there a difference? Yes. Research questions and thesis statements are actually two sides of the same coin. A research question introduces a problem to be solved. A thesis statement is *a tentative answer* to a research question. It is tentative in that your written research project is going to have to test your thesis and hopefully show it to be correct. Thus, if your research question were:

To what extent should the U.S. government have known of the risk of the New York 9/11 disaster before it happened?

Your thesis statement could be:

There was sufficient warning of a New York 9/11-type disaster before it happened, so the U.S. government should have been well prepared for its occurrence.

Or your thesis might be:

Despite the signs of a potential terrorist attack, the U.S. government did not have sufficient information to be prepared for the New York 9/11 disaster.

For either of these possible thesis statements the onus would be on you to provide convincing evidence to support your thesis (as well as giving due consideration to contradicting evidence).

The thesis statement route does have a tendency to create a bias, giving you the temptation to overlook or minimize evidence that does not support your case. Thus, unless you have been told to provide a thesis statement, using a research question is more likely to have you entering the investigation with an open mind.

3.6.4 Research questions: The bad and the ugly

Some research questions simply won't work. They are doomed to failure and will produce research projects that are walking disasters, if they can walk at all. The worse the question, the worse will be your experience all through the research and writing process. One way to recognize a good question is to know what the bad and ugly ones look like, so here are some examples. [The APPENDIX will give you more examples and deeper explanations, so go there next]:

1. **The question that isn't there.** Imagine the horror of someone reading your "research" paper and looking desperately but in vain for a question or even the suggestion of an issue or problem to be addressed, only to discover that there is none. "What's the purpose of your paper?" the professor muses. "To tell me something I could have read in any reference book? To tell me once again what everyone knows already? To put me to sleep with your knowledge of trivia? To punish me for not being your favorite professor?"

2. **The fuzzy question.** Sure, there's a question, but it isn't clear enough to make it possible to answer. Asking something like, "Why do Republicans do the things they do?" is no help at all. What things do they do? Even if you figure this out, you probably have far too much to deal with. Until you clarify your focus, you will find no way to answer your question without simply surveying everything the world knows about Republicans (which would likely overwhelm you, not to mention your poor professor).

3. **The multi-part question.** *You must never let more than one research question intrude into a research project.* The shotgun approach is out. Research identifies *one* question, deals with that question through analytical use of data, and **then quits.** Never *ever* get stuck in the kind of proposal that says, "Why did the financial meltdown of 2008 happen? Should people have foreseen it? Were the governmental measures to solve it the

right ones to use? How can we prevent future meltdowns?" Your second, third and fourth questions are loose torpedoes on your own ship. They will sink you because they'll kill your focus or at least broaden it into something too big to deal with. *One question per research project is all you ever need or want.*

4. **The open-ended question**. This is often expressed as, "What are the implications of..." or "What were the results of...," thus encouraging you to produce a list of possible answers. Open-ended questions tend to be troublesome simply because they can fragment your conclusion into many possible responses and thus destroy any hope of the paper having a single-minded goal. The way to cure this kind of question is to close the end. For example, instead of asking, "What were the implications of the end of WWII?" you could ask, "To what extent was the fact that the car manufacturer, Renault, defied the French *Ministry of Industrial Production* after WWII the reason for its success?" You have set out only one possible area to study instead of many and thus closed up the end or goal for your project. The focus on the implications is now much narrower than it was.

5. **The question that will not fly**. Some questions are amazingly inventive, but they try to answer problems that the data can't answer. Asking, as did an undergraduate in one of my classes, "Is today's generation smarter than the previous one because it knows how to text message?" may look cool, but exactly how would texting ability serve as a measure of intelligence? What data would you provide? If your question is ambitious, ask yourself whether it's even possible to find an answer. If not, curb your enthusiasm.

Summary comment:

In my experience, the best research questions are *simple* ones that still require a good deal of analysis to answer. If you start with a highly complex question, your analysis is going to have to be that much more complex. The ideal is to have a question so simple and clear that you can actually see the goal before you, in your mind's eye, as well as the path you need to take to get there. Yet the path must involve some struggles before you get to the answer or it's not a real research question. And it must be capable of leading you to concrete evidence that supports your answer. You use the evidence that you gather as a means to discover the solution rather than as the solution itself.

[For more on research questions, including many more examples of both the good and the bad, see the APPENDIX. Yes, really. See the APPENDIX. You'll thank yourself later.]

Clearing the Fog: Research is a conversation, not a soliloquy

To be, or not to be, that is the question:
Whether 'tis Nobler in the mind to suffer
The Slings and Arrows of outrageous Fortune,
Or to take Arms against a Sea of troubles... (Shakespeare, Soliloquy from *Hamlet*)

A soliloquy is a revelation of a character's inner thoughts, sometimes reflecting on events of the past but always remaining personal. It is one person speaking his/her own mind in isolation from others. Research is not that.

When you do research, you enter into a conversation. Imagine that you are sitting in a room with several great scholars, each of whom has a perspective on the research question you're addressing. You listen to them and enjoy the way they debate with one another. Then you join in by evaluating their positions and perhaps coming to some conclusions about your own. It's all very civilized but it can get intense. [This idea was first suggested by Kenneth Burke, *The Philosophy of Literary Form*, (Berkeley: University of California Press, 1941), 110–111, and is often called "Burke's Parlor."]

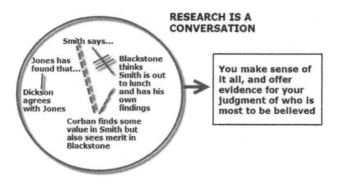

Research is a conversation. In too much of what is called "research" these days, the views of other scholars are just filler built around what you, the writer, want to say (your soliloquy). With such a misguided approach, the only reason to include material from other sources is that your professor said you needed 5 books and 3 articles. You assume they all pretty much say the same thing, and you wonder why you need all this stuff to explain something that maybe needs only two sources.

But that's not "research." Research is a conversation, even a debate. Each of the voices who are speaking though the information you've found has something to contribute, and your task is to make sense of what they are saying, critique it, and come out with your own conclusion on the matter. You pay attention to the differences in positions, and you take seriously the contribution each source is making. In the end, it's your own conclusion that matters most, but you haven't really succeeded at research until you've let the conversation happen.

3.7 The preliminary outline

Chances are that, if you're like most people, you're not in any mood early in a research project to be thinking about an outline for your final product. People who start working on their outline before they've done their first database search are either sick or lost souls, because any sensible person knows that you compose your outline AFTER you write your paper.

Wrong.

If you want to spare yourself a ton of grief, start on a preliminary outline now. Why? Simply because you need to build yourself as clear a roadmap as possible in order to get your research done efficiently (by "efficiently," I mean it will save you time). A research question may be crucial to giving your search a goal, but an outline is crucial to tracing the path you need to follow in order to reach that goal.

What's a preliminary outline? It is simply three to five points that you think you'll need to cover if you want to answer the research question. Don't worry; you won't permanently be bound to the outline, like the albatross around the neck of the Ancient Mariner. It's preliminary and open to modification. Yet, though it may change over time, you need to start on an outline now. It's your roadmap for your research project. Without a roadmap, you'll soon be on some dead end trail with no place to turn around and the search-and-rescue people looking for you.

How do you develop a preliminary outline? Begin with your research question and dig your outline out of terminology in your question. Suppose you have the following question: *Was the American belief that Saddam Hussein had weapons of mass destruction before the beginning of the Iraq War of 2003 based on plausible evidence?* The question itself gives clues to a preliminary outline. You need to look at evidence that he possibly did have such weapons and evidence that he didn't, then look at the plausibility of each side.

Once you have a few basic elements, try to organize them into a rough order. For example:

❖ Introduction to the history of belief in Saddam's weapons of mass destruction
❖ The evidence available at the time that Saddam had weapons of mass destruction

❖ Evaluation of the plausibility of the evidence available

❖ Conclusion

Essentially, the outline is drawn right out of the research question, like this:

Was the American belief that Saddam Hussein had weapons of mass destruction when the Iraq War of 2003 began based on plausible evidence?

- Introduction to the history of belief in Saddam's weapons of mass destruction

- The evidence available at the time that Saddam had weapons of mass destruction

- Evaluation of the plausibility of the information available

- Conclusion

Take note that your preliminary outline is just that—preliminary. You can develop it or change it at will, or even scrap it and create a new one. Your professor only needs to see the final version, so initial blips and failures will stay private. But you do need to get some sort of outline going as soon as you have a research question, because the outline tells you what you need to cover in order to write the paper that answers your research question.

3.8 How about a few good examples?

3.8.1 "The thought of Erasmus of Rotterdam"

Your much beloved philosophy professor has assigned you "The Thought of Erasmus of Rotterdam." Having studied a few philosophy dictionaries (and taken a peek at Wikipedia), you narrow your topic to "The Humanism of Erasmus of Rotterdam." You *could*, at this point, decide to begin your paper with "Erasmus of Rotterdam was born in the year..." You *could* go on to explain what he taught about humanism, and then conclude, "It is clear that Erasmus was an important thinker in the realm of humanism, who deserves more attention."

This method is called "regurgitating your sources." It establishes a conduit between your books/articles and your typing hand without ever really engaging your brain. It also makes for a very dull paper. Professors fall asleep over dull papers.

On the other hand, you could be analytical. Having read your sources and affixed your working knowledge firmly in your mind, you could engage your brain in finding a research question. How about asking this: *Why did Erasmus become increasingly pessimistic about human nature in his later years?* This would certainly demand study of Erasmus' humanism, but it would go further. Now you have the makings of an approach that could contribute something fresh and exciting to the topic.

Outline:
1. Erasmus' humanism
2. His increasing pessimism
3. Potential reasons for his pessimism
4. Conclusion

3.8.2 "Teenage Alcoholism"

You are taking a sociology class and are supposed to write a paper on "Teenage Alcoholism." I suppose you could regurgitate some statistics, recite a few case studies, and then conclude, "This is a serious problem for which we need to find answers." Or you might narrow your topic and ask a genuine research question like this one: *Of the most common school-based models used to address Teenage Alcoholism, which shows the most promise?*

Outline:
1. The problem of teenage alcoholism
2. School-based models that address it
   a.
   b.
   c.
3. Evaluation of models
4. Conclusion

3.8.3 "Climate Change"

For a course on environmental issues, you have been assigned, "Climate Change." You could write up a true horror story about the loss of Arctic ice, along with a warning at the end that "somebody" needs to do something. A descriptive paper like this one would string together quotations from current leaders in the debate who are decrying the way our leaders studiously ignore the problem. Your conclusion could read, "Thus it is clear that governments must change their attitudes." You have narrowed your topic, but you've failed to apply an analytical, problem-solving research question to it. An analytical research paper would go further, perhaps looking at the cost to the world economy that comes from saving a few bucks by ignoring climate change. Your question could be: *Is it ultimately good for the economy in times of economic downturn to devote less money to address climate change?*

Outline:
1. The call to address climate change
2. Argument that addressing climate change is bad for the economy
3. Argument that addressing climate change is ultimately good for the economy
4. Conclusion

3.8.4 "Behaviorism as a model for social engineering"

You have been given a topic which is fairly narrow but still covers a lot of territory. Behaviorism as a social engineering model entails a lot of ins and outs. Why not narrow it down to the Behaviorism model put forward by B.F. Skinner? You might now take the easy way and summarize his book *Walden Two*, which is Skinner's model for social engineering (but easy is the way that leads to destruction). Or you could ask: *How would B.F. Skinner revise his model of human living in Walden Two if darker basic human traits like selfishness, aggressiveness, and deceit were taken into account?* (things which Skinner blissfully ignored).

Outline:
1. Skinner's model of human living in Walden Two
2. The problem of lack of reference to negative human traits
3. How Skinner's model might have been different if negative traits were included.

One final note of caution: **Always clear your narrowed-down topic and brilliant research question with your professor or supervisor**. Disaster could be awaiting you if you don't. Of course, some of us like to flirt with disaster. Do you feel lucky?

3.9 For further study

Study guide

1. What three things do you need to seek if you want to do research well?
2. Name four elements of "inadequate research." Why is each an enemy of "great" research?
3. Define a "working knowledge" of your topic and explain why it's important to have one.
4. What is a "reference source?"

5. What should we do with Wikipedia?
6. What are the steps to finding a good research question?
7. Formulate a definition of genuine research.
8. Describe the difference between a research question and a thesis statement. Why is the former often a safer approach?
9. Describe the following types of bad research questions: The fuzzy question, the multi-part question, the open-ended question, the question that will not fly.
10. Why do you need a preliminary outline early in the research process?

Practice with research questions

Go to the APPENDIX and try *A.2 Practice with Research Questions*

Assignment for a research project of your own

1. Choose a topic of interest to you.
2. Get basic information for a working knowledge of your topic from at least one specialized reference source from the library (not a general encyclopedia but a subject specialized reference source like *Dictionary of Developmental & Educational Psychology*) and from Wikipedia. Compare and contrast the ways in which the library reference source and Wikipedia deal with the topic.
3. Summarize in about half a page what you've learned (your working knowledge), *listing the reference sources you used*.
4. Present three or four possible research questions related to the topic, in question form, which might be suitable for a research essay. These questions should deal with one aspect of the topic, as narrowly as possible. They should not be easy to answer, nor should they be intended to describe what is already known. Try to make them as analytical as you can (seeing them as problem-solving questions rather than as an

attempt to compile existing data). Try turning each of them into a thesis statement.

5. Choose the one question or thesis statement you think is best.
6. Create a preliminary outline based on your question.

Teaching tool

For a short animated tutorial on the research model presented here, go to:

https://www.youtube.com/watch?v=p-qLraS3sGk&feature= youtu.be

4

Database Searching with Keywords and Hierarchies

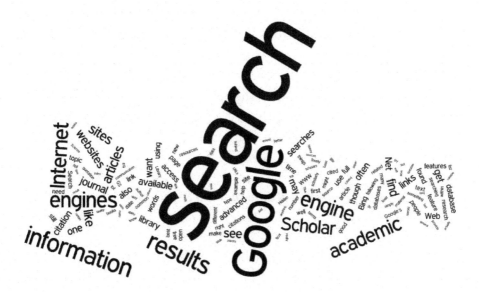

It's time to begin traveling into the realm of e-searching, a land much more complex and (frankly) more exciting than you ever imagined when you first Googled something and actually got what you were looking for. So pack your bags. We're going to be out there in the land of search for at least two chapters. On the plus side, by the end of our exploration you're sure to be a better and wiser searcher.

4.1 What's a database?

Chances are that you fancy yourself as a tech genius and the word "database" doesn't sound like "root canal." But this doesn't mean you have a full perception of what a database does or have learned how to search a database quickly and effectively, coming up with the results you need most of the time.

Then again, you may not yet have warmed to the possibility of search tools beyond Google, nor do you think of journal databases as friendly creatures ever ready to help you, like a big Saint Bernard in avalanche territory. For you, "database" may well be a bad word, a frightening word. If that's your situation, let me give you a soothing message: "Fear not."

Actually, databases are everywhere, and I guarantee you've already searched one or more, though not necessarily with all the skill you needed. When was the last time you Googled anything or searched Amazon for a widget you just have to have? We're talking about databases. Here's a definition:

A database is any collection of data that can be retrieved using organized search procedures.

Many people today are hotshots on various devices. They can make the keys sing, the app activate and the pages scroll. They think that they are also expert searchers, because they know their way around the technology. Not so. In fact, few of us understand database searching well enough to do it effectively, let alone efficiently.

More and more research is pointing to the fact that most students overestimate their abilities in searching for information. They *really* overestimate their abilities. Not good news to hear, but somebody needs to say it: You could probably do with some further guidance in making databases work for you.

Case in point—I once found the dregs of a search on an electronic journal database. The database itself had over 1,000,000 article citations listed in it, and this searcher had typed in the keyword

Johnson, resulting in 4,386 hits. That is, 4,386 descriptive records of journal articles related to the name *Johnson* had become available to him/her. What was worse, the searcher had actually started pulling up each of those 4,386 entries in turn, looking for the right one. Ten hours later, red-eyed, fingers like angry claws...one can only imagine the *angst* that this session created.

You may know how to make technology work for you, but disaster will befall you if you are limited in your ability to search databases. It's a whole lot more than throwing a few words into a search box. Fear not, however. I'm about to show you things you probably never knew you didn't know.

4.2 Keyword searching

The keyword has become the main tool of research in today's electronic database environment, and many people assume that keywords are their friends.

That's not exactly the case. Have you ever had "friends" you trusted only to a certain point, because you had to tell yourself to watch your back when you were around them? You knew they appeared decent and could be helpful, but they could just as easily betray you or do you harm. That's the keyword: Useful, handy, but potentially a backstabber. Keywords represent the Wild West of database searching: bold and exciting, but risky and just as likely to mess up your life.

In the next chapter we'll look at a more civilized and sophisticated way to search many databases (with controlled vocabularies), but for now, let's do what we can to tame the fickle keyword.

4.2.1 Database basics for keyword searching

We start with the principle that every database (collection of data) is made up of words. The search tools we use, though inherently unintelligent when it comes to real thinking, are experts at recognizing words. To understand how keyword searching works, you need to know that most academic databases contain descriptive *records* that stand in the place of actual content when you search. That is, you are not actually searching the content but descriptions of the content. For example, every time a new book is added to a library, it is processed by creating a descriptive **catalog record,** which might look something like this:

Author:	Smith, Gary, 1945- author.
Title:	Standard deviations: flawed assumptions, tortured data, and other ways to lie with statistics / Gary Smith.
Publisher:	New York : Overlook Duckworth, 2014.
Edition:	First edition.
Description:	326 pages : illustrations ; 24 cm
LC Call No.:	QA279.S638 2014
Book Number:	PSY000000
Dewey No.:	519.5 23
ISBN:	9781468309201 (hardback)
	146830920X (hardback)
Notes:	Includes bibliographical references (pages 299-319) and index.
Subjects:	Standard deviations.

This is a description of the main details that the database needs to have available in order for you to identify and find the book. When you search the database by keyword, you will be looking for *significant words* in this record. You are actually searching the descriptive records, not the book content itself, at this stage. Now, imagine that there are thousands of records, and you're interested in finding a list of books about interactive aspects of the Internet. You should be able to think of important words (= *keywords*) and input them into a search box. The database search program will then look for those words in each of the **records** in the database and will download to your screen any records that have the words you've asked for.

To find books, for example, on interactive aspects of Internet use, you might search book titles in the database like this:

Interact* and Internet (Don't worry about the search form yet. We'll get to the details below).

You will get records for books with titles like:

- *Interaction and collective intelligence in **Internet** computing*
- *Digital borderlands : cultural studies of identity and **interactivity** on the **Internet***
- *Murder on the Net : a guide to logging on and using the **Internet** via an **interactive** murder mystery adventure*

(All of the above are real book titles.)

Insight #1: *With keyword searching, what you type is what you get. The search program you use cannot do much to interpret your request or give you the next best solution (though some may search on a few synonyms). All it can do is identify the words you ask for and give you the relevant data. Garbage in, garbage out.*

Notice one little trick I performed above: *truncation* (sometimes inaccurately called *wildcard*). With many keyword searches, you can type part of a word, then add an asterisk (*) or sometimes a question mark (?) or dollar sign ($), depending on what symbol the database uses, and the search software will look for every word that begins with the letters you typed. E.g., **interact*** will ask create a search for search for **interact**, **interactive**, **interaction**, even **interactivity**. (Take note: Most search engines on the Net do not use truncation.)

You can also sometimes do **middle truncation** (the real meaning of "wildcards"), in which truncation is done within a word (e.g., Wom*n for Woman or Women).

Even given the variations allowed through truncation, keyword searching demands a whole lot of precision. The search function in the database will only find the exact thing you want it to find. If you mistakenly type **intract★** instead of **interact★**, the search function will give you data with words like **intractable**, thus spoiling your whole day and making you grouchy in social environments. So your first grade teacher was right: Spell it right the first time.

4.2.2 Boolean searching

Many years before computers, a man named George Boole invented a mathematical system that enabled people to visualize combinations of various classes of things. Tech people have taken his system into the world of database searching in order to formulate searches where two or more terms are used. Let's look at some of the basic commands used in Boolean searching:

The OR Command

Suppose that you're looking in a database for information about cars. You realize that a keyword search will pull out all information that has the word "cars" in it, but some people use the term "automobiles." How can you tell the database search program to look for *both* words at the same time and give you data whether that data uses the word "cars" *or* the word "automobiles?"

In a situation in which you are searching for synonyms—different words that mean the same thing—use the OR command. Let's visualize it this way:

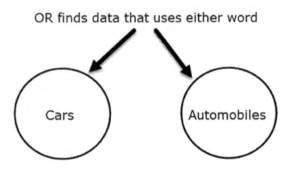

OR finds data that uses either word

Cars   Automobiles

That is, you are saying, "Database Search Program, please give me everything on cars or on automobiles. I don't care which." So you will get all the data with "cars" in it, plus all the data with "automobiles" in it. Both words don't have to be in each of your results. Any one word will do.

In a keyword search in a library catalog or some other database, your search may look like this:

Cars OR Automobiles

Another situation calling for an **OR** search might be that in which two concepts are closely related, and you suspect that finding data on either of them will further your overall goal. For example, in doing a search for "Gestalt Therapy" you might also want to search for the father of Gestalt Therapy—Fritz Perls. You can formulate a search like this:

(Gestalt Therapy) OR (Fritz Perls)

Notice that I've blocked out phrases with parentheses. Some databases, and most Internet search engines, use quotation marks instead: "Gestalt Therapy" OR "Fritz Perls". Check out the help screen in the database to see what it uses. With an **OR** search, you typically get a lot of "hits", that is, citations to relevant data in the database.

Insight #2: *An OR search is usually for synonyms or for keywords that are already closely related. You use it to anticipate the various ways something might be described or approached so that you don't have to do multiple individual searches.*

The only alternative to doing an OR search is to do separate searches on each of your search terms and then compile the sets of results. OR lets you avoid the pain of such an experience.

The AND Command

Probably the most profitable way to use keywords is to combine them so that you can narrow down a search. For example, if you wanted to look at the problem of educating homeless youth, a keyword search could be formulated to produce very precise results.

Let's visualize it with a diagram first. If you're searching for the relationship between homeless youth and education, you don't want every piece of data about homeless youth, nor do you want every piece of data about education. You want the data that comes when homeless youth and education intersect. Thus:

AND finds only the data that uses both terms

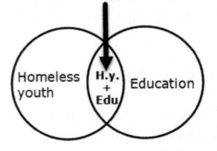

Your formulated keyword search will look like this:

(Homeless youth) AND Education

A tip: Be very careful not to add unnecessary words to AND searches. Suppose that you were searching for material in a database on Osama bin Laden's influence before and during the Iraq War of 2003 (including his supposed alliance with Saddam Hussein). The temptation might be to load up your search with terminology, along the lines of:

(Osama bin Laden) AND (Iraq War)
AND 2003 AND influence

But stop and think: You are searching for *keywords*, probably in a title. Are all these words likely to appear in a title, along the lines of "The Influence of Osama bin Laden on the Iraq War of 2003?" What if the database had an article whose was, "Bin Laden and the Iraq War?" It's on target as far as your search goals are concerned, but your multiword search above is going to eliminate this article from the result list. Why? Because the article doesn't have the words **Osama** and **influence**, nor the date **2003**, in its title. In other words, you eliminated a good article from your results by using too much terminology.

How do you solve a problem like this? You do it by becoming a minimalist.

Insight #3: *With an AND search, always look for the fewest number of terms required to get data that is on target with your search goals. The more unnecessary terms you add, the more you risk screening out good data that does not use those terms.*

For the search above, all you really need is:

(Bin Laden) AND (Iraq War)

You might even be able to get rid of **Bin**. The "2003" isn't needed either, because Bin Laden had little involvement in the 1990 Iraq war (other than wanting his fellow Saudis to handle Saddam themselves instead of letting the Americans do it).

Insight #4: *A keyword AND search is used to search for data that relates two or more topics or concepts together. The data found will show the effect of the relationship between or among these topics.*

An **AND** search is a limiting kind of search. It asks the search program to provide data only when that data contains *all* the keywords linked by **AND**. Thus, you should expect that an **AND** search will give you fewer hits than if you had searched each keyword on its own. This can be a difficult concept to grasp. If you're having trouble with it, go back up to the **AND** search diagram. Or consider the example above: you don't want every piece of data about Bin Laden plus every piece of data about the Iraq War. You want only the data that *relates* Bin Laden to the Iraq War. Thus the **AND** search has set limits for your search. It has narrowed down the data that you want to receive.

Insight #5: *AND searches will narrow or limit your topic. Thus you can expect that you will not get as many "hits" with an AND search as with an OR search.*

Nesting ANDs and ORs

There are times when, within your AND search, several synonyms of key terms are possible. Unless you enjoy doing multiple searches, you can combine synonyms into your search by "nesting" ORs within an AND search:

Homeless AND (youth OR adolescen*)
AND (education OR school*)

This might look like it's contradicting the caution I just gave about avoiding over-complicated searches, but there are actually only three words that are linked with AND. The rest are alternate terminology using OR, which will not eliminate relevant articles.

You can see that I put parentheses around (i.e., "nested") the OR terms that belong together, because search programs can sometimes get confused. The parentheses make it clear to the search engine how to treat this search. Notice as well that I truncated adolescen* so I could include, in one search, "adolescent," "adolescence," and "adolescents." I also truncated "school" to cover both "schools" and "schooling."

The NOT Command

If I'm back to looking for information about cars, but I'm *not* interested in any car made in Europe, a NOT search is what I need (Please don't send me e-mails and texts asking why I have a problem with European cars - it's a long story). With this search, I want to tell the search engine to give me everything about cars but no data about European cars. Here's how to do a NOT search:

*(cars OR automobiles) NOT Europe**

Notice what I've done. First, I took note of the fact that "automobiles" is a synonym for "cars." Thus I included both terms, nesting them with parentheses so as not to confuse the search engine as to what I meant when I added my **NOT** command. Then I added the **NOT** and did a truncation on Europe (using an asterisk) so the search engine could identify "Europe" and "European" with a single search. What I'm saying with my search terms is that I want data about either cars or automobiles as long I don't have to deal with European cars or automobiles.

Exceptions to the Above

Exceptions? Why are there always exceptions? Probably because every database likes to do its own thing. Here are some variations that you may find to the standard Boolean **OR**, **AND**, **NOT** searches:

- ❖ In many databases, you can do an **AND** search simply by leaving a space between words. Thus, instead of:
  homeless youth AND education
  you can type: **homeless youth education**
- ❖ But note that some other databases will see **homeless youth education** as a phrase, thus requiring you to put the AND back in between "youth" and "education.

❖ In some databases, **NOT** has to be expressed as **AND NOT**. In Internet search engines, **NOT** is generally expressed with a hyphen before a word, with no spaces:

–European

❖ Many databases ask you to put quotation marks around words that need to appear together, e.g.:

"apple trees"

❖ Others call for parentheses: ***(apple trees)***.

❖ There are some databases that actually search for synonyms of the term(s) you input so that they can bring up material you might not have found through a simple keyword search.

❖ Some databases provide a choice of search boxes with which to build searches, like the first example below (AND, phrase, OR, and NOT searches). Others will use a search grid with drop-down boxes like the second example below:

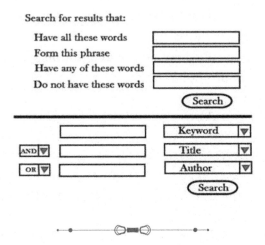

Clearing the Fog: What's the best way to choose keywords?

It's all very well to know how to use keywords, but experience shows that many people struggle with what words to choose in the first place. Here's a common misunderstanding I regularly observe: We want to talk to the database like it's a person. We want to *explain* our goal. This generally results in using too many words. It also produces monstrosities.

For example, you are researching the question, "How well has the government done in tightening bank regulations since the recession that began in 2008?" So you try to explain to your database what you want, and it comes out like this: *Government control of banking so we won't have another recession like 2008.* Nasty business, that. First, you have lots of words that the database won't even look at: "of," "so we won't have," "another," "like." Second, nothing in your search terminology says you are also seeking information on banking regulations. Trying to explain stuff to a database doesn't work, because databases don't think like human beings. They search for words.

So how do you fix your search? As much as possible, use actual words from your research question, or at least synonyms of these words. And keep it simple. Try this out: *"Bank regulations" recession.* If you need to get more precise results, try *"Bank regulations" "since the recession."*

Rule of thumb: If you want results that reflect what you are seeking in your research question, then use search terminology that comes directly out of your research question. And never try to explain to a database. That's usually about as successful as asking your dog where she buried your cell phone.

4.3 Keyword searching with hierarchies

Keywords are flat. What do I mean? Keyword search engines scan across the broad surface of databases looking for matches. I type in "Iraq" and the search engine finds the word "Iraq." In some results, Iraq is the main topic. In others it is incidental to whatever the data is actually about. Sometimes the results are about the culture of Iraq, sometimes the people of Iraq, sometimes the history of Iraq. Because keywords are flat - simply appearing where they appear without revealing the depths of context and meaning - keyword search engines bring up all occurrences of a word, regardless of what surrounding meaning or definition is present. This can be a problem, because real knowledge is not flat but hierarchical.

4.3.1 Hierarchies

I know this is starting to look like hard going, but I'll try not to make it too threatening. Let's start with a brief look at how knowledge is organized. Put quite simply (because I'm only really capable of simplicity), every bit of knowledge has a context within which it fits. Most knowledge can be organized from broad categories (at the top) to narrow categories (at the bottom). The broad categories help to determine the meaning and boundaries of the narrow ones. Let me illustrate:

Can you define the following word?

ROCK

"Sure," you say. "It's a hard object that comes out of the ground."

To which I answer, "How wrong you are! Don't you know that 'rock' is a verb?" My definition, a symptom of my growing age, is that the only rock worth anything is the rock I do in my rocking chair.

"I'm not wrong," you retort. "You're wrong."

To which your friend standing next to us says with a smirk, "You're both wrong. It's music. Classic Rock is real music, and I'd rather be listening to it than wasting time hearing you argue about definitions."

What's the problem here? Why can't we agree on the meaning for one word with only four letters in it? The reason is simple: *Words by themselves don't really mean anything for certain. They need a context.* If I say, "I'm planning to take a whole evening to rock in my rocking chair," you know that my definition of 'rock' is something like 'a back and forth motion.' If, on the other hand, I say, "The rock that went through my window was two inches across," you know that 'rock' is now a noun meaning 'a hard substance taken from the earth.'

Words only have a definite meaning when you put them in a context. Words get their meaning from the sentences surrounding them. In turn, sentences become understandable within their paragraphs, and paragraphs make sense within the larger context of the complete document. The important word here is "context." Meaning is derived from context, and without context we have only confusion.

So what? How do meaning and context relate to research? Exactly like this: All data exists within one or more information hierarchies (contexts). Let me illustrate with the word "rock."

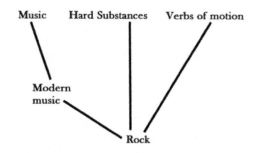

"Rock' is a sub-class of more comprehensive categories. For example, "rock" may be a sub-class of modern music, right alongside other sub-classes like "adult contemporary," "elevator music," and the compositions of John Cage. "Modern music" in turn is a sub-class of the larger category of "music" along with other sub-classes like "classical," "baroque," etc. What we end up with is a hierarchy. Each higher grouping is broader than the one below it.

But notice that "rock" is capable of having several different hierarchies attached to it, depending on the meaning we give to the word. It can also be a sub-class of "hard substances in the earth" or of "verbs indicating motion."

All data comes within a context. Without context the data cannot tell us what we need to know.

Let's now move into an area that better resembles a research topic.

Take something like the Roman emperor Constantine. Depending on how you approach him, he can exist within a number of contexts (= hierarchies):

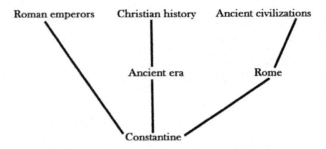

You can deal with him as a sub-class of "Roman emperors" alongside other sub-classes like Julius Caesar and Nero. "Roman emperors" in turn are a subclass of "Roman history", which in turn is a sub-class of "Ancient History." Alternatively, you can deal with him as an important figure within the larger subject of "Early Christian History," since he was the first emperor who affirmed Christianity so that it could eventually become the official Roman religion. Or you can discuss him within the higher class of "Ancient Civilizations," since he ruled one of them. Each of these hierarchies leads to a different approach to the same topic.

Information is hierarchical. The key to making use of this fact is simply this:

Insight #6: *In research, you must always know where you are in the hierarchy. What higher class does your topic belong to? Are there other hierarchies your topic could belong to? Are there sub-classes of your topic that could become factors to consider?*

We live in a time of "sight-bites." Information comes to us in tiny chunks, and Twitter is king. But sight-bites can leave us confused, like a tweet without the thread it belongs to. The more our data is disconnected from its setting (context) the more likely we are not to grasp its full meaning or to misinterpret it. Every time we encounter any kind of search result, we need to be thinking about what it is a part of, what its context is, where it belongs in the larger scheme of things. When you are doing research, you really don't want to be scattered like snowflakes in a blizzard. You want your data to pull together into something that makes sense.

4.3.2 Clustering search tools

Most traditional search engines on the World Wide Web (including Google and Bing) do a flat search for keywords thus separating results from their possible hierarchies. For example, if I search for "William Badke" in Google, I get a bunch of website links to all aspects of me (frightening, isn't it?). But those results don't distinguish between Badke the author, Badke the librarian, Badke the faculty member, Badke the fairly unsuccessful fiction writer, and so on. Badke is always only Badke (sigh).

A few tools are attempting to do something about this. Let's look at some of them:

4.3.2.1 Carrot2 (http://search.carrot2.org/stable/search)

Carrot2 is an example of a clustering search engine. It does a metasearch of a number of standalone search engines and then gathers main topic links in a list. When I search on my name, it includes the expected citations of various websites, and it lists the following linked terms in a side column:

All Topics (85)
    Research Strategies (15)
    Trinity Western University (13)
    Associate Librarian (10)
    Finding Your Way (9)
    Information Literacy (9)
    Edition (6)
    Faculty (4)

High School Sports (4) *[Sorry, not me. Certainly not me]*
Study (4)
Google Books (3)
more | show all

Mercifully, unlike what actually happens with some search engines, Carrot2 doesn't ask me if I mean William Blake, or William Badge (both of which are blows to my ego). Instead, it gives me a way to focus my search on one *aspect*, for example, information literacy (though they got the wrong guy on the "High School Sports" thing).This tool has pulled key subject language out of my initially flat search, subject language that can group my results by the context (hierarchy) within which it exists.

Thus websites related to my book *Research Strategies* (15 of them) are grouped together in that context. Websites about my work in "information literacy" are grouped together as well. Then comes my mythical role in high school sports, and so on. All are aspects of my WWW persona arranged hierarchically from my initial search on my name.

4.3.2.2 Yippy (http://www.yippy.com/)

Yippy is similar in its clustering function to Carrot2, but has a cooler name. This alone makes it worth checking out.

Insight #7: *It is important to think hierarchically. What you are searching for belongs to a higher and broader category and may well have several narrower aspects that come below it. Knowing where you are in the hierarchy is important to enable you to broaden or narrow your searching intelligently.*

4.4 Keyword searching: The good, bad, and ugly

The good part of keyword searching is that it is quick and flexible, as well as giving you the opportunity to narrow down to specific topic areas or combine concepts from more than one subject discipline.

The bad part is that you are controlled by the *treachery of words*. What do I mean? Simply that different words can mean much the same thing, or a single word (e.g., rock) can be capable of a lot of possible meanings. Keywords as search tools can easily betray you.

The ugly part is that keywords are flat. They aren't capable of telling you whether your result is broad or narrow in relation to your topic, nor can they spell out the hierarchical contexts within which your keyword might be found. Clustering search engines try to overcome this problem by suggesting contexts that form hierarchies within which your keyword results can live.

So use keywords, but be aware that they are not superheroes. In fact, that designation may well go to controlled vocabularies, our next topic.

4.5 For further study

Study guide

1. What is a "database?" Name a few examples of familiar databases.
2. What is a "database record?"
3. In keyword searching, what strong ability of computers is used?
4. What is a "truncation" or "wildcard?" Give an example along with the appropriate symbol.
5. Explain the "OR command" in Boolean searching and indicate in what types of searches it works best.
6. Explain the "AND command" in Boolean searching and indicate in what types of searches it works best.
7. Explain the "NOT command" in Boolean searching and indicate in what types of searches it works best.

8. Some databases will allow you to leave out the Boolean AND, and just input keywords with spaces between them. In other databases, if you do this the computer program will understand that you are constructing a _____.

9. Why do words by themselves have no definite meaning? How do they get a meaning?

10. All data comes within a _____.

11. Explain an "information hierarchy." Choose two or three topics and illustrate how each fits into one or more hierarchies (a diagram works best for this).

12. Regarding hierarchies, in research you must know where you are _____ _____ _____.

13. What does it mean to say that keywords are "flat?"

14. How do clustering search tools like Yippy help to resolve the problem of the flatness of keywords?

Practice with keywords and hierarchies

1. How would you formulate a keyword search to get results in a database on the following?
   a. The causes of World War One.
   b. Destruction of the museums in Iraq during the 2003 war.
   c. The role of crime in the novel, *The Great Gatsby*
   d. The problem of fear in patients with the psychological disorder "paranoia."
   e. Teen violence.
   f. The movie, *Vanilla Sky* (as opposed to the painting, *Vanilla Sky*).
   g. Kidney stones in Schnauzers.
   h. Racial conflict in London.
   i. Relationship between unemployment and homelessness in Cleveland.
   j. Stravinsky's musical composition, *The Rite of Spring*.

2. Try a search on Yippy **(http://www.yippy.com/)**, starting with the keyword **Napoleon** and finding sites on the original

Napoleon as opposed to fireplaces and grills (Hint: Use the left column).

3. Create some hierarchical diagrams for the following: *Microsoft, Iraq, Arnold Schwarzenegger,* and *Anorexia.* Indicate three possible higher contexts and three lower.

Suggested key to practice with keywords

1. Keyword Search Terms (My Suggestions)
    a. *The causes of World War One*: This is actually a tough one because you can call this war World War One, World War I, WWI, and even The Great War. Most of these descriptors are actually phrases, and it may be hard to combine them in a search in a database while maintaining their identity as phrases. You may have to search each possibility in turn, e.g., World War One AND Cause* (notice the truncation), World War I AND Cause*, and so on. **Note that Internet search engines don't use truncation well (*), so save truncated searches for library catalogs and journal databases.**
    b. *Destruction of the museums in Iraq during the 2003 war*: Likely you can get by here with as little as Museum* AND Iraq AND War. Don't worry about the 2003, since the 1990 Iraq war did not raise the issue of museums, so the database will have no problem distinguishing the two wars.
    c. *The role of crime in the novel,* The Great Gatsby: The name Gatsby is rare. In this case, you don't need to fill the search with terms. Simply try Gatsby AND Crime.
    d. *The problem of fear in patients with the psychological disorder paranoia*: You have a challenge with the term Paranoia, since it is widely used in contexts other than psychology. Thus, a search like Paranoia AND Fear could create a lot of irrelevant hits, among which will be a few that deal with the psychological disorder variety of paranoia. But don't think that adding terminology like Psychological

Disorder will help the situation. It won't, simply because keyword searches look for *words*. It's unlikely that the writers of an article on fear issues in the psychological disorder of paranoia will use the title, "Fear Issues in the Psychological Disorder of Paranoia." The title will much more likely be "Fear in Paranoia," or something similar. Our discussion of controlled vocabularies in the next chapter will offer an alternative to solve this problem.

- e. *Teen violence*: Try (Teen★ OR Adolescen★ OR Youth) AND violence. Note the use of truncation and the choice of synonyms in an OR search.

- f. *The movie,* Vanilla Sky *(as opposed to the painting,* Vanilla Sky*)*: Try Vanilla Sky AND Movie, or even Vanilla Sky AND Cruise [because the movie starred Tom Cruise.]

- g. *Kidney stones in Schnauzers*: Try Kidney Stones AND Schnauzers. With AND searches, always try to make it as simple a process as possible.

- h. *Racial conflict in London*: Try Race AND London, but there is a potential that "race" may bring up material on racing. Perhaps Racial AND London would work more effectively. Avoid adding terminology like Problems, Issues, and so on, since title terminology of your data rarely uses such terms.

- i. *Relationship between unemployment and homelessness in Cleveland*: Try Unemploy★ AND Homeless★ AND Cleveland. [Remember, if you are trying this in an Internet search engine, most don't use truncation (★), so you will need to spell out the whole word.]

- j. *Stravinsky's musical composition,* The Rite of Spring: For this one, continue the principle that short and simple is better than filling a search with terminology. Since this composition is distinctive, Rite of Spring should be enough. If it's not, add **AND Stravinsky**.

2. To the left of your search results for **Napoleon**, you will find a link to sites for Napoleon Bonaparte.

3. The following are merely suggestions. Other options are possible:

Microsoft—higher categories: computer software, competition laws, successful companies. Lower categories: Office, court cases, Microsoft's emphasis change from computers to smaller devices.

Iraq—higher categories: Archaeology, Arab Nations, History of War. Lower categories: Destruction of museums in Iraq in 2003, Iraq's relations with Iran, the Iraq war of 2003.

Arnold Schwarzenegger—higher categories: Body building, movie actors, politicians. Lower categories: Arnold as actor, the 2003 California recall election, Arnold's movies after his governorship.

Anorexia—higher categories: Weight loss, psychological conditions, eating disorders. Lower categories: The medical consequences of anorexia, the role of self-esteem in Anorexia, the role of "thin culture" in the increase of anorexia cases.

Assignment for a research project of your own

1. State a research question on a topic of your choice. Have a good look at it and determine exactly what you want to search for.
2. Do a *keyword* search for books in a library catalog by:
   a. Choosing important words related to your topic, and doing searches by these words either individually or in Boolean combinations. ***Indicate the actual searches you tried, e.g., (Skinner OR behaviorism) AND Walden.***
   b. Listing 8-10 books, **relevant** to your topic, which you identified through your keyword search. Keep as narrowly focused on your research question goal as possible.

5

Metadata and the Power of
Controlled Vocabularies

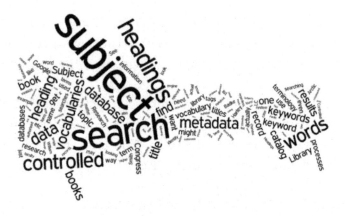

The terminology of this chapter title may have you quivering in dismay, but you're about to learn some cool words to impress your friends and some cooler concepts to make you a better searcher than you ever could have been with keywords alone. I do have to lay a bit of theory on you, though. Sorry about that. Theory seems too often like joining a club with a tough initiation. The task of getting in might be more frightening than the potential membership benefits. In this case, however, understanding a few basics will help the rest of the chapter make sense.

5.1 It's all about the metadata

Research is a quest that can make you trek into mighty strange territory to harvest the information you need. This is the task of "search." If you are devoted Googler (or Bing-er, or whatever) you already know about the joys and sorrows of search. One disturbing fact emerges: search is a messy thing, often leaving us with far more results that we *don't* need than the few we do. So you find yourself saying to your search box, "No, no, no, I want *this*, not *that*, you blockhead search engine."

And it is exactly that: a blockhead, I mean. Search engines are not intelligent creatures. They recognize letters and words, and they can find exactly what you type into the box. But they don't know when the actual results are irrelevant, even though those results contain your search words. In fact, they don't even know what your words mean.

Now imagine that you're trying to discover why Google personalizes search results (more on this later, including a Clearing the Fog vignette from me). So you go to the Google search engine and type in **Google personalization.** A lot of the results are from the Google site, and none of them specifically seem to be addressing the "why" question.

So now you search **Google personalization "why do they do it"** (using quotation marks to search it as a phrase). The results are mostly useless. In fact, the first citation is a Google Books excerpt of an earlier edition of this book. What went wrong? Well, part of the problem is that you are trying to ask Google a question with your **"why do they do it"** phrase. Your question requires Google to work through a complex cognitive task, something it is trying to learn how to do but hasn't quite pulled off yet. Google doesn't reason at all well, despite its claims that it does. A better search term would be **Google personalization rationale** (results will be closer to what you are looking for). A more significant reason for your bad results is that Google isn't functioning with any serious metadata.

In this chapter I want to take you into the heart of the machine to understand why some searches succeed and others fail. I want you to get a grasp of why some databases work better than others and why this has everything to do with the way those databases and their data are constructed. So here goes.

5.2 Understanding metadata

It might seem better for me to avoid throwing complicated terminology at you, because you get enough of that in the normal course of your life, but "metadata" is a cool concept, and knowing what it means can make you a winner at social gatherings. Metadata is simply descriptive terminology that enables a seeker to do more intelligent searches of databases beyond the use of keywords. To understand metadata, you need to grasp how databases are constructed.

Any database is only as useful as its retrieval capability. If you can't retrieve specifically what you need, when you need it, then what you have is a data dump, not a database. For some databases, and for much of the WWW, retrieval is done solely through keywords that are found within the data itself. This, as we will see, is a pretty ineffective way to locate specific pieces of information.

Enter metadata. If a database constructor wants to be successful in setting up data for retrieval, good metadata will do the trick. Consider this fictional listing from an online telephone directory:

Smith, Harley Q.
2947 Olivier Ave.,
Anytown, WA.
699-555-4023

This is a name, address and phone number for one listing in a phone directory. Now, suppose that you're doing what the few people who still use land lines do these days - looking up the number of a friend. Imagine for a moment that the directory you're using only searches on keywords, that is, it searches on the full text of entries like the one above, making no distinctions in categories within the results. Your search is: **Harley Smith,** and it finds:

Boyton, **Harley**, 7690 **Smith** St., Clumpers, MN. 908-555-2956
Harley, John, 2187 Jones St., **Smith**, ND 867-555-4289
Smith, Amos, 2798 **Harley** Rd., Johnstown, AR 223-555-1972

Smith, Douglas, 1197 Samuels Ave., **Harley**, CN. 256-555-6843
Smith, **Harley** Q. 2947 Olivier Ave., Anytown, WA. 699-555-4023

You can see that this database isn't very concerned about word order or word proximity, and that it doesn't know a personal name from a street name. It doesn't even know if Harley is the first name of a person, last name of a person or the name of a town. The keywords are all there, but you got 5 results instead of one, and all but one are not what you were looking for. (For a cool video from Google on the problem some search engines have with giving you everything you *don't* want, see **https://youtu.be/cbtf1oyNg-8**.)

So what was the problem? A lack of metadata. The database search engine simply looked for your search words in a sea of undifferentiated text. It had no way of identifying the name of a person.

Now let me show you how a good phone number database sets itself up:

First Name: Harley
Last Name: Smith
Street: 2947 Olivier Ave.
City: Anytown
State: WA
Phone: 699-555-4023

Each shaded part (or "field") of the above entry serves as an identifier (e.g., Name, Street, City) that distinguishes something you might want to look up. The encoding is metadata: that is, a system of descriptors that come along with the data. The database is constructed so that, when you enter a search in an online version of this phone listing, your search box might look like this:

Find a Person

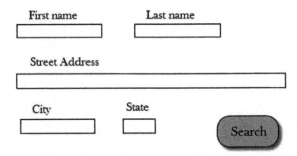

Searching first name Harley and last name Smith will get you:

Smith, Harley Q. 2947 Olivier Ave., Anytown, WA. 699-555-4023

You get only one (correct) result. Why? Because the database creators inserted *metadata* [descriptive labels] into the data to distinguish names from street addresses from cities. Now the database knows the difference between a personal name and a city name, so you get results much closer to what you are actually looking for.

5.3 Metadata in practice: The database record

Let's see how metadata works in the research process. For most databases, but not the searchable part of the WWW, the database search engine doesn't really look for the data itself but searches the metadata. The metadata comes in the form of a data "record," that is, *a short description of the data*. If the data were books in a library, the metadata would be the "records" that describe each book, and the records would be what the catalog's search engine would look through, not the books themselves. The same would be true of an electronic database that searches for journal articles, though these days, because so many journal articles are in electronic form, it is possible to search the full text of articles as well as the metadata records.

Back in 2012 I published a book entitled *Teaching Research Processes: The Faculty Role in the Development of Skilled Student Researchers* (great book by the way; you owe it to yourself to get a copy and make me rich). Shortly after publication, a library catalog record (metadata) was produced for the book. It looked like this:

Local LC call number: ZA3075 .B3385 2012
Personal Author: Badke, William B., 1949-
Title: Teaching research processes : the faculty role in the development of skilled student researchers / William B. Badke.
Publication info: Oxford : Chandos Pub., 2012.
Physical description: xvii, 222 p. : 1 ill. ; 24 cm.
Series Statement: (Chandos information professional series)
Bibliography note:
Includes bibliographical references (p. 195-219) and index.
Contents:
Defining research processes—Research ability inadequacies in higher education—Research processes and faculty understanding—Current initiatives in research processes—The role of disciplinary thinking in research processes—Research processes in the classroom—Tentative case studies in disciplinary research process instruction—Research processes transforming education—Resourcing the enterprise.
Subject term: Information literacy—Study and teaching (Higher)
Subject term: Research—Methodology—Study and teaching (Higher)
Subject term: Academic libraries—Relations with faculty and curriculum.
Series Added Entry-Uniform Title: Chandos information professional series.

This descriptive record is tagged with "fields" such as Personal Author, Title, Contents, and Subject Term. This lets the searcher specify things. For example, "Catalog, I want only the book entitled *Teaching Research Processes*," (title field is searched) or "I want all the books by Badke, William" (author field is searched). The metadata (those field terms like title, author, etc.) allows for precise searching.

Good metadata, unfortunately, is pretty much non-existent on the WWW, so Google, Bing, etc. are forced to search only on keywords. If you do a search on the WWW, it becomes obvious right away that there is no search box to look for authors of websites or for types of websites (e.g., reviews of Toyota cars as opposed to Toyota's corporate website). This isn't the search engine's fault. Most websites just don't have the encoded metadata to enable such a search to be done. The best you can usually do (e.g. with a Google advanced search) is select a search of title words from websites or set a few other limiters.

Without metadata, you usually get tons of search results, but you have to do a large amount sifting to find a match with what you were actually searching for. If you search a library catalog, on the other hand, you will find that there is an available author search, a title search, a subject heading search, etc. that can help you nail down what you are looking for. Why? Because the library catalog is made up of metadata records.

Even with adequate metadata, the big problem with electronic databases is not getting information into them, but *retrieving* the information you need. For this purpose, there are two basic search tools available to you: **keywords** and **controlled vocabularies**. We looked at keywords in the previous chapter, so now we'll turn to the controlled vocabularies, which depend totally on metadata.

5.4 Controlled vocabularies

Several years ago, as people started sharing things on the WWW (photos, favorite bookmarks, etc.), *folksonomies* began to develop. A folksonomy is simply a user-created method of labeling items (tagging) so that you or anyone else in your circle of friends of colleagues can use these labels to find your items. A couple of examples are Flickr (**http://www.flickr.com/**) for photos and del.icio.us (**http://del.icio.us/**) for website bookmarks. The labels or "tags" used in these sites can be displayed as "clouds" of links to actual data. Here is what a "tag cloud" might look like for the City of New York (text size indicating relative popularity of the various tags).

ny newyork nyc newyorkcity

Simply click on the tag you want, and you will get a display of items that have had that tag attached to them. With these clusters of tags (which together form a folksonomy), users can search across one another's collections, pulling out, for example, favorite pictures from Japan or bookmarks to sites on ballroom dancing.

One big problem, though: The tags are user generated. This means that consistency goes out the window. One user tags her photos of New York with the term "newyork." Another uses "nyc," or "newyorkcity" or "ny" (most tagging systems demand that you tag with only one word, or close up the spaces if you use more than word). This means that if you search across the collection for pictures of New York, you need to know all the relevant tags that are being used for the subject. You'll most certainly miss a lot of items just because you didn't use obvious tags.

In some ways, it would be great if some dictator webmaster actually issued a set of standardized tags and insisted that everyone use them instead of making up their own. Hmmm...Actually that's the answer. A set of tags that is uniform so that all the pictures of Japan have to be tagged "JapanPictures," not "JapaneseVacationPictures," nor "PicturesOfJapan." That way, you would find all the Japan-related pictures that are in the collection.

Too bad I can't claim credit for the idea. The Library of Congress in the late 1800s was faced with the prospect of establishing a new method of cataloging by creating descriptive records for its large collection. As part of the process, the librarians determined that the only way to be sure all the books on a particular topic could be identified was to standardize a system of subject headings (tags?) that would be used in the descriptive record (metadata) related to each book. They created records containing these subject headings along with other metadata (authors, titles, etc.). Today, most academic libraries in North America simply use the subject headings created originally by the Library of Congress (why re-invent the wheel?).

5.5 Library of Congress Subject Headings

Earlier I showed you a copy of a database record to one of my books. Now I dare to show it again:

Local LC call number: ZA3075 .B3385 2012
Personal Author: Badke, William B., 1949-
Title: Teaching research processes : the faculty role in the development of skilled student researchers / William B. Badke.
Publication info: Oxford : Chandos Pub., 2012.
Physical description: xvii, 222 p. : 1 ill. ; 24 cm.
Series Statement: (Chandos information professional series)
Bibliography note:
Includes bibliographical references (p. 195–219) and index.
Contents:
Defining research processes—Research ability inadequacies in higher education—Research processes and faculty understanding—Current initiatives in research processes—The role of disciplinary thinking in research processes—Research processes in the classroom—Tentative case studies in disciplinary research process instruction—Research processes transforming education—Resourcing the enterprise.
Subject term: Information literacy—Study and teaching (Higher)
Subject term: Research—Methodology—Study and teaching (Higher)
Subject term: Academic libraries—Relations with faculty and curriculum.
Series Added Entry-Uniform Title: Chandos information professional series.

If you look at the Subject fields just above, you will see terminology like:

Information literacy—Study and teaching (Higher)
Research—Methodology—Study and teaching (Higher)
Academic libraries—Relations with faculty and curriculum.

Each of these is a Library of Congress subject heading related to some aspect of the book's subject matter. They may look a bit complex, but each specifies an aspect of the book's subject matter in a uniform and focused way.

How did the subject heading system originate? Quite simply, the Library of Congress (LC) in Washington, DC created an extensive list of the terminology by which most topics in the world of information would be identified and then it organized these terms in alphabetical lists. Some subject headings were easy: dogs are **DOGS**, sunflowers are **SUNFLOWERS**, and so on. Some were more difficult: What do you call senior citizens? LC chose **AGED**, much to the outrage of senior citizens. Television faith healers are **HEALERS IN MASS MEDIA**. Why? *Because LC said so.* That's the point with controlled vocabularies. These vocabularies are created by people "out there" who then *control* them and don't let you change them.

The fact is that you can't have it both ways. You can either choose your own search terminology (as in keywords or tagging), in which case you can't be sure you'll find everything, or you can let some other agency (in this case, Library of Congress) standardize your subject terminology, meaning that people other than you choose what we are going to call everything. If you use standardized terminology, you have less flexibility than with keyword searching, but you are more likely to find most of what the database has to offer about the topic you are seeking.

Insight #1: *Controlled vocabularies, unlike keywords, get at what the data is actually about, rather than seeking out the words the data uses to describe itself (keywords). Thus, with a controlled vocabulary search, you are more likely to get nearly everything on a topic in the database you're searching, regardless of what words are in titles, etc. The tradeoff is that, with controlled vocabularies, you have to use the subject terms provided by the system. You might not like these terms, but they are what you've got. No variations are allowed.*

How does a controlled vocabulary work? Armed with a set of predetermined subject headings, catalogers (creators of metadata records) decide which subject heading(s) to assign to a particular chunk of data. In the case of LC, every time they get a book to catalog, they write a description of the book (i.e., the catalog record), which then becomes metadata, and one or more controlled subject headings are added to the record.

So a book entitled *Them Television Preachers* may have the subject heading **HEALERS IN MASS MEDIA** assigned to it. A book called *Active Seniors in Today's World* may be labeled with the subject heading **AGED**.

Note something very important here. The book *Them Television Preachers* did not have any of the actual words of the subject heading in its title. The title told you the book was about TV preachers. It said nothing about healers or about mass media. The same was true for the second title—*Active Seniors in Today's World*—the term "aged" is not to be seen anywhere in the title. Why, then, were they given the subject headings they received? *Because some intelligent librarian sat down with these books, determined **what they were about**, and then assigned the closest subject headings from the already existing controlled vocabulary list.* Thus:

Insight #2: *The actual wording in the title of whatever content you are seeking is not important for controlled vocabularies. Subject headings are assigned on the basis of somebody's judgment as to what the item is actually about. Subject headings can thus be the same as some words in the title or they can be radically different.*

Consider the advantages. I have 5 books with the following titles:

Terminal Choices
Choosing Life or Death
Euthanasia
The Practice of Death
The Right to Die

All of them are about euthanasia. You might not have guessed that fact by looking at the titles, but the intelligent LC librarian determined that they are all about the same topic and assigned the same subject heading to all of them: **EUTHANASIA**. Euthanasia describes what these books are actually about regardless of the words used in their titles. One subject term pulls together all five books, even though you would need several keyword searches to find all of them if you searched on their title words. (Good luck thinking up the keywords you need to find the book, *Terminal Choices*).

Controlled vocabularies are a good solution to the problem of *retrieval*. It is a real challenge (and sometimes impossible) to input all the right keyword terminology so that the database will deliver up in a single search the information we need. If we wanted a list of books about euthanasia, it would be nice to have a predetermined word for the *concept* of euthanasia so we could type it into the search engine and get back a list of all the euthanasia books regardless of the wordings of the actual book titles. This is what a controlled vocabulary is designed for. Most of the books **on** euthanasia in a library will be retrieved just by typing in the subject term **EUTHANASIA,** no matter what their titles are.

Insight #3: *Use a controlled vocabulary as a search tool when you want most or all of the data on the same topic regardless of what the data actually says about itself in title words.*

But let's be clear about one thing—controlled vocabularies are "controlled" in the sense that someone other than you has determined what they will be. You as the user can't mess with them by changing their terminology or rearranging their structure the way you can with keywords. You *use* controlled vocabularies; you don't create them, and you can't fool with their form.

Insight #4: *Messing with controlled vocabulary wording or form defeats the purpose of controlled vocabularies. Subject headings are created by someone other than you, and they can't, in most cases, be manipulated or turned into keywords.*

Let's see how the *LC Subject Headings* controlled vocabulary system works in practice. The Library of Congress provides subject headings for the books in its own library collection, but it has also conveniently issued its list of approved headings so that all of us can use their system. Most libraries in North America have chosen to do just that, so that your library's subject headings for book searches are likely derived from the Library of Congress.

The best way to encounter Library of Congress subject headings is online at **http://id.loc.gov/authorities/subjects.html**. Simply give your best guess as to what you think the subject is called and search for it. If you discover that your chosen heading that is not authorized, it will take you to one or more authorized subject headings. If you find an authorized heading, like **Peanuts,** you will get further information (illustrated below but condensed to save space):

▥ Peanuts

Variants
> ▥ Arachides
> ▥ Arachis hypogea
> ▥ Earth nuts
> ▥ Goobers
> ▥ Grass nuts
> ▥ Ground-nuts
> ▥ Groundnuts
> ▥ Monkey nuts
> ▥ Pindars
> ▥ Pindas
> ▥ Pinders

Broader Terms
> ▥ Arachis
> ▥ Oilseed plants

NOTE—*This index is not a library catalog in itself.* It is simply an online guide to subject headings that you can then take to your local college or university catalog and use to find the books you need.

— • ———— ◯▥◯ ———— • —

Clearing the Fog: Subject headings are not keywords. No they're not..

One of the most difficult concepts in academic research is that of the subject heading. Blame it on Google. Most readers of this book have long been avid keyword searchers on the WWW, where subject headings are as scarce as coconut trees in the Alaskan wilds.

Keywords are words that actually exist within the data you are searching (for example, a website on basket weaving in which the words "basket weaving" are actually found). This means that a search engine can be as dumb as a bag of hammers and still seek out a string of letters and bring up the data when it finds the string of letters. It has no clue what the letters mean or even if the word it brought up means the same as the word that is in your mind.

Subject headings require human intervention and thus are smarter than keywords. They are tags or descriptors inserted into descriptive records, and thus are often better ways of explaining what the data is actually about. Subject headings are not words in the data. In fact, their form might be quite different from the words in your data (or possibly the same if the chosen subject heading is common terminology for your topic). They are, instead, preset terminology that *explains what the data is actually about.* They are not words *in* your data but words *above and beyond* your data that describe its subject matter.

Here's an example:

I was researching the ongoing crisis of Arctic Ocean ice melt due to climate change, so I did a *keyword* search in a library catalog on **artic ice**. Here are some of the things I found:

- ❖ Under **ice:** Waldo Lyon and the development of the **Arctic** submarine
- ❖ Art in the **ice** age : Spanish Levant art, **Arctic** art
- ❖ After the **ice** : life, death, and geopolitics in the new **Arctic**

The third one may be on the topic I'm working on. The first two are definitely not. Keyword searches can't read anyone's mind. They just find the words you input.

The subject heading for Arctic Ocean ice is **Sea ice—Arctic regions**. When I search on this librarian-created tag, I get results that are firmly on the concept in my mind:

- ❖ *IceBridge airborne survey data support Arctic sea ice predictions*
- ❖ *Fever at the poles*
- ❖ *Transition in the fractal geometry of Arctic melt ponds*
- ❖ *Arctic report card 2011*

The first result from our subject heading search uses our original keywords: arctic ice. The second one uses neither word but deals with global warming and arctic ice. The third and fourth lack the word ice. Yet all four are on sea ice in the Arctic. The subject heading found all four because it was focusing on what the books were actually about rather than on their title wording. That's smart. Keywords proved dumber than subject headings in this case.

Keywords and subject headings are not the same, no they are not. They do completely different types of searches.

5.6 Working the angles—Identifying controlled vocabularies

Controlled vocabularies can involve more than subject headings. Names can be tricky in databases: Am I "Badke, William" or "Badke, Bill?" Thus many databases also have controlled vocabularies for names, by which they standardize the form of an author's name so you can find everything by that author in the database. Titles of books or articles have their own controlled vocabulary built in: A title takes a unique form in its choice and order of words so that titles tend to be standardized automatically.

But subject headings, whether in a library catalog or some other database, are challenging to identify. Let's look at types of databases that have controlled vocabularies and try to understand how they are organized to provide you information.

5.6.1 Library catalogs

Some library catalogs, where you search for books, may not have guides to subject headings embedded in them, which is why you might need to identify relevant subject headings by using the *Library of Congress Subject Headings* volumes or the online version, described above. Some catalogs do have built in cross reference systems, so you can simply try out a word in a subject search (e.g. "Goobers") and it will link you to the right subject term ("Peanuts").

There is another way to identify subject headings. Being a bit of a purist, I hesitate to share this, because it's not foolproof, and you may end up missing headings you could have used. But here it is:

First, perform a keyword search in the library catalog, choosing words you think might appear in titles of relevant books on the topic you are dealing with. Find a book that is directly on your chosen topic and click on the title of the citation to it to open up the full catalog record. For example, you might be writing on **ecology in Polynesia**, so you use these terms in a keyword search. You discover in your result list the ideal book and open up the full record:

Isles of amnesia : the history, geography, and restoration of America's forgotten Pacific Islands
Author: Mark J Rauzon
Publisher: Honolulu : University of Hawai'i Press, [2016]
Subjects: Island ecology—Polynesia—History.
     Islands—Polynesia—History.
     Coral reefs and islands—Polynesia—History.

Look at the line that says "Subjects." There are three official, authorized forms of the Library of Congress subject heading for this concept: Island ecology—Polynesia—History, Islands—Polynesia—History, and Coral reefs and islands—Polynesia—History. They might not be the subject headings you would have chosen if you were setting up this system, but that doesn't matter, because the choice isn't yours to make. The Library of Congress has made the choice. With these subject headings you have the means to find all the other books on the topic, usually just by clicking on the hyperlinked subject headings in the catalog record. So, click on **Island ecology—Polynesia—History**, and you will get a list of all the rest of the library's books on the history of ecology in Polynesia, even if words in titles would not have led you to them in a keyword search, for example:

Terrestrial biodiversity of the Austral Islands, French Polynesia

Notice that the title above does not use the word "ecology," though "biodiversity" is clearly an ecological concept. The subject heading search found this book on the subject, even when its title words did not reveal its true nature. This method of finding subject headings is relatively simple: Use a keyword search to identify one book on your topic. Open up the citation to get the full catalog record. Go to the LC subject heading(s) used for this book in the catalog record, and click on its (their) link(s) to discover similar books.

5.6.2 Other databases

There are a many databases out there that use controlled vocabularies, including journal databases and institutional repositories. Here are some clues to finding their subject headings systems:

- ❖ A term commonly used is "Thesaurus," that is, a guide to subject headings that not only identifies authorized subjects but also can lead you to broader, narrower or related terms that are also authorized. Sometimes a thesaurus also has "scope notes," that is definitions of what is meant by specific subject headings.
- ❖ At other times in a database you may see a link to "Subjects" or "Descriptors," which mean the same thing.
- ❖ In connection with the options above, or sometimes separate from them, you may find a "browse" function. "Browse" generally involves working with controlled vocabulary terms (subjects, authors, titles, etc.) from alphabetized lists of headings.
- ❖ You can also click on the title of a citation you've found in a database. This will open you up to a larger record that might contain links to related subject headings.

5.7 Getting more creative—combining keyword and controlled vocabulary searching

Let me begin this section by re-emphasizing something: *Keywords and controlled vocabularies are **not the same***. Keywords are constructed by you as best guesses. They are intended to find *actual words* in your data or data record with the hope that those words will guide you to the resources you want. Controlled vocabularies are constructed by someone else, and they exist outside of the data you are searching. They are intended to bring you all the resources on a topic regardless of what terminology is used in the titles, and so on. To ensure that controlled vocabularies provide this service, their form/order/terminology is preset and cannot be changed.

That said, there is a way to construct searches in which a subject heading gets you to the right subject matter, and keywords help you to narrow within that subject area. It's called *faceted searching*. Let's try an example. Consider the following from one of the EBSCOhost journal databases, PsycINFO:

Searching: **PsycINFO** | Choose Databases
☐ Suggest Subject Terms

psychotherapy	Select a Field (optional) ▾	Search
AND ▾	autis*	Select a Field (optional) ▾
AND ▾	child*	Select a Field (optional) ▾	⊕ ⊖

Basic Search   Advanced Search   Search History ▸

Search Results: 1 - 50 of 1,657   Date Newest ▾   Page Opti

1. The Early Start Denver Model: A play-based interventi

I am interested in psychotherapy with autistic children. Thus my three terms "psychotherapy," autis★ (truncation for autism, autistic, etc.) and child★. The initial 1,657 results are more than most searchers want to deal with. This database allows (even encourages) you to do the search in stages. [Note that other types of databases will do this in other ways. The EBSCO example is just that: an example. For other databases, root around in them until you find similar functions.]

In PsycINFO on the EBSCOhost platform, you can go down the column to the left of your results and identify subject headings that move beyond words in titles to identify the central subject matter that you want. This gets you fewer results that are much more focused on what you are looking for:

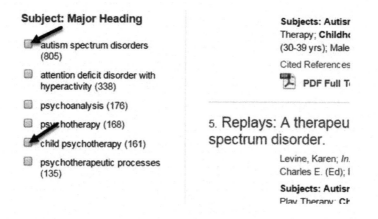

I chose the subject headings "autism" and "child psychotherapy," bringing my results down eventually from 1,657 to 76. I can be sure that the remaining articles are more centrally on the topic, because I used subject headings that didn't depend on words in titles. If I wanted to (and I just might), I could go back to the subject headings in the left column and choose one or two more that would drop the total number of results even further.

5.8 Keeping on track with controlled vocabularies

Some databases today, including most of what is found in Google or Bing, can be searched only by keyword. Keywords have advantages, but the lack of controlled vocabulary search options can be a definite drawback when all you want is a set of data on one subject regardless of what the data says about itself. Thinking of all possible keywords that might give you relevant data can really give you a headache.

Some people have a lot of trouble grasping the essential difference between keywords and controlled vocabularies, especially when the same words can sometimes be used for both. For example, there is a subject heading **Tax evasion,** but that could just as easily be a keyword expression. What's the difference? Well, the keyword search **tax evasion** could bring you up a book like *The Detection of Tax Evasion in the Bronx*. A subject heading search would bring up this title, but it would also find *The Psychology of Escaping the Taxman*, something your keyword search on "tax evasion" would miss completely. Essentially the difference is in the way the database search engine searches for the words. **Tax evasion** as a keyword search will find only those actual words in a title. **Tax evasion** as a subject heading will search for all the database records that have been tagged with the subject "tax evasion," even if their titles don't contain the words "tax evasion." With subject headings, good results will come up even if the title words aren't right.

Keywords are best used if you don't know a subject heading, if your topic has very specific terminology, if it crosses disciplines (like "The education of homeless children"), or if the database you are using has no metadata. Controlled vocabulary subject headings are best when you want to find most of what a database has on a topic, and you are concerned that a keyword search will only reveal some of what is there.

In some situations you can combine the two, but use great care so that the results you get are close to what you wanted.

5.9 For further study

Study guide

1. What is "metadata"?
2. What is a "record," and how does it relate to metadata?
3. Why doesn't the actual title of the book matter a great deal when a cataloger attaches a controlled vocabulary term to it?

4. What are the advantages of controlled vocabularies?

5. Explain the method of starting with a keyword search in order to identify controlled vocabulary subject headings.

6. Define the following:

   Thesaurus

   Descriptor

   Browse function

7. Is it possible to search controlled vocabularies and keywords at the same time? When would you want to do so, if it is possible?

Practice with controlled vocabularies

1. Use Library of Congress Subject Headings (**http:// id.loc.gov/authorities/subjects.html:** click on "Search Authorities") to find the authorized subject heading for each of the following:
   a. LASH ships
   b. Arts, Zen
   c. Clothes hangers
   d. Prevention of Crime
   e. Canadian Religious Poetry
   f. Rookies (Baseball)
   g. Literacy and computers
   h. Pencilflowers
   i. Ancient philosophy
   j. The Roman influences on law in the United States [a tough one to end with. Try various combinations of words.]

2. In the following catalog record, which are controlled vocabulary terms?

   Title: The hitchhiker's guide to the meaning of everything / William Badke.

   Author: Badke, William B., 1949–

   Publisher: Grand Rapids, MI : Kregel Publications, 2005.

Description: 176 p. ; 22 cm.
ISBN: 0825420695
Subjects: Bible—Criticism, interpretation, etc.
Meaning (Philosophy)—Religious aspects—Christianity
Life—Religious aspects—Christianity

Suggested key to practice with controlled vocabularies

1. Library of Congress Subject Headings—Correct Headings
   a. *LASH ships*: See: Barge-carrying ships
   b. *Arts, Zen*: See: Zen arts
   c. *Clothes hangers*: See: Coat hangers
   d. *Prevention of Crime*: See: Crime prevention
   e. *Canadian Religious Poetry*: See: Religious poetry, Canadian
   f. *Rookies (Baseball)*: See: Rookie baseball players
   g. *Literacy and computers*: See: Computers and literacy
   h. *Pencilflowers*: See: Stylosanthes
   i. *Ancient philosophy*: See: Philosophy, Ancient
   j. *The Roman influences on law in the United States*: See: Law—United States—Roman influences [Did you find it?]

2. Clearly the three subject headings are controlled vocabularies: Bible—Criticism, interpretation, etc.; Meaning (Philosophy)—Religious aspects—Christianity; Life—Religious aspects—Christianity. But so is the author's name (because it is pre-formatted for standardization). So is even the title, which comes in a specific, formal order.

Assignment for a research project of your own

Do a *Library of Congress Subject Heading* search on a topic of your choice in a library catalog by:

1. Identifying the best subject heading either through the Library of Congress Subject Headings resource (**http://id.loc.gov/ authorities/subjects.html**) or by starting with a keyword search to find a book on the topic and then locating the subject heading you want through that book's catalog record.

2. Doing the search by using the appropriate search box for subject headings in the catalog or by clicking on the relevant link in a catalog record.

3. Carefully evaluating your results to identify those books most relevant to your topic area.

4. Making a list of 8 to 10 relevant books identified through your controlled vocabulary search.

6

Discovery Searches, Library Catalogs and Journal Databases

Now we move into the area where the rubber meets the road. This chapter is intended to guide you into the major database resources available to you through an academic library, using the keyword and controlled vocabulary methods described in the previous two chapters.

6.1 Discovery Searches

An increasing number of libraries today have discovery search tools, such as Primo, Summon, WorldCat Local, and EBSCO Discovery Service. It may not be easy for you to determine if your library has such a beast, but look for a single search box on your library's home page that enables you to search for books, journal articles and other resources all at the same time. A discovery search tool is essentially one-stop shopping, like a "Google of the Library," bringing you a ton of results of every type with a single search.

Sounds great, doesn't it? Well, depending on what happens next, it can be great or simply more of the information fog you're already used to. Generally, you get a list of results that are either broken out into books, articles, and so on, or you are given a means to choose a particular kind of resource and narrow your results to that type. See such options from example of a search on "climate change" in EBSCO Discovery Search (source types are on the left):

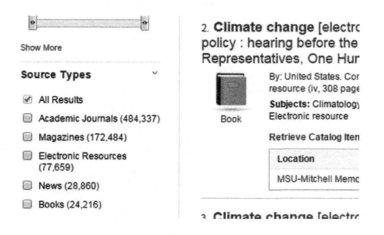

Quite a number of discovery tools used in libraries actually let you start with a choice of the type of resource you are looking for, thus getting the narrowing out of the way early (which is usually a good thing in our era of information glut). Here's an example from Milligan College:

The best way to know if your library is using a discovery tool is to see what's covered in the search you are about to do. You may find labels like, "Search library collections," "Search for articles, books, and more," "Search everything." Or you may be given the opportunity to specify a type of resource from several possible, as in the illustration above. These are solid clues that you have a discovery search in place. If you are still unsure, you can ask a librarian.

As a researcher, I'm not terribly big on discovery searching. Maybe that's because I'm too ancient and set in my ways. But more likely it's because I know that you absolutely don't need, in most cases, a glut of information (think 400,000+ results). A few citations that are dead on target usually beats a great host of results, only some of which are helpful. Discovery tries to be an academic Google, but it often fails to help users enough with getting directly to the few relevant results they need.

Here are some distinctions. Summon™ in its results provides you with a selection of links to articles, books and other resources, each resource type in its own section on the page. Primo, WorldCat and EBSCO Discovery Search mix result types but allow you to select out books, articles, and so on from the left column. A unique feature with EBCO's tool is its commitment to the subject heading as a means to narrow your results.

If your library doesn't use a discovery service, then you can take a breather and get a soda before moving to 6.2. If your library does have a discovery search, try it out and see how it works. Then read on while we look at more specific search tools. Even when you are working with a discovery tool, you can often specify whether you want to use the single big box or search individually for books (the library catalog) or articles (from journal databases).

6.2 Library catalogs

Books tend to create fogs of misunderstanding, because they're blunt instruments. In order to write a book, you need a topic broad enough to be covered in a couple of hundred or more pages, but you also need enough focus to avoid it becoming multi-volume or turning superficial. Thus finding a book on a narrowed down topic that is driven by a research question may well be a challenge. Here information hierarchies can help. If you can't find a book on Bulimia, you might find one on the broader topic Eating Disorders (higher in the hierarchy). If you can't find a book on Constantine, you might find a book on the broader topic of Roman Emperors or Roman History of his era. Generally, you need to assume that few books will be exactly on your topic. That is why strategies are needed.

Library catalogs are electronic search engines for books in physical or electronic format. When you search a library catalog, you are searching the metadata record created for each book, a record that includes the following, among other things: Author, title, publisher, description, subject heading(s), and call number. This is where things can get tricky: Library catalog search interfaces differ widely from one another, so you need to "read" them in order to navigate them well. Common interfaces:

1. A discovery search tool that allows you to narrow your searching to only books if you wish. Here the basic option is a fairly broad keyword search for every type of resource, so you might want to dig around for tabs or an advanced search that can help you develop a more focused search plan.
2. A catalog offering a single search box yet allowing you to specify (through a drop-down) what type of search you want to do (e.g., keyword, title, subject heading, etc.).
3. A catalog that opens in an advanced search with several boxes that enable you to specify the type of search you want and then to format it with Boolean operators.

Here's a collage of the three types:

6.2.1 Making the catalog work for you

If your topic is a reasonably standard one, you will probably do best with a controlled vocabulary subject heading search. It's safer in that you know you will find most books that are available on the topic. The only problem is that you may need only a portion of the information found in each book. For example, if your research question is, "How close to attainability is B.F. Skinner's utopian vision found in his book *Walden Two?*" you might well find that there are few books available specifically on *Walden Two*, and you are going to have to do a controlled vocabulary subject search on **Skinner, B.F. (Burrhus Frederic), 1904–** and then find material on *Walden Two* within books describing his thought. Of course, you'll also need to look at the actual book, *Walden Two*, itself.

(For information on how to identify Library of Congress Subject Headings for your search, see Chapter 4, above.)

If your topic is not a standard one or if it combines a couple of subject disciplines (such as the influence of *Walden Two* on the 1960's hippy movement), you may want to go for a keyword approach. Here are a few warnings, however:

❖ Keywords tend to function best when targeting specific and/ or non-traditional approaches to topics. The library you are using may not have enough diversity to meet your particular narrow and quirky need.

❖ Always remember that keyword searching, while it may appear to focus down on exactly what you want, is a very inexact science. You have to input the right word(s) configured in the right way, and you are highly dependent on the actual terminology of titles in the collection.

❖ Be sure you don't use too many keywords at once. Start with one or two, and if that doesn't give you what you want, try one more. Rarely will you need more than three.

❖ Never forget that, in an AND search, every time you add a term you eliminate data from your results. This may be good if you have too many hits, but make sure that the data you are eliminating is not crucial. It's better to get more results to sift through than to have a smaller set of results that doesn't meet your requirements.

Some catalogs will let you combine controlled vocabulary and keyword searching. If you do this, you'll need to keep your wits about you. In general, the subject heading gets you into the right territory, the broad subject area. Then you add keywords to specify, within this subject area, the narrower concept you are looking for. For example, your subject heading might be **Homelessness**. You could then add the keyword, **Canad★** (for **Canada**, **Canada's**, **Canadian**, etc.).

Why not, then, simply make them both keywords? Because "homelessness" can be expressed in a variety of ways. In the catalog you might have titles such as:

Canada's Homeless: An Inquiry
Street Life in a Canadian City
Ain't Got No Place to Call My Own: A Canadian's Story

Two of them don't even use the term **homeless**. Thus, searching with a subject heading that is not dependent on title terminology can get you all the books generally on the subject, and additional keywords will specify which books you want from that broader pool (those dealing with the Canadian setting).

Alternatively, you can combine two or more subject headings, looking for where they overlap, though this method is less likely to get you solid results than a subject heading and keyword combination.

Above all, when catalog searching, keep your wits in place. Thinking hierarchically can also be a help. Ask yourself one or more of the following questions:

❖ What broader subject could this topic be a part of?
❖ If one approach is not working, what are other ways that I might look at the topic? (i.e., what other hierarchies could potentially contain the topic? How could I narrow to only one aspect?)

6.2.2 E-Books

Electronic books are catching on as consumer-friendly products. While many people have little desire to sit in front of a LED screen and read 300 pages of text, portable e-readers, phones, and tablets are making e-books a lot more practical.

Within library catalogs you will find an increasing number of your results to be e-books with web links instead of call numbers. Major suppliers of e-books to libraries are EBSCO and ProQuest Ebook Central, though you will find any variety of platforms. Here begin the challenges. Each e-book platform functions in a different way. But an even bigger difficulty is that library-based e-books tend to be slow to load (I tell my students to think of how long it would have taken them to get the same book in print by visiting the physical library). It may also be a challenge to know how much of any book you can download as, for example, a PDF, as opposed to simply having to navigate through the whole book in its native reader. (Note that a screen capture program can still snag excerpts, even if you can't download much as a PDF).

In most cases you will find links to e-books in the same library catalog you use to find print-based books. If there is not an easy way to separately search for e-books in your catalog, try a keyword search focused on book titles and add the term: **electronic**. Or use an advanced search, which may let you limit to e-books as a search parameter.

Navigating library e-books can be a challenging business. If you want to get to the good stuff quickly, try using these options:

- ❖ Tables of contents with links
- ❖ "Search within the book" links
- ❖ Links to download a portion of the book as an easier-to-navigate PDF. The portion you can download may be as small as 20–60 pages, but it could be the whole book. Clues to your ability to do this include a download or even a "print" link.

The Google Books project (**http://books.google.com/**) has become a mainstay for many researchers, though its limitations abound, the most challenging being the fact that only portions are available for many of the titles, due to copyright restrictions. Its companion, Google Play (**https://play.google.com/store/books**) is the commercial side, which does give you much more access but often at a cost. Google Books itself is searchable by keyword, so the results can be the same sort of mixed bag you find with any other Google search. If you want to discover a particular title, you can get a host of books with the same title words in various word orders, and the one you want may or may not be high in the results.

Google Books has an advanced search, if you can find it (currently it's the wheel in the upper right on your *results* page, though it may well have moved by the time you read this). Or go to **http://books. google.com/advanced_book_search**. If you want to locate an exact book title, you can use the option in the advanced search:

"with this exact phrase." Google Books' advanced search also has a subject search linked to catalog records supplied from various sources. It works fairly well. A better option for searching by subject may be to identify one book, click on the "About this book" link, and find a catalog record near the bottom of the linked page. If there is one, it will have subject links that will direct you to other books on the subject. All of this, of course, is as useful as painting your toenails and putting on sneakers if you don't get access to the full text of the books you were seeking. The "Find in a library" links may help you discover a readable copy locally.

Amazon.com, the bookseller, has a "Look inside" feature that provides access to portions of a lot of books they sell and also offers a keyword search for content. Copyright restrictions prevent full content from being viewable or searchable in most cases.

There are free e-book collections out there, viewable full text, but they are limited in number. Some examples are Directory of Open Access Books (**http://www.doabooks.org/**), ACLS Humanities E-Book Collection (**http://quod.lib.umich.edu/a/acls/browse. html**), and National Academies Press (**http://www.nap.edu/**).

One advantage of electronic format is the ability to search across a book, or even across a whole collection of books, using keywords to find the most relevant passages. While this may be a neat feature, there is always the need for caution to avoid using chunks of information out of context.

An alternative, of course, to using the library for e-books is to buy your own. I only wish I were rich enough to do the masses of e-book buying some people make a regular habit. For more on e-books, go back to section 1.5.1 in chapter one.

Clearing the Fog: How to create in-text citations from e-readers when page numbers are missing

When you want to include e-books from specialized e-reader devices in notes or a bibliography you can run into a challenge, depending on what e-reader you are using: the original page numbers of the print document may have disappeared. Kindle has a "location number" system for such situations, but some other readers do not. So how do you cite a page number from something you are reading on an e-device that has lost the original pagination?

Here is the consensus as it currently stands for the three most common formats:

APA: Use the pattern of citing the section(s) rather than page number(s). Thus an in-text citation might look like this if you are referring to a particular part: (Johnson, 2016, Chapter 3, para. 34). It's a bit nasty, since you might lose track while counting to paragraph 34 of chapter 3, but at least you can explain clearly what part you are citing.

Your note and bibliography entries would look like this:

(Badke, 2003, Chapter 4, para. 26)

Badke, W. B. (2003). *Beyond the answer sheet: Academic success for international students.* Bloomington, IN: iUniverse. Kindle version. [or EPUB version or whatever type it is]

See: **http://blog.apastyle.org/apastyle/2011/06/how-do-you-cite-an-e-book.html.**

MLA: MLA cuts you a break. In the absence of page numbers, you just need to cite the chapter, rather than including the paragraph number. Thus the in-text citation will look like this: (Johnson, ch. 4). Your note and bibliography entries would look like this:

(Badke, ch. 3)

Badke, W. B. (2003). *Beyond the answer sheet: academic success for international students.* Kindle edition. Bloomington, IN: iUniverse.

See: **https://style.mla.org/2016/06/23/citing-an-e-book/**

Chicago/Turabian: This style, while it has an in-text citation variant, tends to prefer footnotes or endnotes. Create the standard footnote, then cite chapter and paragraph, when there are no page numbers: John Jackson, *Finding the Right Word* (New York: Wordfinder Press, 2014), chap. 14, para. 23.

Your note and bibliography entries would look like this:

[1]John Jackson, *Finding the Right Word* (New York: Wordfinder Press, 2014), chap. 14, para. 23, Kindle edition.

Jackson, John. *Finding the Right Word.* New York: Wordfinder Press, 2014. Kindle edition. [or EPUB edition, or whatever type it is]

See: **http://www.chicagomanualofstyle.org/tools_citation guide.html** (Select, "Book published electronically").

6.3 Journal databases

Just when you thought that finding books was trouble enough, someone is sure to suggest to you that there's another world of research materials crying out for attention - *journals*. Actually, the whole category of this type of resource is broader than you might think, and journals are only a portion. Librarians, ever the stuffy folks we are, call the whole field "periodicals," that is, materials that arrive in the library periodically, as opposed to a book that arrives only once. Included in the category is everything from newspapers to popular magazines (or e-zines) to trade magazines to scholarly journals. But I'm going to call them journals anyway, because this term is more familiar to the vast host of people who aren't librarians (and who, strangely, seem thankful for that fact).

Clearing the Fog: Do you know the difference between an article and a journal?

This is a common trick question that I love to ask undergraduates, who almost never know the answer, though their creativity in trying to come up with one is both amazing and (I have to admit it) sometimes a bit amusing. They tell me that an article is general and a journal is more specific, or a journal is general and an article is more specific, or a journal is more personal than an article. Nice tries, but no.

The problem comes from the fact that we encounter most articles as citations in database result lists. We're aware that there are details that describe the article as part of something bigger (such as 43(2):12-32), but the digital world has killed our consciousness of the analog origin of this stuff.

Here's the answer: *Articles are the individual pieces. Journals are the packages within which articles are found.*

Let's think analog for a moment. Back in 1984, if you subscribed to *Journal of Chemical Ecology*, you paid your money, and several times a year a paperback book-like item would be delivered to your (analog) mailbox. When you opened the pages of this issue of the journal, you would see within it individual articles, like chapters in a book. At the end of the year, if you were particularly nerd-like, you would bind all your journal issues into a *volume*. Thus the journal is the package that you hardly ever see these days in the electronic environment. The article is one of the chapters in the journal, a piece in the package.

In the illustration below, you will see a mashup of the actual cover of an issue of a print journal, an article you can find within this issue of the journal, and the form in which you would find that article in an electronic database.

6.3.1 Some background on the journal scene

Before we get to journal databases, let's clarify what makes journals different from books. The most significant difference is that you can't catalog a journal like you catalog a book. When a librarian gets a new book for the collection, the book is cataloged (i.e. has an electronic metadata record created for it) and is put on the shelf. After that, there is nothing to do but sign the book out and check it back in until it falls apart. The cataloger's job is done.

But journal issues *keep on arriving* every week or month or quarter or year. By definition, they are *periodical*. You can't catalog them once and for all like you can a book, because they keep coming as more issues are added to the growing collection (like zombies that attack you in waves). While it might be possible for a librarian to assign a subject heading to each article in each journal as it arrives and then to create a database to enable you to find articles on any given topic, it just wouldn't be practical. No librarian has the time to create a separate database of all the library's journal articles. This is where commercial journal databases come in as alternative catalogs just for journal articles.

Before we get to these databases, let's recognize that the field of what we are calling "journals" is governed by some significant categories:

Popular vs. trade vs. scholarly

Popular magazines generally come out of a different mindset than do scholarly journals. Both are supposed to inform, but popular magazines also need to entertain (for example, *Time Magazine*). They may be intelligent, but they do not pass the tests that scholars demand in scholarly journals. In general, they lack bibliographic notes and at best report on scholarly work rather than actually being scholarly work.

Scholarly journals are usually the territory of academics and students in higher education rather than the general public who read magazines. They tend to have notes and sometimes bibliographies, with a reading level that is advanced (for example, *Journal of Ambulatory Care Management*).

In the middle are *trade magazines* that specialize in some particular industry or technology where information is shared. They are less "popular" in tone (and are, indeed, often highly technical), but they generally look like popular magazines and do not major on footnotes or bibliographies (e.g. *Online Searcher*, a magazine for information professionals).

Scholarly journals use a system of **peer review**, by which manuscripts submitted for possible publication are read and evaluated by other scholars in the field (peers) before they can be published. This gatekeeping process is intended to weed out inferior work. Peer review itself has come under attack as preserving the status quo and preventing younger scholars with fresh ideas from publishing, but it is still the best system we've got for keeping journal article quality as high as possible. (For an alternate view and perceptive assessment of peer review, see Brian Martin, "The Politics of Research," **http://www.uow.edu.au/~bmartin/pubs/98il/il07.pdf.**)

In order to speed up the release of scientific information, new groups of scholars are suggesting the use of preprints, articles posted online for reading and discussion before the peer review process. Such scholars don't oppose peer review, but don't want peer review to hold up the publication of findings. Major sites for preprints are ArXiv.org (**http://arxiv.org/**) and Social Science Research Network (**http://www.ssrn.com/en/**). Examples from biology include ASAPbio (**http://asapbio.org/**) and BioRχiv (**http://biorxiv.org/**).

Several organizations are now trying to facilitate collaboration of scholars through the whole process of research and writing. Recent examples include Open Science Framework (**https://osf.io/**) and Humanities Commons (**http://news.hcommons.org/**).

Print vs. electronic

Journals, now that they have substantially left behind the analog days, live primarily in the electronic world. Most published journals have electronic versions available, even if they continue also to publish in print. In fact, the print format for journals is becoming a rarity, saving thousands of trees and the squirrels that inhabit them. Why? Simply because people really like what e-journal articles can do for them. E-journals are instantly accessible from anywhere that has an Internet connection, you can print or save only what articles you want to keep, and they are much more searchable for key concepts than are print journals.

But there are challenges:

❖ Electronic versions of articles from the past are generally minimal, most of them going back into the 1990s but rarely earlier. An exception to this is JSTOR, a storage database for the most significant academic journals, reaching back decades in many cases.

❖ There are dreaded "embargoes" everywhere. An embargo prevents the release of the electronic version to a database for a period of time. For example "12 months embargo" means that you won't see the electronic version of the article for at least 12 months after the print version has been released.

❖ Not every journal you want electronically is available through your institutional databases. Be alert, though, to the option of doing an interlibrary loan, essentially asking your library to get your article for you from another library.

Many students are tempted to pay attention only to journal articles that are available in electronic full text, bypassing citations to articles the library may have in print or microform. That can be a mistake if the best article on a topic is only available in some hardcopy format. It's wise to avoid taking the easy road in a misguided quest to finish your research early. (Why do I sense that you're not liking what I'm telling you? Really. It's true. Good, thorough research might demand using the occasional print journal or even microfiche, but this is far more satisfying than simply getting the job done fast and missing the best resources).

William Badke

Free journals: Partially an academic myth

What's the point of doing all this database searching from library web pages when there are tons of good journals right on the Internet? Ah, the ever-hoped-for, ever-elusive dream of being able to access the full text of every article you need, right on your screen via Google! Sadly, reality is rarely what we hope it will be.

It's simply not true that every article from every journal in the world is offered in digital form on the open Net for minimal or no cost. Why not? Let me share a brief primer on economics. Our world turns on the ability of people to manufacture things and sell them to other people. If we all worked really hard to produce things and then simply gave away what we produced, the world would stop spinning on its axis and life as we know it would disappear. Economics makes the world go around.

Thus journal publishers, before they make their material available to vendors of full text indexes, demand to be paid and paid handsomely (too handsomely, I would suggest). If a journal publisher cannot (or will not) come to an agreement with the database vendor, the full text for that journal will not be available except for a fee through the journal publisher's website. Full text is rarely free: It is either paid for by your library's expensive subscriptions to journal databases or you have to pay for your own journal subscriptions online.

The production of journal and popular magazine articles is big business in our world. While lots of people put up websites at no charge to you, few publishers of journals are even remotely as generous (except for those who are part of the open access movement described in Chapter One). The vast majority of journal articles, even those that are electronic, can only be accessed after someone (you or your library) pays a hefty price. Sure, you can find some really good articles for free, but that's not true for most of them. The databases you use through your library are password-protected for a reason—your library has paid big money to give you "free" access to them. And it's in those databases where most of the articles are.

Clearing the Fog: Some tips on journal article citations

A journal article citation is the description of an article needed to help you find it. While the format of a citation may vary, here is what is usually provided in an article's metadata:

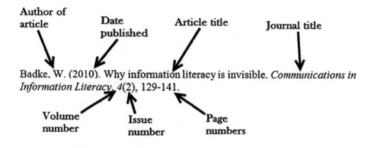

Citation error alert: Some students record the ISSN within database records of articles, thinking that the ISSN is like a call number for a book and thus can work as a citation. The ISSN looks like this: 4562-8793. It is a code number to identify the journal the article came from but is *useless* to help you find any particular article. For the most part ignore it. Instead, record these features:

- author
- date
- article title
- journal name
- volume number
- issue number
- and page numbers

(I should turn this list into a song for all of us to learn. In fact, I actually did).

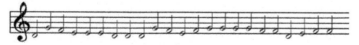

Author - date - article title - journal name - volume number - issue number and page numbers

6.3.2 Introduction to journal databases

Even thinking of using journal articles in a research project may give you a shudder of horror. You imagine Googling for something (anything!) on the "The Implications for Generation Y of Max Weber's Approach to the Sociology of Cities." Hours later, in bitterness of heart and soul, you emerge, red-eyed, with one article that is only vaguely relevant. Or you go to Google Scholar, only to discover that you have to pay for most stuff you find.

Academic research is not supposed to be like that at all. We have better tools for most of what you need: Databases that are specialized for the searches you want to do, and which are more sophisticated than web search engines.

Academic databases are created this way: Specialists sit down in front of piles of articles or, more likely, their electronic equivalents (often related to a specific subject discipline, such as psychology or history or religion) and create a metadata record for each article. The metadata is loaded into the database, thus making it searchable. By doing a search, you can generate a list of article citations from various journals that are relevant to the subject you are studying. Often the whole article is right there as a PDF. You can also, if you want, search within the full text of the electronic articles themselves in many databases.

Approaching a journal database means first being able to "read" its *interface*. The interface is what you actually see on your screen when you search for the data. It includes the screen display, search methods, and so on. Interfaces change constantly. Data doesn't. What this means is that the screen may look different the next time you use the database. The instructions on use may be different. Even the methods you need to follow to search the database may be different. The data inside it is the same, so *do not panic.*

How to read an interface

❖ *Go over the features visible on the screen.* There is likely a basic search available, but is there also an advanced search? Are there ways to limit your results by date, audience, type of resource, and so on? Can you search within a single journal? Is there a subject heading search available (sometimes described as a "thesaurus" or a "browse" function)?

❖ *Look for anything that says "search tips," "help," or "how to use this index."* Most people generally skip instructions, which is why their new lawnmower blows up or their software freezes on the screen. If you are one of those people, at least keep my suggestion in mind when you (inevitably) lose your way at some point. There really are times when it is a good idea to use the help screen

❖ *Start with a keyword search and identify two or three results that look like they are relevant to your research question/thesis.*

❖ *Click on the titles of these relevant articles, one by one, to open the full record.* Is the author's name hyperlinked (allowing you to find other articles by the same author)? Are there subject heading links within the record that you can click on? Do these headings seem specific or are they very broad in their coverage (and thus less useful)?

❖ *Can you locate subject heading links somewhere else on the results page, in a column to the left or right of the results or somewhere above the list of result citations?* If so, they may help you to take your keyword search results into a more focused subject area. For example, if you've done an initial keyword search on "globalization" and one of the suggested subject headings next to the results is "social justice," you can use it to focus your emphasis down to social justice issues in globalization.

Insight: *Be careful about subject links. Some will take you to results that combine your original keyword search in an AND with the subject heading. Others ignore your original keyword(s) and take you directly to everything on that subject. In this case, you may have to add your keyword(s) to the subject heading later by using AND.*

❖ *Look for a "Thesaurus," "Subjects," "Browse Subjects," or "Indexes" link.* Any of these can take you to authorized subject headings for your database. In this case, you can start with a subject area, then either link it to another subject area or add one or more keywords in an AND search.

❖ *Find out through a help screen how keyword searching is done in the database.* What sorts of Boolean operators are in use? Is phrase searching allowed?

❖ *Try a search on a broad basis first, perhaps inputting a subject heading or only one keyword.* If you get more than about 500 "hits" (citations to individual articles), look for a means to refine or narrow your search by adding more words or a relevant subject heading. But be careful, in doing so, that you don't eliminate good data—it's better to have to wade through more hits than to miss crucial articles because you narrowed with too much vigor. Avoid using narrowing words that you don't really need.

Let's see an example

If you want to learn to swim in the sometimes risky waters of journal database searching, you have to arm yourself and just jump in. Let's look at a sample search using *EBSCO Academic Search Complete*, a user-friendly database with considerable full text content. By the time you read this, the interface may have changed, but the image below gives you a good idea of ways in which sophisticated databases can do a good job of leading you to relevant journals.

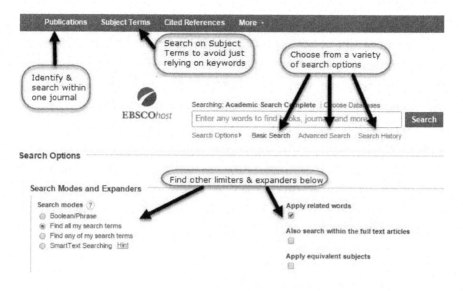

Notice some of the features of this first screen:

❖ The name of this database is "Academic Search Complete."

❖ While there is a basic search box, you can also choose an "advanced search" that allows you to build your investigation using Boolean terms.

❖ You can opt to search within one journal (publication) only. This is generally not recommended unless a professor has told you to do so.

❖ There is also a "Subject Terms" button, indicating that this index has a controlled subject vocabulary. In some databases, this will be called a "Thesaurus."

❖ You can preset search options to specify the kind of keyword searches and the sorts of results you want.

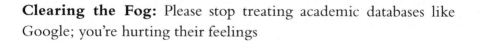

Clearing the Fog: Please stop treating academic databases like Google; you're hurting their feelings

Most of us have keyword fever. Throw some words into a search box and harvest results as fast as you can. But academic databases for books and journals have a distinct advantage over your average Google or Bing: They have metadata that enables you to be very specific about what you are looking for. The better academic databases also have options to search within results, thus letting you facet (or stage) your search. With features like these, you could do an initial keyword search, get hundreds or thousands of results, and then drill down by searching within results until you have a much smaller but much more specific and relevant set of results. Here's an example from the EBSCO Database, PsycINFO:

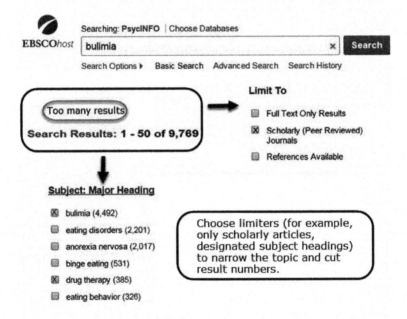

If you want an animated tutorial on how to stage (facet) your searches in this database, go to **https://youtu.be/mzyd3U-4LqQ**.

You need to do the stages. Academic databases are much more sophisticated than Google. Don't treat them like Google. Academic databases have feelings too.

6.3.3 RSS feeds from journal databases

RSS (Really Simple Syndication) feeds enable you to be updated when new material appears in a database. Many databases allow you to identify search terminology you want to track. Every time new articles, related to a specified set of search terms, appear in the selected database, you are notified and given links to find these articles. Look for the RSS icon (an orange square with 3 half circles in the lower left corner), or a link to "RSS" or "E-mail Alert." Recently, some such alerts have hidden under a "Share" link.

6.3.4 Table of contents alerts

If you are a real keener, you might want to keep up with what's being published in a favorite journal or two. A great way to do this is with a journal table of contents alert service like JOURNAL TOCs (**http://www.journaltocs.hw.ac.uk/**). Just register and choose your journal(s). You will get a contents notification (though not the full text of articles) every time a new issue comes out. It's free.

6.4 Approaching journal databases: Tips and hints

6.4.1 Be prepared for challenges.

The journal scene is not nearly as tidy as are books. Journals provide a never-ending supply of issues year after year after year, and they can exist in a variety of formats (PDFs, HTML, open-access on the Net, and even paper and various microforms), but even then you may discover that the very article you need is nowhere to be found in your metropolitan area.

Here's a psychological trick that might help you—*prepare yourself for challenges.* An illustration: If you are aware from long experience that you will face a traffic jam at a certain place every day on the way to work or school, you are ready for it. Only when a traffic jam happens unexpectedly, in an unusual spot, do you get frustrated. In the same way, if you prepare yourself for journal database challenges, you're less likely the mutter to yourself when they happen.

Before you start using a database, say to yourself, "I know this search is going to tax the last fragments of my patience, but it's good for me, it really is, it really, really is, and *I will succeed!"*

6.4.2 Read the interface.

Every journal database is different in the way it searches and the search options it offers, even two databases produced by the same company. Before you simply throw some words at a database and demand articles in return, check out what's available to you. Is there an advanced search? Is there a thesaurus or a subject heading search? In what ways can you limit or expand your search? Is there a tutorial available? (You can find quite a number of short animated tutorials for using various databases from the ANTS project at **http://www. screencast.com/users/ANTS** or **https://www.youtube.com/ user/1LIONTV.**)

6.4.3 Be aware that databases tend to be something of a black box.

You send in a request, and the database tells you what it found (not what it didn't find). The database search program will rarely let you know what you did wrong or what might actually be available if you did a better search. It won't give you three 6.5's and an 8 like Olympic judges do. The data you want could well be in there, but it's hidden in the darkness. You will have to vary your search strategies to draw it out.

6.4.4 Resist the urge to fill the search box with words.

Most keyword searches can be done with two words or, at the most, three. Remember this simple insight—the more words you throw into a search box the more strain you're putting on your search. If it's an AND search, you are telling the database that you want *only* those articles that have *every* word you've entered (which often results in few or zero hits). If it's an OR search, each and every article that has any one of your words will appear (sometimes resulting in thousands of hits). Get focused. *Use as few words as you need to define your topic, no more.*

6.4.5 Think about staging (faceting) your search.

Unlike Google, where you do a search and then pull in your results like you're fishing with a net, a journal database allows you the option of starting broadly and then narrowing in stages. "Stages?" you ask, bewildered that I would even suggest that you might not get great results on the first try. Yes, stages. Like a video game requires stages or like most any activity in life requires steps to be taken. In our example of a real search below, I'll show you how to stage (or facet) a search.

6.4.6 Look for controlled vocabularies and advanced searches.

Tools like controlled vocabularies and advanced searches can help you to specify what you want, especially when keywords could be ambiguous. For example, if I searched EBSCO's *Academic Search Complete* for "paranoia," I would get a host of articles on all kinds of paranoia—political, social, spouses who hire detectives, people claiming to have been kidnapped by aliens, folks suspicious of luncheon meats, and so on. If I could find a subject heading within *Academic Search* for the psychological disorder of paranoia (and I could), I would limit the scope of possible results considerably. Now, if I tried an advanced search—SUBJECT Paranoia and KEYWORD

Fear, I would find articles on the issue of fear among people with the psychological disorder of paranoia. It is that kind of fiddling with features that gets you the *best* results instead of merely a bunch of results.

6.4.7 Think before you search.

Even when you figure out how a journal database actually works, you need to think deeply about the terms you input. Search is strategic. What will uniquely identify your topic in the minimum number of words? If your results show hit rates of 1,000 to 100,000 articles, you're aiming too broadly in your search, and you need to narrow down your terminology. If you are getting only one or two hits, you're probably too narrow: You've been inputting too many search terms or asking for something so minute that there's only one scholar in the whole world who's remotely interested in the topic, and she's on vacation. A tip: As often as you can, use actual terminology from your research question, or synonyms of that terminology.

6.4.8 Retrace your steps.

Be prepared to go back and figure out what you did wrong or how you could get better results. Look for "Refine Search" or "Search Again" options. Journal database searching often demands experimentation to find just the right combination of terms that will nail down what you are looking for.

6.4.9 When in doubt, use the instructions.

Every journal database worth its salt has instructions to guide you through the process of searching. After you've exhausted your own common sense, use the instructions. Different databases have different capabilities and search techniques. You may find that the reason you get 354,000 hits one time and zero the next is that you are abusing the database by trying to make it do things it's not prepared even to contemplate.

6.4.10 Remain calm and get help if you need it.

What's the most terrible thing that could happen if you blew a search? You might have to try again or (worst case scenario) one of your friends will have watched you fail. You can't really hurt the database itself, so the only damage is to your time and your ego. If you find yourself hopelessly lost, there is usually a reference librarian to help you out, either personally or via some remote means like e-mail or messaging. Swallow your pride and ask for help. Having a bad day in front of a database isn't the end of the world. Above all, resist those evil thoughts that take up residence in your mind, such as, "I will never ever get this" or, "For people like me, ignorant would be a step up," "I must be a few pepperoni short of a pizza," or, "I want to break something." Cool your heart and try again.

6.4.11 Sometimes problems arise because you're using the wrong database.

A database for agriculture won't help you with a psychology project. A history database won't be much good if you're researching cockroaches. The right database for the right job is a rule not to be forgotten. If you can't find one for the subject area you're working on, try a larger, broadly based database that covers a number of different topics. These types of databases, however, have their own problems in that their coverage of any one subject area is limited.

Insight: *For specialized topics, start with specialized databases (e.g. for mental illnesses use a psychology database) and resort to more broadly based all-topic databases only if the specialized ones don't deliver enough of what you need or if you need an interdisciplinary emphasis.*

6.4.12 Check out the possibilities of interlibrary loan.

A database may provide a citation to an article you really want, but the electronic full text is not available, nor does the library have the article in any other format. Fret not. While not all academic libraries offer interlibrary loans (the ability to get the article from somewhere else), yours very well may. Have a look at your library web page for information about interlibrary loans or ask a librarian. Do you feel better now?

6.5 Citation searches, related articles and reference lists: Alternative ways of searching

6.5.1 Citation searches

In the sciences and to some extent the social sciences, the relative importance of journal articles (and their authors) is measured by the number of citations to them found in other articles. If an article is cited often within a few years, it is often viewed as being more important than if it is seldom or never cited.

What is more, citations to a key earlier article within several later articles can form a history of how the earlier article has been used by other scholars since it was published. Finding out who have cited a key earlier article can be a good way to add to your own resources.

The traditional tool used in citation searching is Web of Knowledge's three part citation index system: *Science Citation Index*, *Social Sciences Citation Index*, and *Arts and Humanities Citation Index*. While fairly complex to use, you can start with a keyword search, get a list of results, and then sort the list by "Times Cited." When you find an oft-cited (sounds Shakespearean, doesn't it?) article, you can click on the "Times Cited" link to get a list of all the literature that has cited it. Not only does this tool help you determine the relative importance of articles, but it can get you a lot of resources that have cited an important one, thus building up your own bibliography.

Google Scholar (**http://scholar.google.com**) offers a "cited by" link below many of the scholarly works in its results list. It works quite well to track citations and is becoming a serious challenge to Web of Science, though some argue that the actual citation numbers in Google Scholar are inflated. Google Scholar is freely available on the Net while libraries have to subscribe to Web of Science.

6.5.2 Related articles

For quite a number of journal databases, when you open the full record of one of the results of your search, you will find a link to "related articles," or "find more like this one." A feature like this can be of great help when you really want to add to resources. Google Scholar also has this feature.

6.5.3 Reference lists

Once you have a relevant article in hand, a great way to find others like it is simply to look over the notes, bibliography or reference list in that article. What one writer cites tends to be relevant to the topic or issue overall. Advanced researchers often use this method more often than even the searching of databases. But be aware of a couple of things. First, a reference list will always have resources that are older than the original article. Second, what any author cites may not be all that is actually out there. Reference lists can be quite selective and limited in scope. Still, they can be an effective source to mine for additional resources.

A number of databases provide, right in their citations, a list of all the sources a particular article used in its notes or bibliography. Thus, even if you can't get the article itself, you can discover the books, articles, etc. to which that article referred.

Clearing the Fog: What's a doi?

Journals in the sciences and social sciences, with the humanities coming along too, have embraced the doi (digital object identifier) system which, in essence, stamps a barcode-like number on each article a journal publishes. That doi then remains attached to that article, no matter in what format the article is found. Here is an example of an article citation with a doi:

Badke, W. B. (2005). Can't get no respect: Helping faculty to understand the educational power of information literacy. *Reference Librarian, 43*(89/90), 63–80. doi:10.1300/J120v43n8905

How can you find the doi for an article from a database when you want to cite the article properly?

❖ You can click on the citation's title in your result list and look through the full record for that article to locate the doi.
❖ If your database has a citing feature, the citations it creates will have the doi in them.

Here is an example of the open record and citing feature from an EBSCO database:

Can't Get No Respect: Helping Faculty to Understand the Educational

Authors:	Badke, William B.[1] *badke@twu.ca*
Source:	Reference Librarian. 2005, Vol. 43 Issue 89/90, p63-80. 18p.
Document Type:	Article
Author Affiliations:	[1]Associate Librarian, Trinity Western University, Associated Canadian Theological Schoc
ISSN:	0276-3877
DOI:	10.1300/J120v43n8905

The doi is especially important for citations in APA format. An interesting but challenging style note is that APA format *demands* that you include the doi, rather than providing the name of the database you got the article from.

So what if an article has no doi? APA requires you to Google the journal title (not the title of the article, but the journal it came from). Find the journal home page URL and add it to the basic citation, as in this example:

Badke, W. (2001). Questia.com: Implications of the new McLibrary. *Internet Reference Services Quarterly*, *5*(3), 61-71. Retrieved from http://www.tandfonline.com/loi/wirs.

6.6 Trying out a live journal database

Let's test-drive a real journal database, remembering that interfaces and features vary, depending on which one you use. In our case, you will be taking EBSCO's broad-based *Academic Search Complete* for a spin around the block, because the topic we will be approaching is quite interdisciplinary rather than limited to one subject discipline.

Let's begin with the question, "What is the best way for scientists to address the problems of climate change in the arctic?"

We can start with a simple keyword search, just to see what's out there. In this case, the terms *climate change arctic* should do the trick. We end up with 4,356 results. Too many, but there are ways to narrow your search and cut down the result numbers:

Let's have a look at some clues in the image above:

- ❖ 4356 results, even having limited only to scholarly articles, are too much to handle. It may well be that some of the results have the right words but don't deal centrally with arctic climate change.
- ❖ Obviously we need to cut down the total number of results, using a combination of subject headings and a narrowing of our topic.

We can dive further down the column to the left of the results and find Subject: Thesaurus term. Clicking on it identifies a few subject headings. Clicking on the "Show more" link identifies further subject headings. We decide to narrow our topic while cutting results by choosing the subject "polar bear." This means we are now searching on the plight of the polar bear, due to arctic climate change, as the climate change problem we want to address.

Subject: Thesaurus Term   X

	Name ⇕	Hit Count ▾
☐	meteorology	70
☐	global environmental change	69
☐	marine ecology	69
☐	north atlantic oscillation	69
☑	polar bear	67
☐	biomass	64
☐	remote sensing	64
☐	simulation methods & models	64
☐	snow	64
☐	food chains (ecology)	62
☐	holocene paleoclimatology	62

Update Cancel   ▲ ▼

And the results (ta dah!):

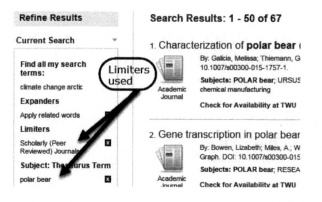

Note that now have 67 results, rather than our initial 4,356, and they are both scholarly and focused on a narrower topic: plight of polar bears in the arctic due to climate change. A new research question could be: "What is the best way for scientists to address the challenges to polar bears brought about by climate change?"

Additional strategy:

Another way to find subject headings to help narrow your search is to open the citation to one of the articles in the results (by clicking on its title). Authors and Subject headings will be hyperlinked in the full record, enabling you to click on an author to find more by the same person or on a subject to find everything on the subject. For example:

Diet of female polar bears in the southern Beaufort Sea of Alaska: evidence for an emerging alternative foraging strategy in response to environmental change.
   Authors:
   Rogers, M.[1]
   Peacock, E.[2]
   Simac, K.[2]
   O'Dell, M.
   Welker, J.
   Source:
   Polar Biology. Jul2015, Vol. 38 Issue 7, p1035–1047. 13p. 3 Charts, 4 Graphs, 2 Maps.
   Document Type: Article
   Subject Terms:
   ★POLAR bear
   ★BIOTELEMETRY
   ★STABLE isotopes
   ★BEARS
   ★HEALTH
   ★BOWHEAD whale
   ★FORAGING behavior (Animals)

Clicking on an author's name or a subject heading opens up new sets of results that can help you focus even more specifically on what you need.

6.7 Varieties of the journal database

It's now virtually impossible to keep up with the number and types of journal databases available, let alone keep up with their ever changing interfaces. Staying in touch with research libraries and librarians seems to be the only way to remain up to date. Of course, for many people even the thought of keeping in touch with a librarian may seem unusual, despite the fact that we're the kindest (and coolest) people in the world.

Most library home pages now have links to their journal databases, using wording like "Find articles," "Find journals," and so on. In most cases, you can look up journal databases by the title of the database (e.g. PsycINFO) or by the subject area you are interested in (e.g. Psychology).

If you expect constant change in the area of electronic research, you won't be disappointed. Despite the fact that it's hard for most of us to keep up, the capabilities of these newer databases are amazing, and you can benefit greatly from them as long as you keep your wits about you. Just don't treat them like Google. They'll remember what you did and not be so kind to you the next time you use them.

6.8 Final pep talk

Don't be afraid of journal databases and articles. They want to be strong and effective resources for you, if you'll let them. Scholarly articles in journals will provide you with a wealth of current and specific information that you dare not ignore. Most journal databases have sophisticated ways for you to focus on the search results you actually need rather than leaving you floundering in a sea of less than relevant articles.

More and more libraries are providing short guides or animated tutorials to their individual databases. Spending 5 minutes or less watching an explanatory animation is probably worth it, especially if you fear you are going to muddle for a couple of hours, saying things to yourself that would make even your dog blush if he could understand you. For a great site to find short tutorials on a number of databases, go to ANTS project at Screencast.com: **http://www. screencast.com/users/ANTS** or **https://www.youtube.com/ user/1LIONTV.**

Just heed the following pieces of advice, and you will survive the journal maze:

- ❖ Stay calm.
- ❖ Stay focused.
- ❖ Read the directions.
- ❖ Plan your searches well.
- ❖ Ask for help when you need it.

6.9 For further study

Study guide

1. What is discovery search? What are its advantages and disadvantages?
2. In a library catalog, when would you use controlled vocabulary subject headings, and when would you use keywords?
3. How can hierarchies help you when you are searching a library catalog for a topic?
4. Why is it futile to believe that the electronic full text of every book you want will be available to you for free?
5. How are journal databases created, and what are they intended to do?
6. Explain the difference between "data" and "interface."
7. Identify each part of the following journal citation:
   Badke, William. (2010). Why information literacy is invisible. *Communications in Information Literacy 4(2)*, 129-141.

8. In journal database searching you should be prepared for
   _____. How does such preparation help you?
9. Why should you resist the urge to fill the search box with words?
10. What are the advantages of thinking before you search?
11. Why is it often better to stage (facet) your search with keywords as well as subject headings and other limiters rather than simply to do a one-stage keyword search?
12. Many journal articles are available in electronic "full text" format. What are some of the advantages and difficulties with accessing full text?

Practice with journal databases

Go to one of your institution's databases and "read" the interface, trying to figure out what search features it provides. Try searches on the same topic using different features. What did you learn about the value of enhanced search features to get you the results you need?

Assignment for a project of your own

1. Choose a topic of interest to you.
2. Choose two journal databases. If you do not have access to university databases like those produced by EBSCO, ProQuest, Sage, and so on, choose from the following free Internet-based databases: **http://www.ingentaconnect. com/** or **http://magportal.com/** (but note that their interfaces are not nearly as sophisticated as commercial products available through your library).
3. Do a search for journal articles on your topic with each database.
4. Indicate what subject terms or keywords you used in your searches.
5. List 6 articles from each database that are relevant to your topic - author, date, article title, title of journal, volume number, page numbers. **Note: Be sure the databases you use are relevant to your topic.**

7

Internet Research

The early 1990s saw the beginning of an information revolution as dramatic as the introduction of the printing press in Europe in 1440 (though we dare not miss the fact that the Chinese people had a printing press 400 years earlier). The printing press made it possible to replace the normal copying of documents by hand with a process that produced multiple copies at the same time. All of a sudden, the availability of written information increased dramatically. The creation of the World Wide Web in the 1990s led to the same kind of revolution, but on a larger scale.

With the rise of the WWW, an information delivery system primarily concerned with paper and print (libraries, bookstores, hard copy journal subscriptions and so on) became an electronic universe available to anyone with a device and a service provider. Today, the average student gets well over two-thirds of his/her information from search engines like Google or Bing.

Please supply your own answer to the following question: **The World Wide Web is an environment where:**_____

Stumped? Let me supply some possibilities:

The World Wide Web is an environment where:

- ❖ you can freely interact with the rest of humanity
- ❖ you can find information on virtually any topic
- ❖ almost everyone is trying to sell you something
- ❖ you can surf until your eyes fall out
- ❖ anything that's worth anything costs *money* to retrieve (or else you're told that access is "forbidden!")
- ❖ you can meet new friends or pick up predators
- ❖ you can't absolutely trust anyone or any piece of information
- ❖ you can get flamed and trolled at will by people who don't even know you
- ❖ you can get your questions answered
- ❖ you can spend a lot of time you don't really have to spare

Maybe your response should be "all of the above." The WWW is wonderful and frustrating, helpful and potentially deceptive, beneficial and a real time-sink. And it has become the common denominator of our daily lives. As the phenomenon of doing things electronically grows, the only common medium that can meet its needs is the WWW. It has become the basis for the things we need to get done. It is the number one vehicle for all informational research, whether through a search engine or a specialized subscription database.

True, some people are calling for us to start over with this thing, using what we have learned to create a new World Wide Web that works more efficiently (see, for example, the Named Data Networking Project: **http://www.named-data.net/**). But no one is advocating that we abandon it.

7.1 A brief introduction to the Net

I hesitate to recite history, but there are a lot of people who grew up with the Net and really don't appreciate its back story. In the late 1960s, the US military developed a worldwide computer network in order to remain in communication with everybody involved in the space program and defense research. This network (really a network of networks) eventually came into the hands of non-military people - scientists, computer buffs, and so on. It lacked a common communication language that was easy to use, so only specialists could profit from it. In the early 1990s, a common communication language (html) and a common communication protocol (http) were created and made public so that anyone who had access to this network could move around it with ease. This resulted in the formation of the World Wide Web (WWW). Essentially, the WWW is a subset of the larger Internet, though in common language the two terms are often used interchangeably.

The following sites on the Internet will provide you with good information about using it for research purposes:

https://developer.mozilla.org/en-US/Learn/How_the_ Internet_works
This site, from the people who developed the Firefox Internet browser, provides a lot of information on the basics of the Net.

https://owl.english.purdue.edu/owl/resource/558/01/
This is a tutorial from the Purdue Online Writing Lab.

Disclaimer: In the pages that follow, several URLs will be provided. Addresses change rapidly on the WWW, so I make no guarantee that you will find what you're seeking by inputting the URLs given. Sorry, but that's life, raw and nasty, though still interesting. Keep these URLs up to date with my live links page: **http://williambadke. com/links.htm**

7.2 Google Scholar and other free academic search engines on the Net

7.2.1 Why start with academic search engines?

We have Google. Why get all stuffy and start our discussion with academic search engines like Google Scholar? Well, my motive is partly based on the fact that this book is about academic research. Another part is the fact that most readers are already familiar with Google (though I'll happily reveal a few things later in this chapter that you possibly did not know).

The other part of my purpose comes from a lingering concern that a lot of students are using general search engines without much regard for evaluation of the websites they find. Academic search engines at least get you to information that has often gone through some sort of gatekeeping process, or so we hope.

But fear not, we'll deal with more broadly based search engines soon. For now, we'll look at academic research tools, whose result lists are most often academic journal articles, books and conference proceedings rather than websites.

7.2.2 Google Scholar (http://scholar.google.com)

Google Scholar, though an increasingly significant player in the academic world, isn't really a subset of the Google search engine. It is for the most part a separate resource devoted to scholarly literature: Books, journal articles, conference proceedings and academic websites found on the WWW. Think of it as a type of academic one-stop shopping center. Yet, before you come to believe that you've found paradise, be aware that GS does have its challenges:

❖ It is limited to the standard basic search box and some rather elementary advanced search features. Thus any sophisticated search techniques using controlled vocabularies or clustering are out of the question.

❖ Not all publishers of academic information are included, though GS is getting more comprehensive all the time.

❖ The definition of "academic" is fairly broad. I've found second year undergraduate student papers through GS as well as articles from second-rate journals.

❖ It's unclear how the results are ranked. What qualifies your results to be on the first page as opposed to being on the fifth or twentieth? In GS, you can rearrange your results by date (though the results only go back a year), or you can set a date range for results. But you can't organize your results by type of material (articles, books, conference proceedings and academic websites). Citations of every type are jumbled together.

❖ The quest for actual full text is a frustrating one. Increasingly, there are links to full text posted by authors, but more often than not, following a link to a journal article will get you only to an abstract of it. The full text will cost you significant coin. This can be offset in a couple of ways: first, check to see if your academic library has linked its journal holdings to GS through the "library links" process (ask your librarian about this or go to **http://scholar.google.com/intl/en/ scholar/librarylinks.html**), and second, check your own library's journal list to see if it subscribes to the journal named in a citation you found in Scholar. A number of database providers like EBSCO and JSTOR have begun including links to full text articles if the searcher is logged in to GS through his/her library and if the library subscribes to those databases.

All of that said, Google Scholar can be a very useful resource, especially for helping to identify something about which you have only partial information, for finding other articles by an important author on your topic (use the "cited by" and "related articles" links under each citation), or simply as one more place to search for resources. It will not, however, usually serve as first choice ahead of the journal databases available through your library.

Google Scholar's help system (**http://scholar.google.com/intl/en/scholar/help.html**) is very good, so I won't take time to explain all of its functions. I would urge you, however, to make use of the advanced search feature, which has some useful limiters. (If you can find the advanced search, that is. When last seen it was that little upside down triangle in the right end of the basic search box). You should also know that, under Scholar Settings (the wheel in the top right of the first Google Scholar screen), you can set yourself up to be able to download citations from GS to a bibliographic manager like RefWorks or EndNote (more on bibliographic managers in chapter 8).

Here are some of the common types of citations you can expect to find in Google Scholar:

- ❖ Journal articles: Look for the journal name just under the title link in the citation. There is no specific descriptor, like [Journal], used to identify journal articles.
- ❖ Books: Not the full text in most cases; designated by [Book].
- ❖ Citations: This is a bit tricky; a citation is a reference to a scholarly article or book found within one of the articles or books in the GS database. So it's a reference to a reference. As such, *it has no link* to take you to a place where you can obtain it, though you can link to the source that referred to it, as well as do a search on Google to see if it's available on the open Net. This type of result is designated as [Citation].
- ❖ Conference proceedings: Conference proceedings have no special designation to tell them apart from journal articles, so you have to look at how they are described under the title link in the citation. Here's an example:

> <u>Time division duplex for preventing reflection interference in visible light communication</u>
> YF Liu, CW Chow, CH Yeh – ... **Conference** (WOCC), 2012 21st ..., 2012 - ieeexplore.ieee.org**...** **Conference**

> **Proceeding** 2012 21st Annual Wireless and Optical Communications **Conference** (WOCC)-April 19-21, Kaohsiung, Taiwan
> Related articles Import into EndNote More

Note that the name of the conference is stated. As long as we are looking at this entry, you can see that it is also possible to identify related (= similar) articles, and you can import the citation into a bibliographic manager (if you set this up in Scholar Settings).

❖ Academic and government websites: These will have URLs (instead of journal names or descriptions like [Book] or [Citation]).

Google Scholar appears to be going up against two large commercial databases: Web of Science and LexisNexis. The former lets scholars see how many times and in what publications a particular article has been cited (referred to) by others. This helps determine the relative importance of that original article. Google Scholar has a fairly sophisticated "Cited by" feature that, in many cases, pulls up more citations than Web of Science does. This is probably because GS has a broader definition what "academic literature" than does Web of Science. Google Scholar has also geared itself up to search for legal opinions and legal cases, something that was once the major turf of the database LexisNexis.

An interesting twist on using Google Scholar arises from the dilemma that users get such a variety of results of varying quality. As "predatory journals" (journals that are published open access with very limited peer review and poor quality) are increasing, Google Scholar, with its emphasis on including everything that looks scholarly, is being somewhat infiltrated with junk. This is still a small percentage of its search results, but is raising concerns (see **https://web.archive.org/web/20161110004415/https://scholarlyoa.com/2014/11/04/google-scholar-is-filled-with-junk-science/.**

What if it were possible to focus Scholar searches on only the best articles? With the "library links" option in Google Scholar, if you log in through your institution, you can limit your search to a specific type of database. For example, you can do your search and add the term JSTOR to it, to focus on results only from the JSTOR database.

Clearing the Fog: Google Scholar may be more valuable for what surrounds a citation than for what is in it.

A few features on the Google Scholar results page, beyond merely the citations, are worth checking out, as seen in citation example below:

Can't get no respect: Helping faculty to understand the educational power of information literacy
WB Badke - The Reference Librarian, 2005 - Taylor & Francis
SUMMARY While there is much discussion today about information literacy, proper implementation of it within university campuses is still a struggle, often due to the fact that librarians and teaching faculty have different "cultures" that create different priorities. ...
Cited by 74 Related articles All 7 versions Import into EndNote Cite Save

* ❖ **Cited by** (under result citations): This will tell you how many times a resource has been cited (referred to) by other sources, and it will give you a list of which sources have cited it. The more citations (in general), the more highly regarded a resource will be. But there are some cautions: a. you need to see how old the resource is (older resources have had the opportunity to be cited more often but may not be more important than an equally cited newer resource); b. you need to recognize that authors may cite themselves from their earlier writing, thus inflating the number of citations for their works; and, c. on rare occasions a source has been cited many times simply because everyone hates it.
* ❖ **Related articles** (under each search result citation): A link to resources that have similar words in them and thus may be

on the same topic. Great for expanding your bibliography (as long as you actually read the things you cite. Not reading at least some of everything in your bibliography is an academic crime akin to mocking a professor on Twitter).

❖ **All ___ versions**: This might be helpful in locating a full text copy if one doesn't seem readily available.

❖ **Import**: You can select what bibliographic manager you want to send your citation to. The one above is set for EndNote

❖ **Cite**: Create citations in one of three bibliographic styles. But be careful. Google Scholar information is often incomplete, so your citation may not have all the parts it needs. You can usually fill in the missing data by clicking on the title of the article and seeing more complete citation data.

❖ **Save**: Google Scholar has a feature called My Library, which you need to enable (**https://scholar.google.ca/intl/en/ scholar/help.html#library**). Once you have enabled My Library, you will see a Save link under each citation and a My Library link to the left. Clicking "Save" puts the citation into My Library. You can also create labels that will let you group your citations. What is more, you can do a Google Scholar search of the full text within My Library.

❖ **Full text?:** As the open access movement grows and more scholars post copies of their published work on their own websites, the availability of full text right in Google Scholar is growing. Watch for links to the right of citations that say "PDF" or "html." If you logged in through your library you may find links to your library's journal subscriptions.

7.2.3 BASE (http://www.base-search.net/)

BASE, produced by Bielefeld University Library, is a large search engine that covers academic open access web resources mainly found in university electronic repositories. Thus it focuses only on academic literature that is openly available on the Net. A couple of advantages of this tool over Google Scholar are that the academic sources are humanly selected (rather than computer selected) and that BASE offers a full list of the academic publishers from whom it selects (Google Scholar doesn't). The disadvantage is that it covers only open access (freely available) resources and does not search commercial/password-protected academic material as Google Scholar does.

7.2.4 Microsoft Academic (https://academic.microsoft.com/)

Following upon the failure of Windows Live Academic, Microsoft renewed its academic search under the name Microsoft Academic Search but stopped adding anything after 2012. In 2016, a ramped up version was developed under the name Microsoft Academic. It boasts that it is adding one million academic documents to its base per week. Though it is still smaller than Google Scholar and produces fewer results, it has a pretty sophisticated set of limiters to the left of search results, giving you: Ability to search by a particular author, journal, conference, date and doi (Digital Object Identifier); ability for users to correct errors in the information; and availability of larger records which are profile pages for content or authors.

7.2.5 CiteSeerX (http://citeseerx.ist.psu.edu/)

CiteSeerX is a search engine for open access (freely available) academic scientific information. As such, it offers the full text of more than 2 million scholarly articles. But it does a lot more. In the scientific and social scientific worlds, the value of research papers is often determined by how many other papers refer to (cite) them. If your paper has a hundred citations to it in other people's papers, it will be considered to be more valuable to the scientific community than if it only has one citation. CiteSeer is able to break down the details of the articles it lists so that you can see what sources each article cited and which articles have cited that article. Helpful charts demonstrate citation history. There are also a number of sort features to reorganize search results.

Citations to an existing paper can also help scholars follow a trail of research on a topic: Paper A, published in 2001, was cited by paper B in 2003, paper C in 2004, paper D in 2013, and so on. The later papers demonstrate how the research in Paper A has been used in new ways to expand knowledge, thus creating a history of the conversation related to the development of the topic.

7.2.6 Scirius [now defunct]

This search engine from Elsevier was retired by the company in 2014. Elsevier recommends you try its database, ScienceDirect, which is only available through subscriptions and logins. So long, Scirius.

7.2.7 getCITED [now defunct]

Clearly 2014 was the year to kill off free and useful academic databases. This one is gone too. R.I.P., getCITED.

7.2.8 Others

Here are a few of the many other academic search engines giving access to freely available resources on the Net:

- ❖ **Academia (https://www.academia.edu/):** An academic social media site that allows scholars to share their articles, conference papers, and so on with everyone. It has millions of such resources in it, but you need to join (for free) to benefit fully.
- ❖ **arXiv (http://arxiv.org/):** Open access to over a million e-prints in "Physics, Mathematics, Computer Science, Quantitative Biology, Quantitative Finance and Statistics" (from the website).

❖ **Directory of Open Access Journals (http://www.doaj. org/):** database of thousands of open access (thus freely available) academic journals.

❖ **Directory of Open Access Books (http://www. doabooks.org/)**

❖ **OAIster (http://oaister.worldcat.org/):** database of academic websites (also available within the larger **Worldcat. org** database)

❖ **ResearchGate (https://www.researchgate.net/home):** academic social media site that allows scholars to post their work. Searchable by everyone.

❖ **Social Science Research Network (http://ssrn.com/):** database that includes over half a million articles in various branches of the social sciences. Now owned by Elsevier, a commercial academic publisher that promises not to mess with it.

❖ **Wolfram Alpha (http://www.wolframalpha.com/):** OK, this one is not a journal search engine, but it's so cool that I had to include it. Billed as a "computational knowledge engine," this tool will do a wide variety of mathematical calculations, but much more. As the site itself tells us: "We aim to collect and curate all objective data; implement every known model, method, and algorithm; and make it possible to compute whatever can be computed about anything. Our goal is to build on the achievements of science and other systematizations of knowledge to provide a single source that can be relied on by everyone for definitive answers to factual queries." Whew! Try it out. For example, input your birth date and it will tell you how many days you have lived upon this earth (though not how many you have left to go). Really quite amazing.

Wolfram Alpha also has an image identification function. Drag an image to its search box at **https://www. imageidentify.com/**.

More of these types of free online academic search tools will emerge over time, fueled in part by the growing open access movement that is making a lot of academic information available for free. But be warned: Much of what you want is found within the journal databases your library pays for. The myth that most journal articles are freely available on the open Web is as believable as the alligators in New York City sewers.

Be aware, as well, that none of the free online academic databases above do searches nearly as well as do commercial academic databases available through your library. While they cost nothing and look cool, their level of sophistication is pretty low. It's like trying to compare a sundial with a Rolex. The Rolex wins.

7.3 Search engines for the rest of humanity: Google and friends

7.3.1 Searching by search engine, using keywords

In the most common Internet research situation, you want information on a topic, but you don't have a specific address (URL). This is where a search engine can help you by taking the keyword(s) you input and searching the WWW for data that is relevant. As you will soon discover, each search engine does the job a bit differently and with different results.

Some search engines are better for certain searches than for others. Most *rank* their results so that, by their algorithms, the most relevant, useful results will come first. But be careful with this. Some sites (often in a different script or with a colored background) are at the top of the results list because they have paid to be there. Ranking is done by complex software functions, but it is still ranking-by-computer. Not wanting to seem anti-tech or anything, humans are still smarter than our devices in evaluating the usefulness of data, so we should not simply trust the ranking assigned by a search engine.

In general, most students commit two great errors when using a search engine. First, they don't go deeper into results than one or two pages. A lot of searchers, in fact, don't look beyond the first five results. This means that they are relying on search engine ranking rather than using their superior brains to probe deeper and find the really good result that might be on the third page of results. Second, they fail to evaluate the websites they choose from their results, somehow assuming that search engine results are all pretty good and have probably been checked out by someone (they haven't).

Insight: *If you want to rise above basic level as a researcher, vow to spend more time after initial searches, especially Internet searches, looking over and carefully evaluating your results. You need to aim to check out 4 or more pages of results before you give up. And assume that your results are a mixed bag when it comes to both quality and relevance. Evaluation is a must. If you haven't found what you want, it's not that hard to modify your search terms and try again.*

What options do we have available to us for creating effective searches? That depends. Each search engine has its own set of search paradigms. Search engines usually have a **"tips"** or **"help"** or **"about"** link you can click on to be guided on the best ways to input keywords for that search engine.

- ❖ In most cases, search engines automatically create an AND search. Use quotation marks if you want to include words that would normally be ignored like "the," or "of," (e.g. **"The" Office** for the TV series, which, like MASH and Seinfeld, will be forever in reruns.).
- ❖ OR is usually required for "or" searches, but make it OR in capital letters.
- ❖ NOT is often done with a dash in front of a word (**-trees** [no space]).

❖ Most search engines allow you to group words that normally belong together. To do this, use quotation marks (**"accountability groups"**). If you don't use the quotation marks, it's often OK, since most initial results will have the words in close proximity. But the search engine could also bring you sites that use the two words even though they are not related, as in: "The president is calling for more *accountability.* This has been rejected by several banking *groups* that insist ..."

❖ Most search engines *do not use* truncation or wildcards (e.g. Freud★ for Freud, Freudian, etc.)

As a skilled researcher, always check the search tips for a search engine and make sure you know what you're dealing with. Most will allow you to refine your search somewhat if you're not finding what you want or you have too many hits.

7.3.2 A basic introduction to the best search engines

Truth to tell (and I usually try to be truthful, because I'm not a convincing liar), you could likely get by with Google and never use another search engine. But it's a good idea to keep a number of engines in your garage. Each engine creates its own index of the Internet, so that, while Google's is the biggest, it may not have included sites that are found in another search engine's index.

You need to be aware that, though the following search engines are currently the best around for the WWW, the quality of the actual websites they cover varies from the most scholarly to a page created by some guy who thinks he's a duck. *You* are the gatekeeper now, and evaluation is all important (more on this later in the chapter). Many professors simply won't accept websites in bibliographies unless you can prove that the material has been produced by reputable scholars or at least people who have advanced knowledge of the topic.

Virtually every search engine now uses personalization, especially if you log in (more on this below). You will have to decide whether or not you want to be tracked.

Every time I bring out a new edition of this book, the list of best search engines is different. Inevitably some merge with others, some change their foci, and some just die. I remain hopeful that the list below will survive this edition, but by the time you read this, a great new search engine may well have arisen and the features of those described below may have changed. Yet, I dare to introduce them to you anyway, brave and foolhardy soul that I am. Here goes:

Google (https://www.google.com/)

Google has the biggest index of the Net and consistently does the best job of locating what you're searching for. Here are some key features:

❖ As you input keywords to use as search tools, Google automatically forms them into an AND search and seeks to bring you websites that contain those words in close proximity to one another.

❖ Google uses a technique called PageRank that prioritizes your results by giving you first those sites that are most often found as links on other websites. This "popularity" measure seems to work well in searches so that the most relevant sites often appear in the first 20 or so results (but not always). There are other things going on in Google's algorithm box, but Google isn't talking in public about most of them.

❖ If you look at the bottom of the search page, you will see your location listed. *Your location*; how does it know where you are? See the "Clearing the Fog" section below for this dark and mysterious side of Google.

❖ Google offers simple techniques to create Boolean searches:
  • AND is automatic
  • You can create an OR by inputting OR. Google will nest searches with () as in Freud (ego OR id), but if you are not sure it's working, use the advanced search, putting

Freud into "with all of the words" and **ego id** into "with at least one of the words." (More on the advanced search below).

- Phrases can be searched by putting quotation marks around them, e.g., "apple trees." Or you can use Google's phrase search option – "this exact word or phrase" – among advanced search features.

- You can't truncate search words, e.g., educat★ for education, educator, etc. This feature simply doesn't work in Google or most other search engines. Educat★ might get you sites on education, but it might not produce what you want.

- Google used to allow you to put a plus sign before words that had to be included. That no longer works. Now, Google uses quotation marks around words that must be included in the search or which must be searched as given. Thus you need to search **"The" Office**, so that Google will include **The** in the search. You can search **"Latina"** (with quotation marks) so that Google will find only **Latina**, not related words, such as **Latino**.

❖ Google has links on its search page to allow you to toggle among various formats for its results: Web, Images, Maps, and so on.

❖ Google has a "Search Tools" button above your search results that allows you to limit to a time range or specify only sites updated in the past hour, day, week, month or year.

❖ Google has a pretty good "Advanced Search" feature that helps you do all sorts of things, *if you can find the advanced search.* For some unstated reason, Google is burying its advanced search function deeper and deeper all the time. You first have to do a basic search. On the results page, upper right, you will see a wheel. Click on it and the advanced search function will appear as a link. Here are some things you can do with it:

  - The "Find pages with..." options let you build complex Boolean searches.

- You can specify the languages of the websites you want returned.

- You can define the region from which your results will come.

- You can ask for return of results only in specified formats (PDF, MS Word, PowerPoint, etc.).

- You can select only the most recently updated websites.

- You can specify where you want your search terms to appear in the documents you retrieve (e.g. anywhere, or in the title, links or URL).

- You can ask for only those sites belonging to a certain domain (registered Internet name, like .com or .edu).

- You can filter by the license type (i.e. the types of usage allowed by a website).

❖ Google has a small inverted triangle next to the URL in each search result. Click on it, and you will find options to see a cache of the site (what it looked like the last time Google added it to its search index).

❖ If you sign in, using the box on the upper right of results, you will be prompted to set up an account with your g-mail ID. This will give you a few other features, like the ability to share websites with others. Google also provides automatic enhancements to your searches to improve results if you are logged in. But be cautious: *Logging in gives Google more of an opportunity to retain information about what you are searching. If you have privacy concerns, go to the Google privacy policy statement at* **https://www.google.com/policies/privacy/.**

❖ Google Instant is a feature that lists possible terminology under the search box while you are typing, so that you don't always have to type in the whole search; just select the search terms from the list below the search box. This feature may also give you clues to a better way to formulate your search terms. There is further information at **https://support. google.com/websearch/answer/186645?hl=en.**

Google offers separate search engines for books (Google Books: **https://books.google.com**), scholarly material (Google Scholar: **https://scholar.google.com**), things to buy (Google Product Search: **https://www.google.com/prdhp?tab=wf&ie=UTF-8**), and so on.

In October 2013, Google search moved into the next phase of its development with a new algorithm (method of gathering and delivering search results) called Hummingbird (because it's "precise and fast"). The goal is to move away from mere keyword-matching and deliver what the user is really looking for. All of this is wrapped around a better ability for Google to handle real questions. Thus, instead of searching on <climate change arctic>, Google wants to be able to handle a question like, <What's happening in the arctic because of climate change?>

Google, in fact, has made no secret of its ambition to create the "Star Trek computer," a system that moves beyond search (put in words and get results) to an interactive experience in which the search engine anticipates your needs, answers your questions directly, and does it all without the need for clunky search words. All of this will take years, but that is the goal. For more, see **http://slate.me/ JKuG4c**.

Google remains the biggest and best Internet search engine. Try out some of its extra features to improve your searches.

Clearing the Fog: While you are searching Google, Google is searching you

Eli Pariser, in a celebrated TED Talk in 2011 (**http://www.youtube. com/watch?v=B8ofWFx525s**) pointed out the risks found in the "personalization" of search engines. He was describing the growing ability of search engines to track your preferences and provide you with personalized results. When you do a Google search and click on the top button "Search Tools," you see your location boldly stated.

Google knows where you live. How scary is that? But knowing your location is only the beginning of the challenge.

Did you know that, if you and I use the same search terms in Google or several other search engines, our results will be different? Yes, different. Your results will reflect your location and also your "search history," which Google collects over time. That is, Google is compiling your preferences – the topics you are interested in – so that it can get a snapshot of you. Google's reason for personalizing, at least on the surface, is that the search engine is "helping" you by providing results that better meet your preferences. But it probably has a lot more to do with Google's ability to send you *personalized ads* which target your preferences.

Don't get all paranoid, though. There are indications that Google is not doing so much personalization that you can't find what you need when you need it. Variations in results among different users are not all that extreme. Still, it's helpful to be aware of the potential to be taken in a direction that has more to do with you and your preferences than with the keywords you used to search. For a counterargument, see the blog by Jacob Weisberg at **http://www.slate.com/articles/ news_and_politics/the_big_idea/2011/06/bubble_trouble. html.**

Google helps make personalization easier by encouraging you along the way to "sign in." Once you do, Google has all the information you have provided to it, including your data in Google+.

Sure, you can turn off some aspects of personalization (see **http://support.google.com/accounts/bin/answer. py?hl=en&answer=54048**), but not all. My own view is that personalization does more harm than good for the researcher. Just because I searched for a topic yesterday does not mean that I will not take a different slant on that topic today or even search for a new topic. Limiting my options (e.g. bringing me sites in my own region before farther away sites come up) is not something I want from a search engine. It makes me frustrated and sad that my beloved

Google, along with Bing and most other search engines have chosen to go this route. There, now I feel better.

———•———⊙▬⊙———•———

Bing (http://www.bing.com/)

Microsoft's search engine, "Bing," is known for its changed-daily full screen photos. Bing is intent on taking market share from Google. At this point, Bing is definitely the leader in coolness if not in search results themselves, where Google still leads. If you are using Windows 10 and the Edge Internet browser, Bing is quite locked into them. You may need to do some working around if you prefer Google. Bing's significant features:

- ❖ The basic search uses conventions similar to Google's.
- ❖ In the new version of Bing, the advanced search is gone, something we've already seen as the likely sad future of most search engines. First they hide the advanced search, then they kill it altogether. This, in my estimation, is a very bad idea. To its credit (somewhat), Bing has a web page detailing operators you can add to the basic search box to do advanced searching: **http://bingtricks.com/bing-advanced-search**
- ❖ When you do a search in Bing, you will get links to "Related searches" on the right. This can help you narrow or redirect your focus.
- ❖ From the bars at the top of the screen, you can track your search history, narrow to websites updated in a date range like "past month" or "past week," as well as opening the same search to other media like images and video. There are also "related searches" links provided on the right.
- ❖ Bing displays the latest news in icons along the bottom of the screen
- ❖ Bing's image and video search results are superior graphically and functionally to Google's. Bing promises a non-text image

search (put an image into the search box instead of words) similar to that already available through Google.

Yahoo! Search (http://search.yahoo.com/)

While Yahoo! Search uses Bing as its search engine, Yahoo! does have an advanced search, accessed through the wheel image in the top right. Advanced searching is quite Google-like.

Ask.com (http://www.ask.com/)

Then we have Ask.com, formerly Ask Jeeves, that is built on the Teoma search engine. It has become very "bare bones" over the years but remains a useful engine and still seems to encourage formatting searches as questions. **To the right of your results you may find news stories related to your search as well as answers to common questions about your topic and the (inevitable) ads.**

Blekko [Defunct]

Like other search engines with promise, this one, described in the 5th edition, has been bought out (by IBM Watson) and has vanished from public view. R.I.P. Blekko.

7.3.3 RSS feeds from search engines

If you are interested in staying up to date with recent results from a search you have done, many search engines allow you to set up RSS feeds that will notify you by e-mail when new sites with your search terms appear.

7.3.4 Semantic search engines

Semantic search is often promised as the future for search engines, though it is still in the early stages. It essentially means that a search engine discerns what you are actually looking for, thus going beyond the mere words in your searches. Often this is described as artificial intelligence. Most search engine providers are working very hard on semantic search development and have gone at least some way towards making their searches semantic.

Google has a growing feature called the "Knowledge Graph" that will provide information related to a search you have done and put it to the right of your results. For example, a search on Leonardo Da Vinci creates a Knowledge Graph that provides pertinent facts about him, links to his paintings and links to other Renaissance paintings. For more information about this feature see **https://www.google.com/intl/es419/insidesearch/features/search/knowledge.html.**

You might also want to try out SenseBot (**http://www.sensebot.net/**).

It appears that the development of new semantic search engines is stalling as existing engines like Google and Bing become more and more semantic. Still, semantic search remains, like most politicians, full of promise but short on delivery.

7.4 Searching by subject tree

All information exists within hierarchies. For example, cell phones are a subclass of telephones, which are a subclass of electronic communication devices, which are a subclass of all communication devices. (For a review of this concept, see section 4.3.1, above)

Information hierarchies form tree-like structures. There are certain sites on the Internet where you can search down various hierarchies or subject trees from more general categories to specific ones. Many of the portal-type sites provide such hierarchies (see below).

7.5 Portals

A helpful though diminishing research tool on the Internet is the "portal," which serves as an introduction to important sites on a subject. Typically, its main feature is a collection of links to sites that have been checked out for quality. What you end up with is a hierarchical way of searching the Net without a search engine. Its advantage is that someone has evaluated the sites, so you have a better chance of finding material that you can actually use (though your own critical thinking skills still need to be engaged).

Many portals are organized by subject. Here are a few examples:

❖ Psych Web (**http://www.psywww.com/**) is a psychology portal to websites categorized by type. Locate a category like Scholarly Issues, and it will lead you to a page that subcategorizes web links under headings like Cross-Cultural Psychology, Hypnosis, etc.

❖ History Subject Guide (**http://guides.lib.washington. edu/history**)

❖ Voice of the Shuttle: Literature (In English): **http://vos. ucsb.edu/browse.asp?id=3**

❖ Biology Online (**http://www.biology-online.org/ dictionary/Main_Pageeric**)

❖ Wabash Center Internet Guide to Religion (**http://www. wabashcenter.wabash.edu/resources/guide-headings.aspx**)

But how do you locate such sites in the first place? Here's where a more general portal can help. A general portal is usually much larger, and often serves as a doorway to more specific subject portals. For example:

Multimedia Educational Resource for Learning and Online Teaching (**http://www.merlot.org/**). This is a project of several universities and academic organizations to organize and peer review websites valuable for higher education. You can search it directly or hierarchically by subject categories.

7.6 The Hidden Internet

You may have heard of the so-called "Hidden Internet," "Invisible Web" or "Deep Web." It's billed as that portion of the Net that only the chosen few can see. Before you start thinking in terms of nasty conspiracies, you should recognize that there could be legitimate reasons why certain Web information would not be easy to find.

7.6.1 What do we mean by "Hidden?"

A simple definition of "hidden" in this context would be: "Any information carried on the WWW that can't easily be found by a Web search engine." Considering the fact that all search engines must first "discover" information before they can index it, there is always a strong possibility that some sites will be hidden at any particular time. Beyond this are sites that search engines did find but that have deeper portions accessible only through a password or a search by a site's own search engine (for example, an online library catalog).

7.6.2 What's in the Hidden Internet?

The Hidden Internet includes the following:

❖ Sites that are password protected—corporate intranets, subscription databases, online banking, e-mail accounts, spy agencies, and so on. These are protected to maintain security and restrict access only to patrons who are entitled to be there.

❖ On the darker side, cybercrime, nastier forms of criminal activity (like child porn, hate conspiracy, terrorism, and organized crime) find ways to block access so that only their authorized users can get in. This is where creepy aspects of the so-called "dark web" can be found. Most ordinary folks never encounter that world.

❖ Information can be buried within non-restricted databases such as library catalogs. A search engine might find a library catalog or other database, but it won't get past the front door to identify/view individual records within that database. Why? Because the Internet search engine can't actually search the database, which has its own search engine. So you might find the catalog of a university library with Google, but Google can't search that catalog automatically to find a record for a certain book. You have to search it yourself.

❖ New or obscure sites not yet indexed by a search engine.

7.6.3 How do I find information on the Hidden Internet?

That depends. If it's a password-protected site, you need to be authorized or you'll need to pay to get access. Don't hack! Many searchable databases can be identified either by a search engine or by hierarchical searches on the Net (see 7.3 and 7.5 above), and then you can search them directly.

The Hidden Internet lives, but there's no conspiracy (usually). Really!

7.7 Evaluating information from the Internet

Let's be realistic for a moment (aren't we always?) and ask the question: *Why would people with data want to put it up for free on the Internet?* The answers are varied:

- ❖ They want to sell you something, and their web page is simply an advertisement or a doorway to a credit card purchase.

- ❖ They have something they want to say, and this a cheap and easy way to do it. Here you can have anything from, *"Hi, I'm Tim, and here are some pictures of my iguana Frank,"* to *"I was abducted by Martians, and I want to warn the world before they eat our brains."* Here too are the blogs and social networking sites like Facebook, Twitter, and Pinterest, as well as human rights sites seeking to tell the world of abuses.

- ❖ A government or public agency will often not charge for its information because it wants to make that information freely available. Here you can find everything from the ERIC Database to government documents, directory information, census data, and so on.

- ❖ An academic or educational body may see providing information as part of its mandate. Here you may get open access journal articles, electronic editions of out-of-print books, guides to this and that, occasionally even electronic dictionaries or encyclopedias.

- ❖ Sincere scholars and other individuals will have valuable information to share and want to make that information freely available for the edification of everyone.

But take careful note of one foundational rule of life: ***Few people, except those related to the last three reasons above, provide information for free on the Net unless they want to make money from it, they can't find anyone to pay for it, or they have the financial resources to give it away freely.***

What does that mean for you, the Internet searcher? It means several things:

- ❖ A lot of what you hoped might be on the Net is not there or you have to pay for it - the full text of most journal articles, the full text of recent books, a vast array of reference tools, etc.

❖ Keyword searches through search engines can bring you a lot of less-than-wonderful websites that you have to wade through to find a few gems.

❖ It's difficult to evaluate the quality of the material you find on the Net. Let's consider this point a bit more closely. In normal publishing, there are gatekeepers to make sure that material that is inferior doesn't get published (at least we hope there are gatekeepers). On the Internet, anybody who wants to say anything has the chance to say it. Unless it is criminally obscene, violently racist, or a clear and present danger to society, no one challenges it. Thus people can tell lies or spread false news on the Net, and they probably won't suffer any nasty consequences.

So what happens when you download a document that has no clearly named author but seems to be reliable information about B.F. Skinner's behaviorism? How do you determine whether it's good or bad information? Here are some clues:

❖ Dig deeper for the name of an author and/or organization responsible for the information. One way to do this is to recognize that Internet URLs are hierarchical and that the slashes in an address (/) define levels of the hierarchy. For example, a PDF of an article on race and the war on drugs is found at **http://scholarship.law.ufl.edu/cgi/viewcontent. cgi?article=1178&context=facultypub**. If I chop off the **cgi/ viewcontent.cgi?article=1178&context=facultypub**, I have the root left: **http://scholarship.law.ufl.edu**, which tells me that it comes from the University of Florida Levin School of Law and is located in a repository of faculty publications. Chopping back on a URL will often lead you to the source behind the document you're interested in, though sometimes it just reveals the name of a person's Internet service provider, which, if it's some generic vendor of web space, will give you no help at all.

- ❖ Look for signs of scholarship—good language level, analytical thinking, bibliography and/or footnotes, logical organization.
- ❖ Look for signs of a **lack** of scholarship—lots of opinion without the support of evidence, indications of paranoia (as in *somebody's out to get us,* or *we're victims of a conspiracy*), poor spelling and grammar, lack of references to other sources, poor organization.
- ❖ Ask yourself—does the author of this site have a vested interest in promoting a viewpoint or is he/she simply sharing information? Vested interests may be OK as long as you are well aware of what they are. A site selling Toyotas is going to be different in its very nature from a site offering independent reviews of Toyotas.

Ultimately, you will have to evaluate the information itself. Does it make sense? Does it ring true? Is there sufficient backing for viewpoints presented? Have you or your professor ever heard of the people involved? Remember that Internet data may lack all the proper signposts of good scholarly work and yet still be valuable. On the other hand, it may have footnotes and a bibliography but be totally uninformed. For proper evaluation, the buck stops with you actually reading the material and making sense of it.

7.8 Some more Internet addresses valuable for research purposes

In presenting the following addresses, I must warn you again that URLs, like phone numbers, go out of date fairly quickly. On the Net, something you found today might not be there tomorrow. So, some of these URLs might not work. If you have a problem, try searching for the title of the source, using a search engine. Or go to **http://williambadke.com/links.htm**, where I will try to keep all the web links for this book alive and current.

7.8.1 Reference sources

❖ *Refdesk*: **http://www.refdesk.com/** (an amazingly detailed site that bills itself as "Fact checker for the Internet")

❖ A biography encyclopedia: **http://www.biography.com/**

7.8.2 Searchable library catalogs

❖ *WorldCat:* **http://www.worldcat.org/** (a union catalog representing holdings from a large number of libraries)

❖ *Library of Congress searchable catalog:* **https://catalog.loc.gov/**

❖ *LibWeb:* **http://www.lib–web.org/** (A directory of library catalogs worldwide that you can identify by country)

7.8.3 Phone directories (for anyone still using a home phone)

❖ *Switchboard*: **http://www.switchboard.com/** (Addresses & phone numbers—US plus Yellow Pages)

❖ *Canada 411*: **http://www.canada411.ca/** (Canadian phone numbers & addresses)

❖ A portal to international phone directories: **http://www. infobel.com/en/world/**

7.9 For further study

Study guide

1. What is the Internet? How does it relate to the World Wide Web?
2. Why are free journals not a prominent feature in the academic world?
3. What's the difference between a scholarly search engine and ordinary search engines? What are the names of some scholarly search engines, and what do they provide?

4. What are a few of the top search engines on the Net?

5. What are "subject trees" on the Internet, and how can they help you?

6. What are Internet portals, and how can they help you?

7. What is the Hidden Internet? How do you find information within it?

8. What are the key means by which you can evaluate the quality of information on Internet sites? What should you check first when evaluating a website? Why is more evaluation required for Internet sites than for regularly published books and articles?

Practice with the Internet

Try an identical search on several search engines (e.g., Google, Bing, Yahoo! Search, Ask.com). Why do some search engines come up with different results than others? Is it a correct assumption that **google.com** will most often produce better results than other search engines? [If you can't think of topics to search try the following: Skinner and behaviorism and Walden; Lucrezia Borgia (or is it Lucretia Borgia?); Bill Gates and antitrust.]

Assignment

1. Try a search on Google Scholar (**https://scholar.google. com**), using the topic: The March 2011 Tsunami in Japan. If your institution has links from Google Scholar to its own journals (called Library Links), make use of this feature (ask a librarian if unsure). Identify 6 journal articles or academic websites that are relevant to your topic.

2. Answer the following questions, using one of these search engines: Google, Google Scholar, Bing, Yahoo! Search or ask.com. In each case indicate the keywords you searched with and URL(s) of the site(s) that had the answer:

a. Where did the saying come from: "It takes a village to raise a child?" Can you find authoritative evidence to demonstrate that this is the source? How certain are you that the websites you looked at gave you an accurate answer?

b. The following is a real question asked by an academic library user. Find the correct citation, including author, title, journal, volume number, date, and page numbers:

> A professor here needs help clarifying a citation. He already has a photocopy of the article, but needs to know the volume, issue, and date in which the piece was published. The information we have is:
> Author: Joachim Begrich
> Title: Das priesterliche Heilsorakel
> Journal: Zeitschrift fur die altestamentliche Wissenschaft (ZAW)

c. Find the website for "Skeptical Science." What is the goal of this site? What would lead you to believe that the credentials of the authors on this site are strong or weak? What link did you use to find the list of authors?

d. The following quotation is plagiarized from a source on the Internet. Identify the author and title of the original source:

> "Jack the Ripper! Few names in history are as instantly recognizable. Fewer still evoke such vivid images: noisome courts and alleys, hansom cabs and gaslights, swirling fog, prostitutes decked out in the tawdriest of finery, the shrill cry of newsboys—and silent, cruel death personified in the capeshrouded figure of a faceless prowler of the night, armed with a long knife and carrying a black Gladstone bag."

How easy/difficult was it to identify the quotation? What does this tell you about the fate of those who plagiarize from the Net when a keen professor suspects some of their words are not their own? (Sorry to sound preachy, but it really is pretty easy to root out Internet plagiarists.)

8

Other Resources and Case Studies in Research

Sometimes you get desperate. All the normal research avenues narrow down to footpaths and then disappear entirely. You're running out of time and you have nothing to show for the hours you've spent. Now is the time for innovative action. This chapter will try to steer you in new and potentially fascinating directions. Then, this being the most loosely organized chapter in the book, we'll look at some other helpful resources and try out a couple of case studies with actual research projects.

8.1 Seeing where you've been

Before you launch into new sources for research data, it's probably a good idea to rehearse where you've been. Maybe you've missed some important resources. Here's a strategies list to help you go back over your research methods to this point and check out possibilities that may have eluded you the first time you went through.

The Strategies We've Covered (Now for the First Time in One Place):

❖ *Get a working knowledge of your topic* (You want to use reference sources, print or online, and became familiar with the basics.) Ask yourself: Did your reference sources suggest related topics or give a bibliography item that you've overlooked? Are there other sources of reference information to consider? (see below)

❖ *Assess the research topic, narrow it, come up with an analytical research question, and suggest a preliminary outline:* Did you set the topic so narrowly that you have a shortage of resources? Or, did you fail to set it narrowly enough, and now you have a fuzzy view of what your topic is? Often the problem with finding relevant sources is that you are not focusing clearly on what the research project is setting out to do. You need to be able to express your research question or thesis statement in **one sentence** that deals with **one issue or problem that you're trying to solve**. Your outline, in turn, needs to be drawn directly out of your research question/thesis. More on all this in the APPENDIX.

❖ *Do a book search in a library catalog or discovery tool, using keywords and controlled vocabularies as needed:* Did you find everything that was relevant? If you began with a keyword search, you need to look closely at the catalog records you brought up. What controlled vocabulary subject headings were attached to the books you found? If you started with subject headings, did you identify the best ones for your topic? Looking at the records you've brought up may help you to discover other possible subject headings or narrower approaches to the topic. Did you consider more broadly based books that might *contain* information relevant to you? E.g., for a paper on euthanasia, perhaps some key works in medical ethics might have relevant chapters on euthanasia.

❖ *Do a search for journal articles:* Did you use the right journal databases for the topic? Did you investigate the searching requirements for those databases? Did you choose narrow enough keywords and use controlled vocabulary terms? Have you checked your library's journal holdings carefully to be sure the library either did or did not have the articles you wanted? Did you take the extra step of enlisting interlibrary loan (in which your library obtains resources from another library) to get the full text of articles you didn't find in the databases you were searching?

❖ *Make a judicious search of Internet resources.* Here, use your best evaluative skills and be sure you know what your professor will allow you to include in your research project.

Does all this sound a bit too mechanical? A bit too much like "Five Steps to your Next Research Paper" which doesn't take into the account the reality that you may need to go back to earlier steps, skip a step, or do things in another order? Read Clearing the Fog below.

Clearing the Fog: Step by step may not always be the best approach, but it can help you find your way

Throughout this book I have suggested a step-by-step approach to research. Why? Because learning a task often works best if you follow the same pathway every time until you master all the parts. Having steps to follow helps you succeed until you know the path well enough to branch out a bit.

But there also comes a time, with the steps to good research clearly and solidly within your consciousness, when you may want to live a little more dangerously. Maybe you will initially entertain two or three possible research questions and then explore a bit more before you settle on the final one you will use. Maybe you will minimize the use of books and move quickly on to journal articles. Maybe you will feel the need to go back to earlier steps and do them again or revise what you did. The research process can thus become a glorious tangle of adventurous moves in many directions at once.

Warning: If you try out this more risky approach to research too early, before you've understood the steps you ultimately must cover, you'll end up with what you had before you began learning how to do research: a tangled mess. Remember when you were running around like the proverbial headless chicken, banging into walls of confusion and disappearing down rabbit trails?

So master the essential steps first. Then, if you want to get adventurous and mix things up a bit, you'll actually still know where you are.

Now let's consider some further options you may not have thought of:

8.2 ERIC

One of the great untapped resources for research is ERIC (**https://www.eric.ed.gov/**). No, this is not a professional hockey player with a lot of missing teeth. ERIC stands for Education Resources Information Center, a clearinghouse that makes available studies, reports, curriculum helps, etc. produced by educational institutions.

But don't think of it just as an educational database. Educators are concerned about virtually anything that might be related to education, from the effects of early poverty on graduates students' job performance, to the ramifications of teen alcohol use. This means that a wide range of topics in the social sciences are covered, as well as quite a few areas of the humanities.

Rather than have schools, colleges and universities put their studies on the issues affecting their work into hard drives or filing cabinets, never to be seen again, the U.S. government arranged to collect these studies and make them available to libraries. To do this, ERIC needed to have a two part approach:

❖ The reports themselves. They could be anything from a study of the effects of TV violence on high schoolers in Salem, Oregon, to an analysis of dyslexia in relation to reading speed in Podunk, Vermont. Such reports could be under 50 pages in length, though they might sometimes go to 100 pages or more. Pre-1992 ERIC documents (i.e., these gathered reports) were once only available on microfiche. Now most of them have been digitized and, along with documents 1993 to present, are freely available in PDF full text.

❖ A database with which to search the ERIC documents for topics of interest. Here the government had a stroke of genius—why not put the database for free on the Internet so that anyone could search it from anywhere without a password? What is more, all ERIC documents for which electronic full text was available could be linked to the citations in the databases and downloaded by users for free.

One further feature that sometimes baffles users: As ERIC grew, the database added a journals component to enable people to identify journal articles in education. The confusing part is that *ERIC itself does not provide the electronic full text of many of these journal articles. You will need to locate the actual articles yourself.* Thus you have two databases in one: a documents database and a journals database. To distinguish ERIC Documents from ERIC journals, the former were designated ED, so that each ERIC Document has a code number that looks like this: ED213562. ERIC Journals are designated EJ, as in: EJ498231. You can find both EJs and EDS in a single search, though it's possible to pre-set your search for only journals or only documents.

The ERIC interface at **http://www.eric.ed.gov/** begins with a keyword search and then provides limiter links on the results page (similar to what the EBSCO databases do). You can narrow down the search by date range, subject heading (descriptor) and so on. You can also limit just to peer reviewed resources and just to those citations that provide full text:

Alternatively, you can do a Thesaurus (subject heading) search. ERIC's thesaurus is very well constructed and can really help you formulate a focused search.

ERIC has now also begun creating "brief, plain-language summaries of key education issues and topics" (from the ERIC Database). These documents will be written by leaders in the field and will provide links to other resources in the ERIC database.

In recent years ERIC has updated some of its search features. Here's a summary:

- ❖ Its servers have now moved to the "cloud" and search is faster.
- ❖ You can limit to only peer reviewed material and to only full text results from the initial search box.
- ❖ The advanced search is gone, but there is a link for advanced search tips. ERIC argues that field codes such as author:Smith do no better searches than ordinary keywords.
- ❖ ERIC claims that quotation marks are not really needed around phrases in the keyword search now that its search function has been improved.

❖ The two main search options left are "Collection" (keyword search of ERIC), and "Thesaurus" (ERIC subject headings search).

❖ You can search by keyword within in the Thesaurus option to find all the subject headings relevant to that keyword.

❖ At the bottom of the ERIC home page is a "downloads" link. This allows you to get a copy of the ERIC Thesaurus (index of subject headings) and all the citations ERIC has added in a particular month.

Some database vendors (e.g. EBSCO) provide their own interface for ERIC, with additional search options.

Don't ignore ERIC. It is a very good resource for many kinds of research. The fact that you can access its index and much of its full text for free on the Internet makes it all the more helpful.

8.3 Government documents

Governments produce vast hosts of information which can often be found in libraries, be purchased, or be discovered free on the Internet (depending on what the information is). Publications put out by governments cover potentially every area of life. The only problem is that they are notoriously difficult to find. If you are in a library that has government documents, rely on your reference librarian to guide you through the maze.

For US government information on the Internet, the site to go to is "govinfo": **https://www.govinfo.gov/**. There you can find materials by keyword searching (basic and advanced searches available) or by browsing through various categories. For state and local government information, try the portal produced by the Library of Congress: **http://www.loc.gov/rr/news/stategov/stategov. html.**

If you are blessed enough to live in Canada, as I am, the Internet site you want is: **http://publications.gc.ca/site/eng/home.html**.

For other country governments, try: **http://www.politicsresources.net/official.htm**.

Census data can be hard to find and interpret. For a helpful American site try **http://factfinder.census.gov/** and for Canada: **http://www.statcan.gc.ca/eng/start**.

For all kinds of public data from the US, go to Data USA: **https://datausa.io/**

Not everything you need in government information, however, is on the Net. As with every other source of information, some is online and some is only accessible in print. Certain libraries are designated as depository collections that receive print and digital versions of government information. To locate the depository library near you in the US, go to **http://www.gpo.gov/libraries/**, and in Canada to **http://publications.gc.ca/site/eng/home.html**.

8.4 Doctoral dissertations

It sounds so intriguing, so right. If you want the best cutting edge research on a topic, why not locate a few doctoral dissertations? But the realities can be a mixed bag.

The primary searching tool for dissertations is *ProQuest Dissertations & Theses Database,* an electronic tool available in larger libraries but few small ones. It's fully searchable and you can easily locate citations and abstracts (summaries) of doctoral work on your topic. ProQuest offers with its databases the full text of close to a million dissertations, for those libraries that can afford to provide this feature. (There is a tutorial at **http://proquest.libguides.com/pqdt/pqdt**). For older dissertations not available in full text, you may be able to use interlibrary loan (not always successful) or buy the dissertation yourself from ProQuest.

Increasingly, doctoral dissertations are migrating to the WWW. Here are a few places to look for them:

- ❖ Open Access Theses and Dissertations: **http://oatd.org/** (over 3 million full text dissertations)
- ❖ PQDT Open: **http://pqdtopen.proquest.com/** (ProQuest dissertations that have been released to open access)
- ❖ Networked Digital Library of Theses and Dissertations: **http://www.ndltd.org/resources/find-etds** (hundreds of thousands of dissertations, mostly in English but a number in other languages; click on titles to access full text; get links to other electronic dissertation sites as well)
- ❖ OpenThesis: **http://www.openthesis.org/**
- ❖ DART-Europe: **http://www.dart-europe.eu/basic-search.php** (several hundred thousand dissertations from European universities)
- ❖ EThOS (UK): **http://ethos.bl.uk/** (British dissertations; opened padlock symbol next to a citation indicates that free full text is available)
- ❖ Google Scholar (a good source for dissertations if you can wade through all the stuff that is not dissertations). Note that a dissertation may be cited without the full text actually being available, so GS is a spotty resource for finding dissertations.

A suggestion: Before you go on a long quest for a dissertation, search for the author's name in your catalog and/or a larger catalog like WorldCat (**http://www.worldcat.org/**). It's possible that the dissertation was later published as an academic book which might even be in your library collection.

8.5 Bibliographic managers

For some time now there have been programs and apps available to help you save your citations to books, articles, websites, and so on. These *bibliographic managers* enable you to collect citations in specified folders and generate bibliographies in most any format you want. What is more, many of them are not only web-based, but offer the option of adding a plug-in to your word processing program so that you can create automatic citations and bibliographies without having to type in the information yourself. Let's take a quick look at a few of them:

8.5.1 EndNote (http://www.myendnoteweb.com/)

EndNote offers both a free online version and a for-pay downloadable software version that is avidly used by quite a number of scholars (**http://endnote.com/**). These tools allow you to import citations from various databases, search databases from within EndNote (though the search interface is not as sophisticated as searching a database directly), store citations in designated folders and even attach PDFs to citations. Since the free web version is all Internet-based, it doesn't take up room on your hard drive (leaving you space for a few more videos). You can configure Google Scholar to create an export link to EndNote (click the wheel icon to the right of Scholar results). Most journal databases support downloads to EndNote.

What is more, you can download Word templates from EndNote to help you format a research paper properly. Even better, you can download a plug-in that enables you to zap citations right into your research paper and format them as well as create a bibliography in the bibliographic format of your choice.

8.5.2 RefWorks (http://refworks.com/)

RefWorks provides most of the features of EndNote except the Word templates. It also has a plug-in to download WWW citations. Many library catalogs and most journal databases have direct download to RefWorks functionality. Like EndNote, you can configure Google Scholar settings to export citations to it, and it has a word processing plug-in to insert citations into your paper as well as create a bibliography. Most people use RefWorks as part of an institutional site license, though individual paid subscriptions are available. If you start with RefWorks as part of an institutional license, you are automatically given lifetime access as long as your institution subscribes, so you can continue using this tool even after you graduate.

8.5.3 Zotero (http://www.zotero.org/)

If your institution doesn't have access to RefWorks, and you want to use a bibliographic manager, do not fear. You can use EndNote Basic, or try out Zotero, which is free and offers most of the strong features provided by commercial bibliographic managers. It will capture book, article and website citations and will even store PDF full text. Like the other two managers above, it has a download for working with Word documents. Zotero operates as a plug-in on the Firefox browser, for which there's a free download on the Zotero home page. It is also available as Zotero Standalone, a download that allows you to use it in other browsers, like Chrome and Safari (search <Zotero Standalone> in your favorite Internet search engine).

8.5.4 Mendeley (https://www.mendeley.com/)

Mendeley has many of the features of the other free bibliographic managers, but offers a few unique perks. First, it is very well set up for sharing and collaboration so that you and your fellow researchers can easily work together or pool resources. Second, beyond offering lots of space for PDF storage, it allows you to annotate and mark up your PDFs. On the down side, it doesn't import directly from all databases. To make up for this, you can export citations in Bib TeX format and import them into Mendeley, or you can sync from Zotero to Mendeley. If Mendeley won't import from a specific database, Zotero might, and your results will also appear in Mendeley.

For lists and comparisons of reference managers see **https:// en.wikipedia.org/wiki/Comparison_of_reference_ management_software**

8.6 Consulting with friends, mentors and librarians

We live in a highly collaborative age, and the tendency to run our ideas past other people is pretty strong. There are real and obvious reasons why trying out aspects of your project on others can bring fresh perspectives and help you make early or mid-course correctives. Being more of a solitary researcher myself, I may be too anti-social to write about collaboration, but here goes anyway.

8.6.1 What are good friends for?

Meetings of minds are usually helpful, at least in theory. Running ideas past your friends is generally a good idea. Be open to their suggestions. At the same time, recognize that you may already know more about the subject matter than your friends do. Thus taking advice from a friend because he/she seems smarter than you, or more experienced, or whatever, may not be the best choice. Trust your instincts and filter advice from friends carefully.

8.6.2 Consulting professors

Your profs are a breed to themselves: Intelligent and articulate, but they usually have far too much to do (which, I think, leads to the mythology of the absent-minded professor). If you are going to consult with a professor, have a clear question in mind and focus on being brief and to the point. For example, you might ask something like this: "You listed a research topic as 'Charlemagne,' and I was wondering what you'd think of me approaching it this way..." Consult your professor if you are unsure of what to do or unclear about what is being demanded, if you have thought of an approach to an assignment which may not be exactly what the professor is asking for, or if you are stuck somewhere in the research process and need advice to help you get unstuck.

Avoid the false assumption that, if you don't understand a professor's assignment, you are a dimmer bulb than are your fellow students. Professors, at least in the belief of their students, are notorious for setting assignments that are confusing and for not being clear enough on ultimate expectations. It may not be at all surprising that you need clarification.

8.6.3 Finding shelter among librarians

Research shows that many students have a very limited perspective on what librarians can do for them. Some believe librarians are basically semi-skilled clerks. Untrue. Some believe librarians are helpful only for book and paper issues, because they know almost nothing about technology. Not so. Most academic librarians are techno-geniuses. Others see librarians as "generalists" who know a little bit about everything but, unlike professors, don't know a lot about any specific topic. Not so again. Actually, most librarians have a good idea how most subject disciplines work. If you need to use almost any database, a librarian is likely to offer more help than anyone else can. And if you are working on a highly specialized topic, a librarian has the skills to help you manipulate that topic so you can actually advance significantly beyond where you are. Librarians are amazing people. Consult them frequently. They don't bite. And they can usually do a good job of guiding you through the fog.

8.7 Case studies in research

It's all very well to read about the theory of research, but hands-on experience teaches us that we live in a complex world. Methods that may have worked perfectly well in one research project are useless in another. A keen mind and a brave heart are needed if you want to succeed in actually carrying out a research project. The moment you've been waiting for all along is here. Let's do some research.

8.7.1 "Arctic Ice Issues Resulting from Climate Change"

There is no question that the loss of Artic ice is creating serious problems, from rising sea levels to serious challenges for humans and animals in Artic regions and around the globe. You could compile a survey of all these problems, along with a suitably pious call for more action on climate change, but that would be similar to gathering books and articles, then giving a monkey some scissors, paste and blank paper. You need something much more dramatic.

What you do depends on what subject discipline you are working in. Possible research questions, each of which would be its own topic:

❖ Why are governments so slow to act on climate change, when the evidence from loss of Artic ice is so compelling? (Political Science, Economics)

❖ What process is required to enable former hunters in the Eskimo (we Canadians call them Inuit) communities to find a viable way to sustain their lives in the north? (Geography, Sociology, Economics)

❖ How can the Arctic polar bears be saved in light of diminishing Arctic ice due to climate change? (Ecology, Zoology)

❖ Or, if you really want to go down this much traveled road again: Is the loss of Arctic ice in recent years primarily the result of human activity or of natural phenomena over which humans have little control? (Not sure what discipline this falls into)

Since I like polar bears (though I would not want to meet one face to face, since they are nasty and unreasonable), let's go with the question: **How can the Arctic polar bear population be saved in light of diminishing Arctic ice?**

Reference Sources

The natural temptation is to go first to Wikipedia. And that may indeed be a helpful first step. The Wikipedia article on "Polar Bears," has a section on climate change, along with some high powered citations of recent studies.

But let's balance that with something created in a more traditionally peer-reviewed manner: *Encyclopedia of Global Warming & Climate Change* (2012). Sure, it's a bit dated, but there is a cool picture of an iceberg on the front cover, a feast for the eyes on a hot day.

Topic Analysis

We seem to have a fairly firm research question, but we need to determine what we actually need to accomplish in order to answer it. This is a "problem to solution" kind of project, which usually demands that you determine what the problem is, then look at options for a solution.

In the case of our topic, we need to establish that climate change is, indeed, creating a problem for the survival of the polar bear population (there's nothing as bad as getting deeply into a project, only to find out there is no problem at all). In the case of polar bears, some people are claiming that bear numbers are actually increasing. Is that the case? An article by Peter Dykstra (**http://www.sejarchive. org/pub/SEJournal_Excerpts_Su08.htm**) argues that the view that populations are growing is tainted by the fact that there were no accurate counts of polar bears in earlier decades. More recent research, however, is showing that, while the bears have adapted to hunting more land-based food, due to loss of ice, the food they are eating is not nutritious enough to sustain the population.

Having determined that there is a problem (or at least a potential one) we need to discover the extent of that problem and determine what negative effects on polar bears result from climate change. Only then can we begin looking at solutions, which might range from "do nothing," to "create supported refuges for polar bears," to "send them to Antarctica."

The best way to visualize this is with a preliminary outline:

Introduction: The Current Plight of the Polar Bear Due to Climate Change
I.   The Effects of Climate Change on Polar Bears
    A.
    B.
    C.
II. The Seriousness of the Problem
    A. Not a problem?
    B. Yes a problem?
III. Possible Solutions
    A.
    B.
    C.
    D.
Conclusion: A Proposed Protection Plan for Arctic Polar Bears

Why go to all this work? Because we now have a road map for the things we need to discover, and the things we need to think about, on our way to answering our initial question: "How can the Arctic polar bears be saved in light of diminishing Arctic ice due to climate change?" No road map, and you will be lost before you gather your first book or article.

Book Search

Having the most recent stuff is important, so I apologize in advance. By the time you read this, two or three years may have passed. In any case, the results below were fairly up to date when I put them together. Focus on my method more than the actual titles as you read on.

If you are searching a library catalog or using a discovery search tool, you are likely going to start with keywords. So what keywords should you use? Let me suggest that you choose words right out of your research question, e.g. **"polar bears" and (climate change OR global warming)**. I left out "Arctic ice" so as not to overload the search and eliminate good sources that might have great things to say about the effect of climate change on polar bears, even though the topic of "ice" doesn't come up specifically.

Here are some results from a keyword search for books:

❖ Derocher, A. E., Cherry, S. G., Hamilton, S., Pilfold, N. W., Pongracz, J., Thiemann, G. W., University of Alberta., ... United States. (2013). *Populations and sources of recruitment in polar bears*. Anchorage, Alaska: BOEM Alaska Region.

❖ Derocher, A. E., & Lynch, W. (2012). *Polar bears: A complete guide to their biology and behavior*. Baltimore: Johns Hopkins University Press.

❖ Ellis, R. (2009). *On thin ice: The changing world of the polar bear*. New York: Alfred A. Knopf.

❖ Northwest Territories Species at Risk Committee,, & Northwest Territories. (2014). *Species status report: Polar bear (Ursus maritimus) : Nanuq, Shih Dagaii, Ours polaire in the Northwest Territories*. Beaconsfield, Quebec : Canadian Electronic Library.

❖ Waring, R. (2009). *Polar bears in trouble*. Boston: Heinle/ Cengage Learning.

Some of the books are more directly relevant to the species threat situation, but all of them should be useful in some way or other. The problem is that we can't be sure we've found everything we could. Keywords are tricky and may have us missing out on some good titles. This is where opening up the full catalog record for one of the relevant books above may lead us to a strong subject heading. I chose the title: *On thin ice: The changing world of the polar bear*, and I identified these subject headings, which I probably wouldn't have thought of otherwise (lacking imagination):

Polar bear—Effect of human beings on
Polar bear—Climatic factors—Arctic regions

With these subject headings in hand, we should be well placed to identify relevant books whose titles might not clearly reveal their subject matter.

Journal Article Search

Half the battle with finding journal articles is identifying the right database to use. That's not as much of a problem if your library has a discovery search tool like Summon, Primo, or EBSCO Discovery Search, but focusing on a database relevant to the subject area you are working with can really help when the discovery search has pulled in 352,498 results, most of them not relevant (that does happen). In this case, a tool like the database ScienceDirect should work well to cover aspects of ecology, biology and so on in the problem of threatened polar bears.

A search on **"polar bears,"** along with some narrowing in the left column, produces articles like these:

- ❖ Elvin, S. S. (2014). The large marine ecosystem approach to assessment and management of polar bears during climate change. *Environmental Development, 11*, 67-83.
- ❖ Stapleton, S., Atkinson, S., Hedman, D., & Garshelis, D. (2014). Revisiting Western Hudson Bay: Using aerial surveys to update polar bear abundance in a sentinel population. *Biological Conservation, 170*, 38-47.
- ❖ Tartu, S., Bourgeon, S., Aars, J., Andersen, M., Ehrich, D., Thiemann, G. W.... & Routti, H. (2016). Geographical area and life history traits influence diet in an Arctic marine predator. *PloS one, 11*(5), e0155980.
- ❖ Tyrrell, M., & Clark, D. A. (2014). What happened to climate change? CITES and the reconfiguration of polar

bear conservation discourse. *Global Environmental Change, 24*, 363–372.

These, and the other articles I found, looked promising as I did my searches. But I wasn't really getting at the issue of a solution to the polar bear survival problem. So I tried **Polar Bears AND management**, but I found nothing new. Then I tried **Polar Bears AND survival**, and again found nothing new. Clearly, I am going to have to go through my existing resources and pull out what they suggest about possible solutions. As with many things in research, the answer is not just going to fall easily into my hands (sigh...)

Google Scholar may actually have some promise. A search on **Polar Bears AND survival** got me, among other citations:

❖ Jenssen, B. M., Villanger, G. D., Gabrielsen, K. M., Bytingsvik, J., Bechshoft, T., Ciesielski, T. M. & Dietz, R. (2015). Anthropogenic flank attack on polar bears: interacting consequences of climate warming and pollutant exposure. *Frontiers in Ecology and Evolution, 13*(3), 1–5.

❖ Regehr, E. V., Wilson, R. R., Rode, K. D., & Runge, M. C. (2015). *Resilience and risk: a demographic model to inform conservation planning for polar bears* (No. 2015-1029). US Geological Survey. [Note that this one is a scholarly research report that wouldn't have been found in a journal database].

❖ Rode, K. D., Robbins, C. T., Nelson, L., & Amstrup, S. C. (2015). Can polar bears use terrestrial foods to offset lost ice-based hunting opportunities? *Frontiers in Ecology and the Environment, 13*(3), 138–145.

❖ Rode, K. D., Wilson, R. R., Regehr, E. V., Martin, M. S., Douglas, D. C., & Olson, J. (2015). Increased land use by Chukchi Sea polar bears in relation to changing sea ice conditions. *PloS one, 10*(11), e0142213.

Summary

There appear to be sufficient resources out there, though not everything deals directly with a solution to the problem. That will require more digging, but more digging is what the fun of research is all about.

Let's try another topic, this time in the area of history:

8.7.2 "The First Crusade"

For a course on Medieval History, you've been asked to write a research paper on the First Crusade. Since the issue of the Crusades in general is a hot-spot in international politics these days (long memories and ongoing tensions, etc.), you decide to work on the research question: *"Was the actual motivation for the First Crusade primarily religious or political/economic?"*

The rationale here is that the first of the crusades may have been guided by a quest for territory and money rather than liberation of the "Holy Land" from Islam. That would speak to current debate regarding the Crusades and their goals. You could, of course, find another topic, because this one is awfully controversial, but the key to solving problems in our world is understanding the issues as well as you can. So it's probably a good idea to press on.

Reference sources.

For a topic like this, any number of reference sources would give you a working knowledge, even general encyclopedias like *Americana* or *Britannica*. There are also specific dictionaries and encyclopedias related to the era of the Middle Ages. In this case, we have access to something even more direct: *The Crusades: An Encyclopedia* (2006). This resource has detailed information on the rise and carrying out of the First Crusade. As can be expected, there is also a fairly lengthy Wikipedia article (though don't forget the usual cautions about Wikipedia). The above sources have abundant citations to other works that should be checked out.

Topical analysis.

My initial research question suggestion – *Was the actual motivation for the First Crusade primarily religious or political/economic* – now needs some nuancing. It appears that there are multiple suggestions as to the motivation, so we can now move to a more basic question that does not prejudge the options: *What was the primary motivation behind the First Crusade?*

A preliminary outline at this point needs to be quite open until we have nailed down the three or four most likely options. That's fine as long as we can fill in the blanks as soon as possible:

Introduction (Basics of the First Crusade)
I.   The Statement of Pope Urban (which initiated this crusade)
II. Alternative Motivations
    A.
    B.
    C. etc.
Conclusion

Book search.

While there are many books on the Crusades in general, it's better to attempt a narrower approach initially and search for books on the First Crusade. Amazingly we find success from the beginning; how rare is that? A keyword search brings up a number of books specifically on the First Crusade (at this point, because books are blunt instruments, I won't seek for books more specifically on the *purpose* of the First Crusade). What is more, there are a number of primary sources: actual accounts of the First Crusade from people of that time. History professors love primary sources, so you will look good just by having them in your bibliography. Here are some titles:

- ❖ *The First Crusade: the call from the East* (2012)
- ❖ *The Chanson d'Antioche: an old-French account of the First Crusade* (2011: primary source)
- ❖ *The social structure of the First Crusade* (2008)
- ❖ *The Gesta Tancredi of Ralph of Caen: a history of the Normans on the First Crusade* (2005: primary source)
- ❖ *Fighting for Christendom : holy war and the crusades* (2004)
- ❖ *The First Crusade and the idea of crusading* (2003)

And so on.

There are many volumes specifically on the First Crusade. If we fall short, books on the Crusades in general will fill the gap. What is missing, however, is specific material on the motivations for the First Crusade, though most of the books above will include information on that issue. Journal articles, however, being more specific to particular aspects of a topic, may be more fruitful.

Journal databases

We have lots of choices for journal databases, from a religious source like ATLA Religion Database, to various historical databases to a broad search tool like JSTOR or EBSCO's Academic Search. Let's choose the latter in this case, because there is the potential for a number of motivations for the Crusades, coming from different areas of study like religion, political science, geography, and history. The broad subject coverage of Academic Search (or a similar database from another database company) is more likely to provide lots of good options to consider.

In the case of Academic Search, we want to do more than treat it like Google, so we'll start with a keyword search and see if we can narrow down our results. The initial keyword search is First Crusade. I had hoped we could try a narrower search, First Crusade AND (motivation OR purpose), but it brought disappointment (databases can do that).

Initially we have close to 700 results. Too many. So we use EBSCO's left column features and limit to the subject heading – **Crusades (middle ages) – first, 1096-1099** – and to academic journals only. Always look for limiters if you have more than 50-100 results. In this case, we get down to 30 quite focused journal articles. Looking at them, we can see why the (purpose OR motivation) limiter didn't work. The article titles are much more subtle in looking at motivations. Consider these article titles from the set of results:

❖ "A Warlord's Wisdom: Literacy and Propaganda at the Time of the First Crusade" [**Propaganda** implies a motivation that was being promoted.]

❖ "Christians, Muslims, and the `liberation' of the Holy Land." [**Liberation** is a loaded term, since it has quotation marks around it, implying a motive that was promoted.]

❖ "Destruction or Conversion Intention and Reaction, Crusaders and Jews, in 1096." [Notice term **Intention**, as a substitute for "motivation".]

❖ Iuvenes and the First Crusade (1096-99): Knights in Search of Glory? [**In search of glory** as a motivation.]

❖ "'Let Not a Remnant or a Residue Escape': Millenarian Enthusiasm in the First Crusade." [**Millenarian Enthusiasm** as a motive.]

❖ "The Call of the Crusades." [**Call** implies motive.]

❖ "The Pilgrimage Origins of the First Crusade." [**Pilgrimage** as motive.]

❖ "The Roots of Lay Enthusiasm for the First Crusade." ["**Roots**" implies a motive.]

While bound to be a lot more complicated in its results, you might want to try, with Google Scholar, the narrower search we first attempted on Academic Search (which failed, much to our embarrassment): "First Crusade" AND (motivation OR purpose).

A search on these terms in GS's advanced search, limiting only to title words, gets us a few more articles, a second year undergraduate student essay (sigh...), and a couple of doctoral dissertations, one of them with the whole of it available online. Searching on full text rather than title words, we find a bunch of books and a number of journal articles.

A further element remains: Locating a copy of the sermon by Pope Urban II that largely initiated crusade activity. Sadly, the actual sermon is lost to history (as in "gone forever"), but there are firsthand accounts of the sermon from observers and a copy of Urban's letter of further instructions. Here Wikipedia helps direct us to *The Medieval Sourcebook* where there are five such accounts with bibliographic data for the published volumes in which these translations first appeared: **http://www.fordham.edu/halsall/source/urban2-5vers. html**.

Conclusion

In the examples above, you probably hoped for easy and tidy results. Research isn't like that. Every project has its hazards and obstacles. There's rarely anything tidy about gathering information on a narrowed down topic. That's why we've looked at so many strategies. While you won't use them all in every research project, you need to have them in your arsenal just in case your next research adventure turns into a fight for your very life. Who said research is boring?

Clearing the Fog: Research is like a box of chocolates

"My momma always said, 'Life was like a box of chocolates. You never know what you're gonna get.'" - *Forrest Gump* (Movie, 1994)

Every new research experience is exactly that: New. While I've provided you with steps to follow, several key principles may help you navigate the reality of the many differences in what you experience, depending on your topic:

- ❖ No author/scholar is obligated to be interested in, or write about, any topic. Thus you may find that some topics bring up fewer resources than you were expecting. A possible solution is to go broader: If you can't find a book on your favorite 1970s rock group, for which you have to write a history, maybe a few books on the history of 1970s rock will contain useful information on your group. Journal articles may be your best option, because they tend to be narrower in focus.
- ❖ Newer topics tend to have much less material on them, and a lot of that material lacks the level of sober reflection and evaluation you may be looking for. This means that you are going to have to provide more of your own analysis of what is going on rather than relying on other scholars to do this for you (this is a good exercise and builds character, so hopefully you'll embrace the opportunity).
- ❖ It's a real challenge to figure out how narrowly or broadly you are working. I have seen students start far too broadly on a topic and end up with a survey instead of an analytical research project. I have also seen researchers start so narrowly that there is little or nothing to be found when it comes to searching for resources. A lot of researchers, as well, have a narrow research question but do searches that are too broad (instead of searching directly on the name of a 1970s rock group, the researcher searches on "Music.") A cure for this is to use search terms, whenever possible, that *actually come out of your research question*. Only if this doesn't succeed should you create slightly broader searches.

8.8 For further study

Study guide

1. Summarize for yourself the research strategies covered so far.
2. What is ERIC, what kinds of documents does it provide access to, and what subject areas does it cover best?
3. Where do you find the ERIC database? In what format is the text of most ERIC documents from the early 1990s to the present?
4. What is the Eric Thesaurus?
5. What's the difference between ED and EJ in ERIC?
6. How useful is the Internet in finding government documents?
7. What's the main problem with locating doctoral dissertations? What avenues can you follow to get your hands on one if you want it?
8. What kind of help can you expect from a librarian as opposed to the help you get from a professor?
9. If you can't find books or articles by a person you are researching, what other option do you have?
10. If you are doing research on a person (like a president of the US), would writings by that person be considered primary or a secondary sources?

Practice with resources introduced in this chapter

Try these searches:

1. From ERIC online, **http://www.gpo.gov/fdsys/**, using the search box, do a search on "fetal alcohol" and use the subjects on the left to narrow to "Fetal alcohol syndrome" and "children." Then go further down in the left column and click on Reports-Research under Publication Type. Have a look at your results.

2. Go to **https://www.govinfo.gov/** and find the most recent edition of the Congressional Record.

3. Go to **http://www.politicsresources.net/official.htm.** Find information on the Estonian president (choose your language on the site from the upper right options of Estonian, English and Russian).

Assignment

1. Do a search for a topic relevant to ERIC using the Thesaurus function, and setting Publication Type to Reports-Research. List several relevant documents that you retrieved in your search.

2. Go through each of the cases above (8.7) and learn what you can.

3. Try out a few of the topics below, narrow them, then locate materials in various formats (books, journals, and credible websites). Obviously you won't have time for a lot of in-depth work, but see what you can accomplish in an hour or two:

Youth crime
Anti-Semitism
Causes of World War One
Anorexia
9/11
The Crusades
The Euthanasia Debate
Family Violence
Homelessness
Issues Facing the Modern City (too broad?)
The Syrian Refugee Crisis
Moral Development of Children

9

Learning How to Read for Research

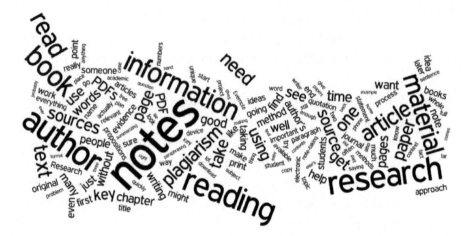

It's all very well to amass an enormous bibliography and have all your sources scattered artfully on your desk or screen. But if you're assuming that your essay or research report is now as good as written, you're going to suffer a grave disappointment. Obtaining the research materials is only half the battle. Now you have to read them and evaluate them. This chapter majors on the joys of reading and note-taking.

9.1 Reading for the connoisseur and the glutton

With a tantalizing heading like the one above, you may want to head for the nearest cafeteria. But read on—food for the mind is better than French fries.

Our generation is very big on what is commonly called "escapist fiction." This kind of book makes no claim to be great literature with deep themes but does promise to take you out of yourself and into a far more exciting world. I, like many librarians, enjoy reading adventure fiction, spy novels, and so on. I've even been known to write and publish such fiction in my spare time. This does get me dubious glances from some people, but I am amazed at how many seemingly sophisticated academics read or write the same stuff.

The advantage of a thriller is that it gives you a way to escape. You can sit back and let it happen without pondering or analyzing too deeply. Let the skilled thriller writer feed you the adventure until you scream for mercy. Escapist fiction is for gluttons.

I do not, however, call a well-crafted mystery novel "escapist" in the same sense. The writer of this kind of work dares you at every point not only to figure out who did it, but why and how whoever did it did it. In other words, such a writer does not want you to swallow the novel whole (as in a thriller) but to read it with discernment, pausing to think over clues with reserve and intelligence. The well-crafted mystery novel is for connoisseurs.

Where is all this leading? Simply to a foundational statement: *Research is not for gluttons.*

Consider the problem you face as a researcher: You have twenty-five scattered sources and seven online articles waiting to be read. They comprise 3,423 pages in total. At an average rate of one page every two minutes, this will take you 6,846 minutes to read, or, in more familiar terms, 114.1 hours. If you skip classes for two weeks (or take a vacation from your job) and read 8.15 hours per day, you will have it all read. But wait a minute (even though you have none of these to spare): I haven't allowed you the time you need to take notes on what you're reading nor to ponder its value. You'd better plan on three weeks.

Before we get too far into the realm of the ridiculous, I think you can see that there is no way you will be able to read and take notes on all 3,423 pages for one research project. The approach that works so well for devouring spy novels - gluttonously reading without much thought – is going to sink you when you try to read research materials. There has to be a way to determine what's important and what's a red herring (or a blue elephant).

Let me show you the connoisseur's approach to reading:

9.1.1 Be ruthless

You may not like what I have to say now, but I do have to say it. *Any book or article you read for research purposes must be used and left behind as quickly as possible, even though you can never take anything out of context.* Forget that the author probably worked long into the night, leaving a weeping spouse and children waiting outside the study door. Forget that for perhaps years the author was utterly consumed by the burden of this topic until it could be rendered into print.

You need information. The source you are reading has information. The problem is that it has too much information that is not relevant to your research topic. Thus you need to use every skill you have to sift quickly through what you don't need and find what you do need.

At this point I must warn you not to show this chapter to anyone with an academic title. Such a person may very well burn your copy of *Research Strategies* right in front of you (if you have the print version) or confiscate your device (if you have an electronic version). Professors are purists, and rightly so. They have written one or more theses for which they actually did read all 3,423 pages plus 74,689 more. They got into the hearts and souls of the authors they were reading.

You, on the other hand, are writing a paper that is due, along with two others, in seven days. *Be ruthless.* Read what you need and abandon the rest. It's your only hope.

One big note of caution: I am not urging you to read out of context. You have to read enough of an author's work to have a good idea of his or her main message. It's all very well to be efficient and discerning (the connoisseur) rather than a mindless sponge (the glutton), but be very sure you have grasped, not only what the author is saying, but why the author is saying it.

9.1.2 Get to know the material without reading it all

No, this is not an incentive to do skimpy research. This is an attempt to show you how to zero in on what you need without missing anything important. Here are the steps to take, first for books, then for articles:

Books

❖ At the start, have a good look at the title page, preface, foreword, and introduction, even if you are planning to keyword search in an e-book. A book is not just a series of paragraphs. It is not just a chunk of content. There is usually a motive and a plan, so the preliminary pages can give you solid clues as to why the book was written and what it intended to do. A lot of readers ignore title pages because they seem to have so little information on them. But they can be important. Be sure to look at both the title and subtitle, since increasingly titles are there just to look cute, while the real purpose of the book is revealed in the subtitle. Consider these gems:

Lifestyle: Conversations with Members of the Unification Church
Passages: Predictable Crises of Adult Life
Sex in the Snow: Canadian Social Values at the End of the Millennium

The preface, foreword, or introduction will often tell you what the author was attempting to do in the book. There you can look for a thesis statement, as well as for a description of the approach to the subject and of the material to be covered.

Reading a good preface could give you all the clues you need to get into the really important data.

❖ **Second**, check out the table of contents. This table forms the skeleton upon which the body is hung, the keystone that supports the building, the street signs that give meaning to the metropolis, the – but why go on? The point is simply that the table of contents provides you with the basic structure of the book in its proper order. Here you find the good, the bad, and the useless for your purposes. There was a time when tables of contents gave you main headings, subdivisions, and even short summaries of the main arguments. Now chances are that most chapter headings you see will be cute but relatively uninformative. Still, it is worth your while to check out the table of contents. It may help you zero in on the chapter that you really want. And it gives you a sense of the writer's whole development of the topic.

❖ **Third**, have a look at the index. Indexes can be good, atrocious, or nonexistent. Their real value (when present) lies in their ability to locate specific information when the book itself covers a broader topic. But beware of two problems:

- Indexes often list many page numbers after each topic heading, forcing you to do a lot of looking up to find what you want. Comparing chapter headings with page numbers in the index might help you speed up the process by identifying the most relevant sections.

- When you have located a relevant page by using an index, beware the natural tendency to take information out of context. Remember that the paragraph you are reading on page 294 was preceded by 293 pages.

- If you are using an e-book, there is usually some sort of "search within" feature which acts like an index so you can input keywords and bring up relevant passages. Be sure you read enough around the keyword results you get so that you understand the context.

❖ **Fourth**, be sure to give the book a run-through, even if you are only going to use a part of it. If you fail to do so, you may miss completely the overall intent of the volume and thus misunderstand what you are reading in one portion of it. A run-through includes:

- Reading opening and concluding portions of each chapter to see what the author intended to cover and what he or she concluded.
- Considering the subheadings in the body of each chapter.
- Going over any summary or conclusion chapter at the end of the book.
- Possibly looking up a book review or two if the book is confusing or potentially controversial.

❖ **Fifth**, when it comes to reading the appropriate portion(s) of the book, be a connoisseur of the argumentation, not a glutton who does not evaluate what s/he's eating as long as there is a lot of food. There's only one way to read when you are doing research—*by asking constant questions*. Questions form absolutely the most useful key to good analysis. Ask yourself:

- What is the author saying?
- What point of view or background is the author coming from that might influence what is being said? Thus, what biases do you discern?
- Is the author really dealing with the issues or are there some things missing or minimized in the argument?
- Is the evidence presented fairly? Is there enough evidence? Does the evidence support the author's case? Is there counter-evidence that needs to be considered before you automatically buy into the author's argument?
- How do this author's approach or beliefs compare/contrast with other things you've been reading? (Here you should be able to group authors by what they believe so that you can see who supports whom and who opposes whom. This supports the concept that scholarship is a conversation).

And so on. Don't merely absorb (gluttony). Analyze. Get involved. Ask probing and constant questions of everything you are reading. It will help your research immeasurably. What's more, your questions will help you start preparing your work for the final writing process.

Articles

With a journal article, or an essay within a book, you lack some of the more familiar signposts—tables of contents, indexes, sometimes even subheadings in the text. To add to the problem, the writer may argue a complex point over several pages without stating a conclusion until the last moment. How do you get a grasp of the article's message in short order and make good use of it?

- ❖ *First*, find an abstract (a summary of the article) if you can locate one quickly. The most generous journals actually provide their own abstracts in the text of their publications. If this is not the case for your article, the article may well be abstracted in a journal database. With a good abstract, you can discern the author's main points and conclusion.
- ❖ *Second*, watch for key propositions. *Key what?* **Key propositions**, despite the strange name, relate to a simple concept: *A key proposition is a statement of what the author believes to be true.* Whether or not it is actually true is something for you to discern, but it is what the author believes to be true. Most pieces of expository writing, whether books or journal articles, have several key propositions dotted throughout with, hopefully, a big key proposition at the end. There are two ways in which an author might present key propositions. Some authors start with a question, present various lines of evidence, then state a key proposition:

Question → Evidence → Key Proposition

Others start with a key proposition (in the form of a thesis statement), present evidence for it, and then re-state the proposition:

**Key Proposition (Thesis) → Evidence
→ Restated Key Proposition**

Your task is to identify how your author presents key propositions, and then *find them*. Key propositions form the foundation or the skeleton of the article. Everything else is introduction or evidence. With the key propositions identified, you can get to the heart of what the author is trying to say. [Note: The above procedure works just as well with books]

❖ *Third*, check out the author's conclusion at the end of the article carefully. What is the author's bottom line as far as beliefs or final thoughts are concerned? Presumably everything else in the article has some relation to that final statement.

❖ *Fourth*, if the article you are reading still gives you very few clues, read the whole thing. There are times when you just have to muddle through, but it won't hurt as much as you think it will. As you go, try to abstract the article for yourself on paper. It will help your understanding, and if you ever have to refer to it again (in a week, by which time you've forgotten you ever read it), you'll be one step ahead.

9.1.3 A final word on analytical reading

We have been dealing with hard realities here—too little time and too much to read. Perhaps professors or employers one day will let students work on fewer but larger projects where they have the hours to do the job right. Until that happens, you will need to know how to practice discriminating reading.

Remember that books and journal articles are sources of data. Develop those skills that will help you extract data with the greatest speed and efficiency. But beware of quoting an author out of context because you did not read enough to get the author's overall message.

Clearing the Fog: On using more than the first three pages

In a study of student research, The Citation Project found that 77% of all student citations relate only to the first three pages of a source, regardless of its length (Sandra Jamieson and Rebecca M. Howard, "The Citation Project: Preventing Plagiarism, Teaching Writing: Initial Data from the Citation Project Study of Student Use of Sources in Researched Papers from Sixteen US Colleges and Universities," 2011).

This means that many students in higher ed are really only interacting enough with sources to get a general idea of what is in them and to (dare I suggest it) mine for a few cool quotations.

In this section of *Research Strategies*, I've offered several efficient ways for you to engage with the whole of your sources without having read everything. So imagine this scenario: The really crucial information is on page 5 but you only read to page 3 and missed the point of what the author was saying. Unknown to you, your professor read the same article last week and remembers it well.

Even if you don't get busted by your prof for only skimming the first three pages, the point is that doing a decent job of research means you actually have to have significant interaction with your sources. Train yourself in the methods I've suggested above, and start reading past page three. It will open up whole new worlds for you.

9.2 Evaluation of research resources

Much of what we might call "evaluation" is part of analytical reading: trying to discern what the author is saying and how credible the author's arguments appear to be. But I also want to provide you with some clues regarding the overall evaluation process.

Evaluation has to do with determining the following:

❖ The qualifications of the author. The first criterion that comes to mind is how many academic degrees an author has, but that may not be the only measure of qualification. If your family doctor starts writing books about medieval art, her medical degree is not going to make her nearly as competent as someone with a degree in medieval art. If an author is writing on a subject area but lacks clear qualifications to be writing in that field, the product is going to be shabby.

❖ The biases of the author. Bias is not necessarily a bad thing, because none of us are 100% objective. It may, indeed, be the bias of the author that is most important to you. For example, if you are writing on prejudice against Chinese-heritage people in 19th century San Francisco, reading primary sources (e.g. newspaper articles) by biased people of the time may well make your case. What is important here is that you *identify* the biases of authors so that you can walk into their works with eyes wide open.

❖ The level of expressed opinion as opposed to evidence. Opinion is not fact, but constitutes views that are unsupported by evidence. As you know, just because you read something in a published work, you can't assume that it's bound to be correct. You need always to ask, "How do you know that to be the case? Where's your evidence?"

❖ Whether or not the material is relevant to the problem you are addressing. Here you should take note of the fact that *relevance is not the same thing as quality*. A book or article may be highly relevant yet not up to par by the measures of scholarship. On the other hand, a book or article may be oozing scholarship but really have nothing much to say directly about the issue you are addressing.

A couple of great resource for evaluation:

http://guides.lib.berkeley.edu/evaluating-resources
http://www.virtualsalt.com/evalu8it.htm

If you are really into this issue, you might have a look at my book chapter (warning, it's a bit complex, but in a good way):

> Badke, William. (2015). "Expertise and Authority in an Age of Crowdsourcing." In *Not Just Where to Click: Teaching Students How to Think about Information* (pp.191-215). Ed. Troy Swanson; Heather Jagman. Chicago: Association of College and Research Libraries. **http://williambadke.com/ BadkeExpertiseAuthority.pdf.**

9.3 Note taking

You may be aware of those rare people who never annotate or take notes on the data they are discovering in research. Instead, they gather all their books and articles around themselves just before they start writing their first draft, then they cite and quote their sources simply by hauling books out of the pile and looking up appropriate passages. Or they open multiple windows of online articles and navigate skillfully among them. Such people, of course, have photographic memories and the organizational skills of Noah loading the ark. Or they are really only using one source for most of their data while occasionally referring to others to cover up the narrowness of their approach. Perhaps (heaven forbid), they're writing their research paper out of their heads and citing the occasional book or article only as some sort of weak signal to the reader that they did some actual research.

For most of us, it's crucial that we distill out of what we are reading the essential things we are going to have to include in our research paper. We don't have the minds, nor the stamina, to retain everything, unaided by notes. Trying to teach someone how to take notes is almost like trying to teach a baby sparrow to fly. Most of what it takes comes from within, not from instructions. I can try to help you by flapping my arms and showing you the motions, but you have to develop the will and skill to soar for yourself.

Generally I recommend taking notes from (or annotating) one source at a time, covering all of that source (book, article, etc.) before moving on to the next one. The alternative is to create note documents for each subject you are dealing with (or separate subject files on your device), then to record notes from various sources into these subject designations. This latter method may be used later in your process but is not recommended as a starting tactic, because it drags your notes out of their original contexts, thus losing the threads of thought of the authors you are reading. It's better to cover one book or article at a time, keeping all the notes for it in one place.

One of the biggest problems most students face is that they take too many notes that will later go unused. The key to this difficulty is to have a good research question and preliminary outline as soon as possible in the research process. If you are one of those people who only discerns your outline for the first time while you are proof-reading the final copy of your paper, you have probably wasted a lot of time taking notes that ended up being junked. After all that needless effort, your paper is probably not very good anyway, because its structure was never planned. On the other hand, if you have a fairly solid idea of what you want to accomplish with your research project, you are less likely to take notes on irrelevant information.

Once you have a clear vision how you want your research materials to help you deal with your question, you next have to decide on a note-taking style.

9.3.1 The determined photo-copier/printer/e-doc highlighter

For some students, note taking is easy. You just annotate or highlight the PDFs you've gathered. Or, if you are doing analog, you arm yourself with fourteen dollars in dimes or a charged up printing account, then photocopy or print everything that looks important, taking all 140 copies home and assembling your essay out of them (though, admittedly, not many people do this anymore). Would that most of us could afford this method. Using the scan-to-e-mail function on many photocopies is often free, making that the better financial option for turning print into PDF. Or people snap pics of their favorite pages with their phone or other mobile device and download the whole mess later. You can also use speech recognition software, available on most devices and operating systems, to read text into a device as visual words. In each case, you end up with the full text of the resource and then must figure out what to do with it.

A bit of advice here:

❖ If you are using a printing device, scanner, phone, or speech recognition to record pages of notes, make sure that you have also recorded the *author, title, place of publication, publisher and date* for every book or article you've retrieved (*author, title, journal name, volume number, date and page numbers* for journals). You'd be surprised at how many people I find wandering the library, wayward copy in hand, looking desperately for whatever source they took it from.

❖ Use a highlight pen on your paper copies or print-offs as soon as you have made them, while the information is still fresh in your mind. PDF in Adobe Reader has a comment function for your e-resources notations. For phone scans, use an OCR app (Apple, Android or Windows) to turn the print into searchable text as PDF. You want to mark the passages that were of the greatest importance to you so that you will not, later on, wonder why you retrieved this material in the first place.

❖ Remember that you are at a disadvantage if you print, scan or snap. "Me?" you grin. "I'm the one who snagged all this stuff in a tenth of the time it takes these longhand scribblers and clickety-click keyboarders around here." Yes, but recognize that you have probably interacted with your material at a far more superficial level than have those "longhand scribblers and clickety-click keyboarders." When you go home tonight and try to wade through all your retrieved stuff, you may find that you've entered a strange and cruel world in which no landmarks make sense to you and the reasons why you printed/copied/digitized/snapped even half of the stuff totally escape you.

❖ Once you have PDFs or other types of docs for your material, make sure you name them consistently and file them for clear and easy retrieval. I prefer using author name as the first part of the PDF file name, then a space–dash–space and the first few words of the title (e.g. **Smith – The apple pie conundrum**).

❖ Sometimes the option of creating separate notes can become attractive. With note-taking, you can copy/paste excerpts from your full text PDFs to a Word document, and add your own comments and summaries, thus establishing a condensed version of the original source (making sure that you stamp each set of notes with the correct bibliographic information.)

Here is an example of notes excerpted from large documents:

There are cool Net-based programs that can help you with note creation. Evernote (**http://evernote.com/**) is a free to use (but you pay for additional features) resource for gathering and accessing your notes. You can also download the app, Evernote Web Clipper, to save anything from the Web without having to leave your browser (**http://evernote.com/webclipper/**). Evernote will enable you to get to your cloud-based notes from any device. For a tool to annotate and store web pages, try Scrible (**http://www.scrible.com/**). The tool "Catch," described in the 4th edition of *Research Strategies*, has shut down. This is a useful lesson for us all: Make sure you subscribe to the e-mail updates most of these free online programs offer you, so that you know what is happening to them and can save your stuff if your free program dies.

If you are using a phone, there are scanner apps available that can turn photos into PDFs. Here are a few options:

- ❖ CamScanner: Scan to PDF (Android, iOS, and Windows: **https://www.camscanner.com/**).
- ❖ Genius Scan: Scan to PDF. One neat feature is that documents scanned at an angle will show up flat in the PDF (Android, iOS, and Windows: **http://thegrizzlylabs.com/**).
- ❖ Google Drive: Allows you to scan with Optical Character Recognition capability and PDF conversion: **https://drive. google.com/.** (Already built into Android devices: See **http://googledrive.blogspot.ca/2013/05/a-smoother-drive-app-for-android.html**).
- ❖ Scanable from Evernote: Scan to readable text and add to Evernote or Dropbox (iOS: **https://evernote.com/ products/scannable/?var=c**).
- ❖ RefME: A phone-based free citation creation tool. Download the app and scan a book barcode to get a citation. Or search by title, author, ISBN, DOI, or URL. There is also a Chrome browser plugin. It works with most bibliographic managers (**https://www.refme.com/**).

Just be careful that you tag or otherwise identify each of your notes consistently so that you can identify them easily. Chapter 10 offers some tips on organizing notes.

One word of caution: Because it is often so easy to input notes, you need to be careful that you keep your notes to a minimum. Simply pulling everything you've been reading into a large pot of notes is probably counterproductive.

9.3.2 The value of going all digital

I've been all digital in my own research work for a few years now, getting PDFs of articles and scanning portions of hardcopy (books, etc.) to PDF. I use a bibliographic manager (see 8.5 above) to keep track of citations, and a separate folder in My Documents, or a cloud storage source like Dropbox, to keep the PDFs. All PDFs are labeled with author-title format (e.g. Smith - Finding reality in the digital world). Then I create a notes file (Word Document) so that I can summarize portions of what I am reading and copy/paste relevant excerpts from my PDFs into my notes, making sure I identify each document in turn and retain page numbers (see illustration above). Some PDFs are image files that won't copy/paste well. For those, I use screen capture (built into most device operating systems) to snare relevant portions that I then put into my notes document. Note that such scans will not be searchable. At the end, I have a collection of key information from my sources without having to type anything.

But be cautious here: If you collect a lot of PDFs without excerpting notes from them, you may have difficulty pulling out the information you need, since you have to search each PDF separately. A free resource to help you with this is Qiqqa (**http://www.qiqqa. com/),** a simply amazing PDF manager that enables you to store and annotate PDFs. It also provides unique search capabilities. If you are working with your original PDFs rather than taking shorter notes, give Qiqqa a try (requires a no-cost software download). Many bibliographic managers also allow you to store PDFs.

9.3.3 The quoter

Some people still prefer a low-tech approach with paper and pen or, lacking a portable scanner, they are using their own fingers to type material into electronic files. Often the plan is to get down information that is verbatim, that is, pull direct quotations out of their sources. There are some advantages to copying material word for word into your notes, and (inevitably) some disadvantages.

Advantages

❖ You won't have to go back to the book or article later on if you need a suitable quotation. It will be right in your notes.

❖ A quotation method can give you greater accuracy, since you have the actual words of your sources. This is especially helpful when a topic is new to you. When you don't fully understand a writer's argument, you can copy out a paragraph that states it. Later, when you are more in tune with the subject, the paragraph may make more sense. If you had tried merely to summarize it before you understood the material, you might have misinterpreted the argument and carried that misinterpretation into your notes.

❖ The mere act of hand or keyboard copying helps you get to know the material more intimately, since copying demands that you read more slowly and, in fact, that you read each word several times. In understanding, you will be far ahead of the photocopier or scanner when your notes are complete.

Disadvantages

❖ The process can become fairly laborious. It's easier to photocopy or scan.

❖ You must be very careful to quote enough to catch the context. Alternatively, you could summarize the context in your notes, then directly copy the portion that is most important to you.

9.3.4 The summarizer

This person reads a chunk of material and then summarizes it in his or her own words. The point is to condense several pages into a paragraph of notes or a paragraph into a sentence.

Advantages:

- ❖ This method is quicker than quoting.
- ❖ The process of summarizing forces you to think about the material and make it your own.

Disadvantages:

- ❖ The method does not work well if you are dealing with difficult material that is hard to condense.
- ❖ You will have to go back to your book or journal article if you find later that you need a quotation.
- ❖ You have to be very careful that you understand the things you are reading. If you misunderstand, you have no way of checking for the accuracy of your summaries later on, other than going back to your source material.

9.3.5 The paraphraser (not recommended in most cases)

The difference between summarizing and paraphrasing is that the former *condenses* material while the latter *rewrites each sentence of the original in the reader's own words.* For example, perhaps the original book or article said:

> *The rate of increase in building costs is rapidly making home ownership impossible for the average middle class family.*

A paraphrase might say:

> *The speed of growth in the cost to build is quickly making owning a home impossible for the average family with a middle income.*

But a summary might say:

> *The rising cost of construction is squeezing out middle class of would-be home owners.* [i.e., an **interpretation** rather than a paraphrase]

With a paraphrase, you can expect that your paragraph of notes will be as long as the book's paragraph, if not longer.

Possible advantage:

This method can be helpful if you are working through difficult material. Sometimes just the task of rewriting each sentence in your own words makes the writer's meaning clear.

Why, in most cases, paraphrasing is a bad idea:

❖ While sometimes recommended by professors, this method leaves you particularly open to a charge of plagiarism (see the end of this chapter), since you are still reproducing the writer's work, thought for thought if not word for word.

❖ In fact, people who paraphrase tend to change far too little of the original to qualify the result as plagiarism-free. Most paraphrasing that I see appearing in research papers is out and out theft of most of the original author's words as well as his/her thoughts.

❖ The method is laborious. Not only do you have to rephrase each sentence, but your notes will be as long as your original source, maybe longer.

So paraphrase only if you need it to explain a piece of writing to yourself. Word to the wise: *Avoid letting paraphrased material appear in an actual research paper you have written. Paraphrased material only puts you at risk of a plagiarism accusation. Summarize instead.*

9.3.6 Which method is best?

You can use any or all of these methods, except paraphrasing, to advantage. I suggest that you keep all methods available, using each as appropriate.

9.4 Further notes on note-taking

❖ Make sure you leave nothing out of your notes. Keep track of full information on author, title, place, publisher, date, volume number, page numbers, etc. You don't want to have to relocate a book or article you've already read. (I recently encountered a student going through exactly this process. He couldn't find his quotations from the original book, and there is no searchable electronic version). Chances are someone else will have the book you used by now, and you'll never find out what page that key quotation came from. Other than a cold shower, there's nothing as subduing as having to throw out perfectly good notes because you don't have enough source information to use them in your bibliography. Bibliographic managers are great resources for keeping track of your bibliographies (7.6 above)

❖ If you are quoting, use quotation marks in your notes. If you copy/paste in an electronic environment, keep track of page numbers. If the material you are reading turns a page in the middle of your quotation, put a slash mark or some other indicator into your notes to tell you where the page turned in the original.

❖ If you are summarizing, conscientiously try to work at using your own wording. If you find that your wording is turning out like a clone of the original, then quote directly or photocopy/print. With summaries, indicate in the margin of the notes the page numbers you are summarizing (in case you want to go back to the book or article later).

❖ If an insight comes to you as you are reading, include it in your notes. Put square brackets around it and end the statement of your insight with a dash and your initials, like this:

[*Schwartzburg agrees with Smith on this point. Does Flutnof?—WB*]

An "insight" is simply anything that occurs to you while you're reading, as, for example, the discovery that this writer agrees or disagrees with someone else, has omitted something, has made a statement that you would like to challenge, has given you a good idea you want to follow up, and so on.

Clearing the Fog: What if I'm not an organized person?

All of this talk of pre-planning to create your notes and use them effectively may have you feeling a bit queasy. You, in fact, may find the whole idea of *method* to be a limiting factor. You are used to glorious chaos out of which emerges fresh ideas. Creating notes by set methods and organizing them (we'll get to note organization in the next chapter) seems much too structured, the kind of thing a librarian might do.

If you are a person who finds organization to be a burden, I suppose you can carry on as before. But how has that been working for you? As projects get bigger and more detailed, are you noticing that the anxiety regarding your "just wing it" approach is growing? Have you wasted a lot of time finding and re-finding material that you know is there somewhere? Do you often feel utterly lost?

Is the problem less that you hate organization than that you struggle with *doing* organization? If so, try this approach. First, before you ever start on a project, say to yourself, "I need to plan and organize my research." Rather than telling yourself that you can't create such a plan, let alone carry it out, ask yourself a set of questions. The answers will create a roadmap for you to follow:

❖ *What format do I intend to use to hold the notes I need to take for this project?* Rather than having some notes in paper, some on PDF and some on your phone, decide on one resource format and then determine how you will convert everything to that format. For example, you may say, "I want to have everything in PDF on my laptop and backed up on Dropbox." Clearly, your article downloads will be PDFs. You can scan print material to PDF (see suggestions above). In the end, you will have only one type of format to deal with. If you use my naming convention (Author, space dash space, First part of title, e.g. Jackson - Finding a Path in Research), all your PDFs will organize in a documents folder in alphabetical order by author.

❖ *Where do I intend to store my notes?* This could be a binder for print, a documents folder for PDFs, one of those note programs like Evernote, or a bibliographic manager. Keep your storage place consistent.

❖ *What rules do I intend to follow in note-taking?* Decide on a method in advance, and follow it. See the examples above.

There, you have a plan. Now all you have to do is stick to it.

9.5 A gentle warning about the horrible crime of plagiarism

Just to end the chapter on a cheery note, let me caution you about the academic crime of *plagiarism*. Plagiarism, to put it simply, is passing off someone else's work as your own. The following examples, if they describe your actions, place you very obviously among the guilty. You are plagiarizing if you:

- ❖ Get your whole essay from a friend or a paper mill online and then pass it off as your own original work.
- ❖ Quote directly from a book, journal, newspaper, friend's essay, etc. without using quotation marks and a note to indicate that the material is not yours;
- ❖ "Borrow" text from the WWW or some other digital source by copy/paste without indicating the source;
- ❖ Paraphrase an author, sentence by sentence, without acknowledging the author as the source of the material;
- ❖ Use a unique idea from an author without indicating the source of the idea. When you can't find the same idea in two or more independent sources, then it's unique and you have to tell the reader of your research project where the idea came from. (Concepts that are unique to an author need to be acknowledged, while more generally known information does not).

Plagiarism is an academic crime because it is the theft of someone else's creativity, and because it gives the impression that someone else's words or ideas are your own. Most astute professors catch offenders quite easily (especially those who skim their papers off the Internet), and then feel hurt that they have been lied to. This can result in anything from a zero for the paper to expulsion from the institution.

9.5.1 Why get stressed about plagiarism?

With easy access to the WWW and to online full text journals, plagiarism is increasing. A lot of students struggle with why plagiarism is such a big deal. We download music all the time, and the WWW is full of free information. What's the difference between downloading a song and downloading text to put into a research paper? The following may provide some answers:

- ❖ There is a difference between free access and your freedom to claim that you are the author of the information you copied from the Net. If you download a song, you may "own" it, but you can't legally claim that you wrote it or sang it. If you download text from a freely available source and then neglect to indicate who authored that text, you're not only taking control of the information, you're executing a fraud by leading the reader to believe you actually wrote the stuff.
- ❖ Intellectual property is a big deal in Western society. As an author, to be able to write something and put my name on it is something I value, and my right to claim ownership is protected by copyright law. When someone else takes my material and puts his/her name on it, my intellectual property has been stolen.
- ❖ When you take someone else's words or ideas and pass them off as your own, you rob those words/ideas of their power, because you've broken the connection between the creator of the information and the information itself. To say that a known authority in the field wrote that: _____ (you fill in the blank) is much more powerful than saying or implying that you wrote the same thing. The power of information often comes from the power of the person who authored that information.
- ❖ Research writing is a conversation. As you address your research question, you know that there are other voices out there who have already expressed points of view about

possible answers to your question (you'll find these in the sources you are using: books, articles, and so on). Research involves dialoguing with those sources, agreeing with some, disagreeing with others. If you steal text or ideas from those sources and pass them off as your own words or ideas, you kill the dialogue and leave yourself as the only authority on the topic. A prof can see through that sort of thing in an instant. It's much more powerful to write, "Jones has argued _____ but Smith has countered with the argument that _____. In considering Jones' view, it appears that she has neglected to take into account the evidence that _____." Focus on the dialogue. That's the key to good research writing.

9.5.2 About getting caught

Just at the time when it's easier than ever to steal electronic text and paste it into your research project, thus deceptively passing it off as your own, it's easier than ever to get caught. If you plagiarize an author's unique ideas, chances are your professor already knows what those unique ideas are. But even if you steal text, your professor can catch you very easily.

For material from the WWW, a simple Google search on a string of text from your paper (using quotation marks) will likely find you out pretty quickly. The same can be done with full text searches in journal databases or Google Scholar. For books, both Google Books and Amazon have a lot of electronic full text available for searching.

Even if you take text from a print book or journal not available electronically, you are still at risk. Case in point: I was reading a student paper that just didn't seem right, so I googled a string of text. The source the student was using wasn't actually available electronically, but the text I googled had been quoted in a website, and there was a citation to the original print source. Once I knew what hardcopy book had been plagiarized, I got it off the library shelf and tracked down the rest of the massive amount of plagiarism in the paper.

Many institutions are using plagiarism detection services like Turnitin. Students submit their papers electronically, and the degree of correspondence between those papers and other electronic sources (including their bank of student papers) is analyzed. The professor gets a report.

So it's getting easier to be caught at the plagiarism game. The results are pretty awful. If your professor is really merciful you'll have to rewrite your paper. Normally the paper gets a zero, with no chance for a rewrite. But many institutions don't just stop there. They record your plagiarism infraction in your academic file, and you may be given a failing mark for the course. You could even be suspended or expelled. Overall, plagiarism can look like an easy way to get a paper done, but the rewards are not worth the penalty.

For my Google Slides presentation on plagiarism: **http://bit. ly/1p00KX3.**

See also the 10-minute video by Conrad van Dyk of Concordia University College: **http://youtu.be/50zeD7uQiQs**.

For an article expanding on my approach to plagiarism, see Badke, William. "Give Plagiarism the Weight It Deserves." *Online* 31.5 (Sep. 2007): 58-60.

9.5.3 International students and plagiarism

International students face some unique challenges with the plagiarism issue. In many cultures, information is perceived as the property of the community more than it is the property of the individual. In fact, when other people in a community copy or freely use the information of a great scholar, they are honoring that scholar. If information is seen as communal property, using someone else's words or ideas does not appear to be a serious problem.

Yet even in societies where information is communal, it remains wrong to pretend that other people's words or ideas are our own. Even information that belongs to the community still had an author. If you leave the impression that you are the author, you are committing fraud.

Unfortunately, international students who struggle with English are more likely to be caught when then plagiarize than native English speakers. Why? Because the style of English in the plagiarized material is obviously different from the style of an English used by a second language writer. It is not that international students plagiarize more often than domestic students. It is that international student plagiarism is easier to detect.

For a handbook to guide you in every aspect of your academic life as an international student, including plagiarism, see William Badke, *Beyond the Answer Sheet: Academic Success for International Students.* Bloomington, IN: iUniverse.com, 2003.

For more information on, and examples of, plagiarism see the APPENDIX, section A.5.4.

9.6 For further study

Study guide

1. What's the difference between connoisseur and glutton reading?
2. In what way do you need to "be ruthless" in research reading?
3. What are the four steps to discovering the overall message of a book quickly?
4. When you get to the fifth step (actually reading material you need), explain the best way to go about it.
5. What is an abstract, and how can it help you?
6. What are "key propositions" and how does finding them help the reading process?
7. What's the secret to avoiding the trap of taking too many notes that you will later not use?
8. What are some of the risks for those who take most of their notes by scanning, copying, or printing their sources?

9. What are the advantages and disadvantages of taking notes using the methods of quoting, summarizing and paraphrasing?
10. What are the 4 further instructions the author gives about key elements of note-taking?
11. Define plagiarism and explain why it is such a serious offence. You might want to supplement your knowledge with the following websites:

http://library.camden.rutgers.edu/Educational Module/Plagiarism/
http://www.hamilton.edu/writing/style/plagiarism/ plagiarism.html

Practice / Assignment

1. How is your research reading going? Is it efficient and effective? Go over the suggestions in the first part of this chapter and discover ways in which you can improve your research reading methods.
2. Assess your methods of note taking. Are they working for you? How would you improve them? Do you see ways to improve efficiency by using your electronic device (phone, tablet, or laptop) in note taking?

10

Organizing Your Resources
to Write your Paper

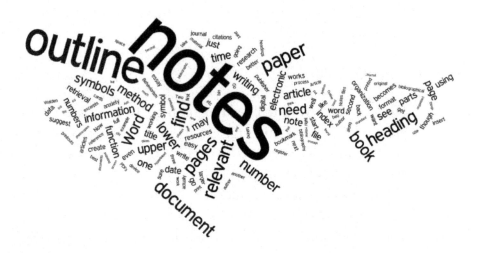

"I have seventy-five pages of notes not counting the photocopy I left in the printer and the two pages which I think fell behind my desk. And I've got at least 7 journal articles printed off, but I haven't highlighted them. I've got a bunch of PDFs, but I forgot to put them in one folder on my hard drive, and their file names tell me nothing about what they are. What a mess! How am I ever going to finish a research project out of this chaos? Will there ever be meaning to my life?"

Yes, there will. Take heart. There is a way to organize your disastrous jumble of resources or the chaos of notes in your laptop, no matter how incomprehensible it now seems to be.

I hesitate whenever I suggest "my" method for organization. What if your mind, heaven forbid, does not correspond with mine?

What if I'm totally out of touch with the logical categories you most enjoy?

Still, someone has to suggest something. Librarians, even though dull, are undoubtedly logical and thus better equipped than, say, Renaissance painters, to suggest methods of organizing information. I am giving you only a couple of approaches to the problem, because throwing too many methods at you can be confusing. If you don't like what I suggest, ask your favorite professor or another librarian to suggest a better plan.

My first system can be called a "register method" of resource organization. A "register" is an index of some sort that enables you to organize data. Consider an auto parts store. The parts are laid out in bins on row after row of shelves. The fact that the water system thermostats are next to the gas caps that are next to the spark plugs is not nearly as relevant as the fact that each bin has a number on it.

When I walk in and ask for a thermostat for a 1949 Wuzzly Roadster, the parts person does not immediately proceed to the shelves and start looking. He or she searches a database to find the bin number for that model of thermostat. Then it's an easy task to find the bin with the right number on it and deliver the part to me.

Here's the point of the analogy: The rows of auto parts are your jumbled mess of notes and printouts, in print or online. The bin numbers are codes you insert into these resources. The parts book or digital index represents an indexed outline by which you can retrieve your notes in a coherent way. This is how it works:

10.1 Your notes, photocopies and printouts

10.1.1 Organizing digital notes

I am presuming here that you have captured excerpts, produced summaries, etc., so that you are working with notes and saved portions rather than with the full documents you acquired in the process of your research. If you are working with full documents, go back to

9.3.3 for some guidance. If you have created a digital document containing notes taken from your original PDFs (through copy/paste, plus your own annotations), take advice from the following:

❖ Some people prefer to print their digital notes onto paper. In this case, your device is just an input medium, and notes should be handled as in 10.1.2 below.

❖ If you are planning to retain your notes in their electronic format, you need to determine how you want to set them up for easy retrieval of the information you need. The best solution here is to create a single Word file of notes, using copy/paste from electronic sources as well as your own summaries and comments. I've created such note documents up to 400+ pages, so I know that they work and that retrieval is still possible, no matter how big the document becomes. *Presumably I don't have to stress the importance of backing up this file as you go along (I'd suggest at least a cloud backup like Google Drive or Dropbox, and maybe a flash drive too). Lose it, and you lose everything.*

❖ Your word processor's "find" function (in the "edit" menu) will become a retrieval tool, though in the organizing process you will need to input some codes (see 10.3 below).

10.1.2 Organizing your paper-based notes

Many students still base their notes in hardcopy, thus printing articles, taking photocopies of book pages and writing or typing/printing summaries. Some write notes on 3 x 5 or 4 x 6 cards. This is, in my humble opinion, a grave error. If God had meant us to write out notes on cards, he would not have allowed us to invent standard notepaper or printers that take standard paper sizes. Does not nature itself tell you that eyes, hands and pens were made for writing boldly on decent sized paper instead of scraping one-sixteenth inch high letters on miniscule cards? Are not printers set to standard size paper by default?

Save your note cards for the next part of my system if you wish (though there are much better ways), and produce your notes (if you are using print or printing electronic notes) on normal paper, hole-punching them and keeping them together in a binder. Be sure, however, to follow a consistent method. As you begin taking notes on each book or article, be very certain that you include full bibliographical information in the notes (author, title, place, publisher, date, volume number, and page numbers).

When you have completed creating your notes for a particular item (even if those notes are ten pages long), simply leave a few lines blank, then start notes on your next book or article, being sure again to enter full bibliographical information first. (If you are using a device, see the alternatives below.)

One of the important things you need to do is *number the pages of your notes consecutively.* If you have fifty pages of notes on ten pages, then number your note pages from one to fifty. (If using an electronic device, see below). If you have photocopies or journal article printouts, put them in the right places in your notes and number them along with the notes, even if you end up with 150 pages numbered consecutively.

10.2 Your bibliography

As you gather sources, you have to keep track of them, including enough bibliographical information so that you won't need to go on a desperate search for a lost date or volume number when you start writing your paper. The best resource for this task is a bibliographic manager like EndNote, RefWorks, Zotero, or Mendeley (See 8.5, above, for an explanation of these tools). If you do not use a bibliographic manager, you may want to enlist a software or online style formatting program or at least construct a separate Word file with the bibliography in proper format (for format and formatting tools, see the APPENDIX: A.6).

Here's the minimal information needed for your citations:

Book: Author(s), title, city of publication, publisher, date.

Journal Article: Author(s) and title of article, journal title, volume, issue number, date (e.g., (2013), (January 1999) or (Spring 2000)), and page numbers where the article is found.

Journal Article from an Electronic Periodical Database: everything listed under Journal Article above plus (possibly) the date you accessed the article, and either the persistent link / journal home page, or the DOI, depending on what bibliographical style you are using. For example:

> Badke, W. (2010). Foundations of information literacy: Learning from Paul Zurkowski. *Online*, *34*(1), 48-50. Retrieved from http://www.infotoday.com/online/.

> Weickert, T., Goldberg, T., Egan, M., Apud, J., Meeter, M., Myers, C., et al. (2010). Relative risk of probabilistic category learning deficits in patients with Schizophrenia and their siblings. *Biological Psychiatry*, *67*(10), 948-955. doi:10.1016/j.biopsych.2009.12.027.

Essay in a Book: Author(s) and title of essay, title of book, editor of book, city of publication, publisher, date, and page numbers where the essay is found.

Reference Book Article: Title of article, author(s) if given (often an abbreviation of the author name is provided at the end of the article), title of reference book, edition of reference book; and (sometimes) city of publication, publisher, date. Note that most basic reference book articles are not cited in bibliographies, though longer articles from substantial reference works may be.

Website: Author (if given), title, publisher (if given), Internet address (URL), and date you most recently accessed the information.

<hr/>

Clearing the Fog: How can I learn to read citations well?

So you've got a bunch of citations, but they are just *so* confusing. It's not only format – MLA, APA, Chicago, etc. – it's the fact that there are so many details. Is this a citation to a book or an article or an essay in a book, or just what? Websites are recognizable for the most part, but other academic literature can be a nightmare to decipher.

Being helpful as always (I'm a librarian, after all), I've compiled a graphic that spells out the main elements of book, essay and journal article citations. Don't worry about the format. Just have a good look at the various parts of the citation and what they mean. I hope this clears out some fog.

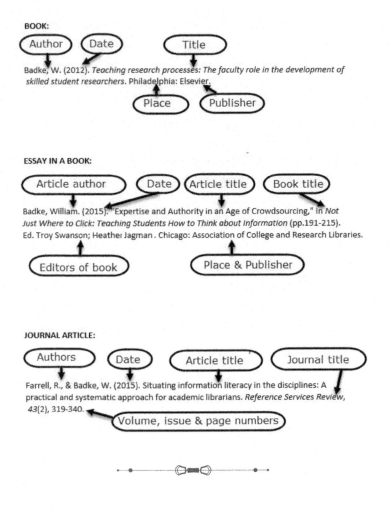

10.3 Your subject index

Note taking and printout gathering are easy. Retrieval is hard. The biggest problem most students face is that they've ended up with a ton of PDFs (or many pages of notes and printouts), but when they want to write the research paper, they can't retrieve the data they need from these resources.

Virtually anyone, even a seasoned author, gets writing anxiety: That moment when you are finally staring at a blank screen (with the cursor blinking in taunting fashion), and your mind tells you that this essay will never happen. You may have written brilliant works in the past (or not), but this one simply will never see the light of day. You are doomed.

Now, imagine that you have the further problems that your full text resources or notes are a mess, you're not sure you did enough research, and you can't find even the data you remember noting down. Writing anxiety now becomes writing crisis. The only way to save yourself from all this *angst* is to get organized before you write.

Sure, I know you're thinking, *"My paper is due in 3 hours. I don't have time to get organized."*

My response is that **you don't have time NOT to get organized.**

Let me suggest a method that will break the back of writing anxiety and actually save you time in the long run. This procedure can be done with physical paper or an electronic document. [For a slide presentation on this, see **http://bit.ly/1SdMRRU**]. Here are the steps:

❖ Open a new Word document (or take a good-sized piece of paper) and type/write your preliminary outline on it, leaving lots of space between each heading and subheading. (This assumes that you actually **do** have a preliminary outline. If not, you've probably already lost a lot of time researching things that aren't relevant to your topic, which may explain in part why your unfinished paper is due in three hours [not meaning to be cruel; just saying].)

❖ Determine a symbol to represent each heading or subheading. These symbols could be the letters and numbers used in your outline (I, A, 1, a, etc.) or special symbols not normally used in written work: #, $ % +, etc. The latter type usually functions better.

❖ If you are working with notes in paper form, read through your notes. Every time you discover data that is relevant to one of your headings in your outline, write the location (page number of notes) under that outline heading. In your notes, insert your symbol for the relevant outline heading so that you can use your outline to find the exact location of the data related to it. (If this is confusing, see the example below.)

❖ If you are working with electronic files, type the symbols (%, #, @ or whatever) into the spots in your online file that are relevant to your outline. The "find" function in your word processor can then locate any symbol and its relevant notes any time you need them.

For example:

% Darwin's approach to natural selection made it possible...etc.

If you are working with a PDF file, use the Comment function on the top right of the screen to insert your symbol where you want it (choose the "Sticky note" icon; you can then see your symbols in the right column and quick connect to the related text).

Thus, with this exercise of organization, you cross-reference your notes with your outline so that you can retrieve the relevant notes as you write your paper. The outline may then look something like this:

The Limits of Behaviorism: *Walden Two* in Perspective
I. An Introduction to Behaviorism
4, 7, 12, 17 [page numbers of relevant notes only needed if your notes are in paper format; for electronic files, just the symbol # is necessary].

II. B.F. Skinner's *Walden Two*
$ 3, 18, 3

III. *Walden Two* as a Demonstration of the Limits of Behaviorism
% 6, 12, 14-17

In the above example, note that my symbols are #, $ and %. If I had subheadings, I could create more complex symbols like &1, &2, and so on. These symbols will also be inserted in the appropriate places in the printed notes or electronic files for easy retrieval of data.

Below is an illustration of a pages of notes, with #, $, and & symbols attached to the relevant parts. If those notes are in digital form, you can use the "Find" function in your word processor to find them (as long as you ensure there is a space after each symbol). If they are in print form, you have page numbers of your notes, and the symbols just tell you where on the page you will find what you need.

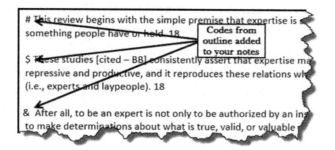

Why go to all this trouble? Simply because it saves time and alleviates writing anxiety. Consider this awful alternative: You begin writing your paper and get to heading number one: "An Introduction to Behaviorism." Now you have to do a keyword search on "behaviorism" with your find function (with unpredictable results) or rummage through all forty-seven pages of your printed notes, looking for material on this aspect. Having found your material and written this section of your paper, you come to your second roadblock: The next heading is "B.F. Skinner's *Walden Two*." Now you have to go through your notes again in a second desperate search for relevant information. Then comes heading number three, and the whole nasty quest starts over again. In the process, you will have plowed through all your notes three times and restarted your writing anxiety three times.

Thus, setting up an outline-based index to your notes before you start writing saves you having to re-read your material every time you start a new section of your paper. Besides, you are left with a warm and comforting sense that you actually know where you are going before you start. When was the last time you had a feeling like that?

10.4 A Second Method for Note Organization

This one is more complex and works best for larger projects up to a thesis or doctoral dissertation. But it takes some effort to make clear. You might find this explanatory PDF helpful: **http://williambadke.com/NoteMethod2.pdf**. Method number two works only if all your resources are digital. That is, you have PDFs of articles, you've digitized book pages, and so on.

The first step is to get all your notes into a single document. This means that, for each source you used, you need to have a citation and notes/excerpts from it in a single Word document. Just do this with each source, one after another.

Second step: Create a second word document. This second word document will place your notes under each heading in your outline. Like this:

Put your outline at the top of this second word document. Then put *another* copy of your outline below it. We will call these the "upper outline" and the "lower outline." The upper outline will serve as a hyperlinked index to the lower outline. The lower outline will have selected notes from your *first* word file pasted into it under each outline heading. The reason you need an index at the top (the upper outline) is that it will become increasingly difficult to find the headings in the lower outline as the space between them becomes filled with notes relevant to each heading. Your upper outline acts as an index to the lower outline. Thus:

Word document #1: Your notes arranged under each resource you are using, e.g.

Smith, The Effects of Viscous Membranes in...
Notes

Jones, The Feasibility Study as a Means....
Notes And so on.

Word document #2: Your notes pulled from Word document #1 and placed under the various headings of your outline, e.g.

Upper Outline which you will hyperlink to your lower outline

Lower Outline Heading 1
Notes, notes, notes

Lower Outline Heading 2
Notes, notes, notes And so on.

Go through your original Word document #1 and find material relevant to your outline. As you find relevant information in your original notes, copy it and paste directly into your Word document #2 under whatever heading is relevant in your lower outline. Make sure you include citations for these excerpts. In essence, you are creating notes for each of your headings, pulling them as excerpts from your original master notes list (Word document #1).

Here is a screen shot of the upper and lower outlines, along with notes:

Preface
**Portion of upper
outline**
PART ONE: The Problem

The Cost of Information Illiteracy
Illiteracy in Academia
The State of the Art in Information Literacy

PART ONE: The Problem
**Lower outline
and notes**
The Cost of Information Illiteracy

Feldman, The Hidden costs of information work (2005)

"With the economy now becoming information-based rather than industrial, the n
is to make information work more productive." (1)

"During the summer of 2004, IDC surveyed 600 U.S. companies in three size cat

In Word document #2 you have two copies of your outline, one above the other (the upper and the lower outlines). Now, you turn the upper outline into a hyperlinked index to the sections in your lower outline. Here are the steps (see **http://williambadke.com/ NoteMethod2.pdf** for illustrations):

1. In front of each heading in the lower outline (the one with excerpts of notes), create a **bookmark**, using the Insert function in Word.
2. Then create a hyperlink to each bookmark in the upper outline so that the upper outline becomes a set of links.

Then, when you need to find the notes below, related to a particular outline heading, you can click on the relevant upper outline heading to launch you into the corresponding notes below.

In summary, it works like this. First click on the "bookmark" tab and insert the bookmark where you want it. Second, create hyperlinks from the upper outline to the lower outline. The upper outline thus becomes a hyperlinked index to your lower outline.

This may be a bit hard to conceptualize. View the PDF (URL above) to see how it is done. It could be a very rewarding method for you, especially if you are doing a larger project.

[Word 2016 has a "Go to" function in its Find and replace area. You just need to create bookmarks for each outline heading in your notes. The "Go to" finction will enable you to go to any bookmark you have made. See **http://tinyurl.com/zjdonlv**.]

10.5 Indexing your notes for larger assignments

There might come a time when you are asked to produce a really large research paper such as a thesis, dissertation, or book. Now the process of note organization becomes crucial, because retrieval is much more complicated.

In general, the procedures described above will work just as well on longer papers as they do on shorter ones, though my method two is better for larger assignments. A few tips for such projects (beyond the obvious that you should always back up your files):

* ❖ Do your indexing as you are going along in your research rather than waiting to the end and being faced with the task of indexing a massive electronic file or dozens (even hundreds) of printed pages of notes.
* ❖ Make especially sure that you are managing your bibliography well. The larger the bibliography, the more the risk of losing things. Here a bibliographic manager (see 8.5 above) is well worth the effort it takes to make it your friend.
* ❖ If your preliminary outline should change as you are going, don't panic. Go back over what you've already indexed and transfer your old indexing, as best you can, to the new outline. Sometimes this will mean going back over your notes again and making changes to symbols embedded in them.

Research may be fun, but nobody said it was easy. Come to think of it, though, isn't the challenge what makes it so much fun?

10.6 For further study

Study guide

1. Write out an explanation of the "register method" of note organization, including a description of each of the parts.
2. If compiling your resources together is easy, what is hard? Why?
3. In using a device as your note-taking tool, what options do you have for retrieval?
4. Why go to all this trouble to organize notes and establish retrieval procedures?

Practice/Assignment

Assess your past method(s) of note organization. Would the register method work for you? Are you ready to go all electronic? Can you think of another method that you'd prefer?

11

Tips on Research Writing

Research doesn't mean much if the presentation of your results is flawed. The kiss of death is to have a final research paper returned with the comment: "Excellent bibliography, but your argument could have been developed more logically."

Two writing problems stand out as the most challenging: Getting your research question and outline straight, and writing persuasively. Let's deal with each in turn.

11.1 The research question and final outline

Earlier, I argued that you need to have a preliminary outline pretty much from the beginning of the research process to act as a guide for the gathering of resources. In the early stages, organizing your outline is not crucial, but eventually you are going to have to put it into final form. Outlining is a major challenge in any research presentation. If you are attempting (in real uneasiness, no doubt) a thesis or dissertation, the problem only compounds itself.

Let's visualize what we're dealing with first and then look at some possible solutions. The reason why the outline is so troublesome is that people receive information in sequence rather than absorbing all of the facts at the same time. Simply because a twenty page paper may take fifteen minutes to read means that some information must be presented before other information is given.

Let's look at it another way. Putting forward an argument (that is, the statement of a response to your research question) is like building a house. You have to lay the foundation before you can move to the upper stories. Everything you build rests upon whatever you've already laid down.

Perhaps the best way to learn outlining technique is to look at specific steps and see these illustrated with examples.

11.1.1 Step one: The research question/thesis statement

As we have seen, the first step toward putting together even a preliminary outline is figuring out what issue you want to deal with. This involves narrowing your topic and stating a *single* research question. For our purposes, let's choose the topic of "Burnout in the Workplace." Our narrower focus will be "preventing burnout," and our research question is, "How can today's office worker use common warning signs to resist burnout in the workplace?" A corresponding thesis statement would be something like: "Today's office worker must be alert to the common signs of burnout and take specific steps to counteract their influence."

11.1.2 Step two: Preliminary outline headings

Now you need to assess your question or thesis statement to determine what data you are going to need to answer it. For our example, presumably you'll need an introduction to burnout, explaining what it is and raising the issue that there must be means to resist it. You might, as well, assume that resisting this problem will involve recognizing the warning signs of coming burnout and taking some counter-measures to overcome those signs or to prevent them happening in the first place. Thus your preliminary outline (in no particular order) has three possible headings already: Knowing the Common Warning Signs of Approaching Burnout, Counter-measures, and An Introduction to the Problem of Burnout.

11.1.3 Step three: Organizing the headings

This is usually the hardest part. What you want is a logical order that is helpful to the reader. Above all, you want to avoid the impression that your paper lacks direction or that the direction it is taking is strange and hard to justify. The transitions in a good outline should not be all that noticeable because your goal is to take the reader from introduction to conclusion as smoothly as possible.

A few tips

- ❖ Get general and introductory matters out of the way first. Just as you needed a working knowledge of the topic when you started your research, you now need to give your reader a similar working knowledge, including background information and a clear statement of the question you're dealing with. In the case of our burnout example, you would probably have to define burnout, demonstrate what a problem it is, and then ask what things could be done to resist burnout in the workplace (your research question).
- ❖ Look for a natural order to your headings, if you can find it. In our burnout example, it seems more natural to discuss first the need to recognize the warning signs of burnout and *then* to consider possible counter-measures to resist burnout (i.e., knowledge before action seems like a natural order).
- ❖ Here are some other possibilities:

- In a historically-oriented paper (e.g., "The Early Conquests of Alexander the Great"), you might simply want to move the paper along chronologically.
- In an analysis of issues related to a topic, you can follow an ascending or climactic order, looking at smaller factors or arguments first, then moving up to the more crucial factors. Your last section could begin,

  "The most serious difficulty with_____, however, is_____."

  Ascending or climactic order adds power to a paper by leading the reader into increasing levels of tension, much like an action movie builds to a climax. Resist giving away the most exciting parts of your paper early on—if you use up the good stuff too soon, you'll have little left to keep the reader interested in the rest of what you have to say.

- You need to include all relevant points of view on an issue, not just the one you support. When a research project ignores opposing arguments, the reader feels cheated, and the case you are making is weakened, not strengthened. An argument that pays no attention to other voices will not stand up to a challenge. Remember, it's all about the conversation.

Comparing and contrasting

If you are comparing or contrasting two or more viewpoints, there are a couple of ways to go about it. Now's a good time to get your wits about you, so go have some coffee or take a walk, then read on.

If the two views you are discussing are relatively simple to explain and analyze, try a *longitudinal method* by which you discuss all aspects of view A and then moved on to discuss all aspects of view B. Suppose, for example, you were dealing human cloning and covering both sides—**<Go Ahead>** and **<Wait a Minute: What Do You Think You're Doing?>**

Your outline might look like this:

I.   Introduction to Human Cloning
II. The Go Ahead Position
    A. All Science is Legitimate.
    B. We Can Trust Scientists Not To Put Us At Risk.
    C. The Benefits of Having Clones Outweigh The Risks.
III. The Wait A Minute Position
    A. Is all Science Legitimate?
    B. Can We Trust Scientists Not To Put Us At Risk?
    C. Do The Benefits Outweigh The Risks?
IV. Conclusion

You can see that you are presenting one position in total, then the other, using your discussion of the second position as a base to deal with the arguments against the first. Thus the Go Ahead position will be described as objectively as possible. The analysis will come with The Wait a Minute Position.

But suppose that the arguments are getting complicated, and you're afraid your reader will have forgotten what the first position said about the legitimacy of science before you have time to discuss it in the second position. In a complex situation, you'll need a *cross-sectional approach*, which deals with both sides of each sub-topic in turn:

I.   Introduction to Human Cloning
II. Is All Science Legitimate?
    A. Yes
    B. Maybe not
III. Can We Trust The Scientists?
    A. Yes
    B. Not always
IV. Do the Benefits of Having Clones Outweigh the Risks?

    A. Yes

    B. Maybe not

V. Conclusion

If you want to see the two approaches side by side, here they are. Note how differently they are structured, despite the fact that they are dealing with the same subject matter:

Longitudinal Approach	Cross-Sectional approach

I. Introduction to Human Cloning
II. The Go Ahead Position
  A. All Science is Legitimate
  B. We can Trust Scientists not to Put us at Risk
  C. The Benefits of Having Clones Outweigh the Risks.
III. The Wait a Minute Position
  A. Is all Science Legitimate?
  B. Can We Trust Scientists not to Put us at Risk?
  C. Do Benefits Outweigh the Risks?
IV. Conclusion
	I. Introduction to Human Cloning
	II. Is all Science Legitimate?
	  A. Yes
	  B. Maybe Not
	III. Can We Trust Scientists?
	  A. Yes
	  B. Not Always
	IV. Do the Benefits of Having Clones Outweigh the Risks?
	  A. Yes
	  B. Maybe Not
	V. Conclusion

Using an outline akin to one of the above examples gives you the chance to deal with both sides of each issue in turn. By the time you get to your conclusion, your reader should have a cumulative understanding of the issues and of the reasons for your position.

A couple of other tips:

❖ Avoid stringing out a list of 7 or more main headings without subheadings, because this tends to obscure the unity and coherence of your paper (just like leading someone down a winding path creates more confusion than leading the same person down a straight city block with sights to see on all sides). How do you cover the ground without multiplying your outline headings? You do it by using fewer main headings and adding subheadings to them. Thus you *group* your points, arguments, etc. within 3 to 5 main categories and let subheadings pick up the detail. This makes a tighter structure that has more of a chance of achieving unity in the paper. See the outlines above for examples of useful ways to do this.

❖ Attempt objectivity at the beginning and do your analysis later. Here I need to get on a soapbox for a few moments:

Why does objectivity come before analysis? Because every view needs to be heard before you criticize it. Suppose you are doing a paper on the well-known (at least to me, since I invented him) social scientist Horace Q. Blowhard, who has had the audacity to argue that the death penalty should be instituted for traffic offenses in order to restore public order. Your paper, entitled, "Why Don't You Stand In Front of *My* Car, Horace?" intends to say terrible things. But how can you do this most effectively?

If you are still unclear about the fine points of research maturity, you may want to begin your paper with the words, "Horace Q. Blowhard truly lives up to his name. If there were ever a reason for tar and feathers, Horace (no friend of yours or mine) would be it." From here, your outline would be:

I. Condemnation of Blowhard
II. Some of the Vilest of his Views
III. Concluding condemnation.

But this is utterly the wrong approach. O ye contenders for justice and all it for which it stands, halt and listen: *No one deserves to be torched verbally or in print before he or she has been given a fair and objective hearing.* Not even Horace Q. Blowhard.

I know what you're thinking now—When did true objectivity ever exist? All of us are subjective, so why not just state our personal views without worrying about truth and fairness to other viewpoints? Why try to give anyone an objective hearing? My answer is that, while this is neither the time nor the place to get into the murky depths of Postmodernism, all of us know that it's possible to hear someone, understand that person, and treat that person's views fairly. Sure, our presuppositions will get in the way to some extent, but our goal still needs to be to understand the positions of others as best we can *before* we level either praise or crushing criticism. A good measure of objectivity is still possible for most of us.

Remember that scholarship is a conversation. The essence of being able to deal with an issue is determining and paying attention to what others have been saying about it, even when you encounter positions you don't like. You have to get into the conversation if you want to be seen as having any credibility as a player in the issue.

Devastating attacks do not come before we have explained the position of our opponents. They come after, when both you and the reader have enough knowledge of the opposing position to determine whether you are launching the right missiles. Anything less than this is poor sportsmanship, bad form, bigotry, whatever you want to call it. Mature writing makes sure every view has been heard fairly before it is analyzed.

Clearing the Fog: What about creativity?

All this planning, let alone outlining, before you write the paper, may seem to be stifling those creative urges that make for great writing. My pre-planning process might look like one of those adult coloring books that are such a big deal these days. Restful, but you have to stay within the lines, and that's just boring and uncreative.

If you have to plan everything in advance, isn't the writing going to be a pretty dull process of filling in the blanks? What about people who actually learn by writing or who problem-solve best in the act of writing up the final project? Won't all of that creativity just be suppressed?

Surprisingly, no. And this for one strong reason: your research question/thesis/outline are works in progress until you turn in the final project. Only then is it too late to change them. There is still ample scope for creativity as you write. You can come up with new ideas, revamp your outline, and even tweak your research question or thesis. No one will see earlier versions of your planning elements, so if you want to change them as you write, do so (but carefully, and with a lot of thought).

Why plan anyway? Simply because, when you aim at nothing, you are bound to hit it. You don't want your goal to be mush, because the chances that your creativity will then turn the mush into substance are slim to none. Having a clear goal in mind gives you a product to revise as need be, without having to re-invent everything from the beginning.

Please do plan and organize. It won't hurt your ability to be creative. Only a novelist writes with a murky outcome in mind (and I think it's the rare novelist who has no idea where the story will end up.)

11.2 Some tips on research writing

11.2.1 Introduce your paper well

Introductions serve two purposes:

- ❖ They give you a chance to provide your reader with a working knowledge of your topic.
- ❖ They let you state your (*single*) research question or thesis statement.

Something to avoid here is the temptation to multiply your research questions along the lines of:

> "Why, then, did Skinner write *Walden Two?* Did he indeed believe that he could create Utopia with

behavioristic methods? Was he blind to the problems in his approach? Did he later change his mind?"

What you've done is create a shotgun blast heard around the world, not one goal but many. You reader has no idea what your real intention is because you have so many of them. The paper itself will be as superficial and as scattered as your introduction. Keep your goal singular.

Sometimes a real life illustration is helpful to get the topic going. For example, if you are doing a paper on a historical figure, you might want to begin with an anecdote from that person's life to illuminate what you want to say about him/her. Beyond that, stick with the purposes of an introduction: To provide a working knowledge and to state your research question or thesis.

11.2.2 Be focused at all times

There is something almost magical about creating a successful research paper. If you have a solid, narrowly-focused, analytical research question, you can pretty much see in your mind's eye the problem to be addressed. If you have a well-structured outline, you can also see the path through the paper to a conclusion before you even start writing it. Don't begin writing the paper until everything comes into focus and you have that "Aha" experience that tells you that you know pretty clearly what you need to do. If it's all fuzzy, it will remain fuzzy through the writing process, and the product will be fuzzy too (a triple fuzzy can't be a good thing).

If you keep the narrow focus on what you are doing, magic will happen.

11.2.3 Always describe before you analyze.

You thought I had long since fallen off my soapbox. Don't worry. I won't bring it up again. But do it. Your writing will look more mature.

11.2.4 Avoid ridicule.

When you disagree with a certain author or viewpoint, you need to maintain a level of respect and decorum. Your opponent is not a "moron," "idiot," "stupid" or "useless." (Believe it or not, I've seen all of these terms in student papers). This kind of language reminds me of an elementary schoolyard with two kids arguing about an issue until one of them runs out of ideas and says, "Oh yeah? Well, I think you're just stupid." Ridicule is the lowest form of argument. It reveals a lack of ability to address the issues in a mature, intelligent manner. Such language only reflects badly on you.

11.2.5 Be logical.

By this, I mean that, whenever you are traveling along a certain train of thought, make sure your reader is in the caboose behind you (sorry, I forgot that trains don't have cabooses anymore). Don't flit around. Don't jump to another track without warning. Always remember that you are writing for someone who doesn't know where you're going. Lead your reader along gently, step by step. Stay on track. For example, when you move on to a new area of discussion, use a transitional clause such as, "Turning to the issue of...," "Having considered Smith's approach, it is necessary to go on to that of Brown, who...." For guidance on creating transitions, see the absolutely fabulous site for academic writing: The Academic Phrasebank (**http://www.phrasebank.manchester.ac.uk/**) and choose "Signaling transitions" from the left column.

Keeping a clear sense of your research question and outline is a great help here. If you have a single focus for your paper and understand the steps you need to take from question to solution, it's easier to help your reader stay with you. To make sure you're really on track, ask yourself with each paragraph in your paper:

❖ Is this paragraph in the right place in my paper (i.e., does it match the heading it's under)?

❖ Does this paragraph contribute to the solution for my research question?

There are times when I come across a research paper with a "bulge" in it. What's a bulge? It's a chunk of information that has very little relationship to the paper topic. How did it get there? The researcher worked for a long time on something that, as it turned out, didn't really fit into the final paper. But no one wants to admit to wasting time, so the researcher simply plugged the less-than-relevant material into the paper anyway. This turned what might have been a lean and mean research essay into an ugly project with an unsightly bulge in the middle of it. The poor reader is left to figure out what the bulge has to do with anything else.

11.2.6 Be explicit.

I don't know how many students there are out there (good, otherwise intelligent students) who believe in ESP. They assume that their professors can read their every thought even if it is never expressed. Thus we get a gem that looks something like this:

> "In looking at the issues of Nicaea, we must focus on the Arian Debate. The facts are well known and thus we move to the specific role of the famous Athanasius in dealing with..."

What's a Nicaea? What's an Arian Debate? Who's Athanasius and, if he's so famous, why have I never heard of him? Be clear.

You might counter-argue, being a clever person, that if this were a paper, say, in pre-medieval European history, the professor indeed would know all this. If you're writing for your professor, why would you have to explain these terms? But consider the problem of the professor, who has two options when reading a sentence like the one above: Either you know what you're talking about and you're sparing the prof a tedious explanation, or you don't understand the topic at all, so you're throwing in jargon to convince the prof that you do. In the face of no clear explanation, your professor may well choose the second option and think you're trying to hide your lack of understanding with bafflegab. It is better to be clear about what you know, even if you know the professor already knows it.

There's a balance, of course. You have limited space to get your ideas down, so too much explanation can be counterproductive. Find a healthy mid–point where you show what you know without showing *off* what you know.

11.2.7 Aim for clear writing rather than big words and complex sentences.

The mark of an educated person is not the length of words and sentences used but *the ability to communicate complicated information in plain language*. Be concise. Say what you mean. Avoid like the plague every long word where a shorter word would work as well. Try never to be ambiguous. Writers often struggle with just what sort of language to use in order to be clear to the reader. You can get all sorts of help from The Academic Phrasebank (**http://www. phrasebank.manchester.ac.uk/**).

11.2.8 Watch out for flawed arguments.

These include:

* ❖ *Misrepresenting authorities*. If you are appealing to someone's work as support for your argument, be very sure that you represent that person accurately. Don't quote out of context, suppress information that would give a more honest picture, or do anything similar. This sort of misrepresentation is best left to the tabloid newspapers, which do it with better skill than the rest of us.
* ❖ *Arguments from origins*. Just because a viewpoint arose from a dubious source, it does not necessarily mean that the idea

itself is wrong. If a nasty government that exploits the poor of its nation comes up with a wonderful invention to help end famine in the world, is the invention of no value simply because the government it came from is exploitative? Of course not. Those who know about such things are going to have to examine this invention and make their own assessment, regardless of its origin. Similarly, we can't always determine the value of an idea simply by considering the person who suggested it. While it might seem legitimate to doubt the advice on marital harmony put forward by someone who has been divorced seven times, you have to look at the person's material itself. The concepts may be sound even though the author does not exemplify them.

❖ *Arguments from insufficient evidence.* I am constantly amazed at the way some researchers skip over weighty problems without making their case. They use expressions like, "It is obvious that…" or "Nobody believes that today…" or "In my opinion…" even though much more effort is needed to convince the reader to buy into what they are saying. My reaction when I see statements without sufficient evidence is to assume one of three things: the writer hasn't done enough research to discover that a controversy exists, the writer has no evidence to offer and is trying to bluff through the problem, or the writer is has inflated sense of self and believes that merely stating an opinion is all any reader needs to be convinced. Only if a writer is a seasoned scholar in the field should you consider accepting a controversial or unproven idea without evidence. Even then, that seasoned scholar could be biased.

How much evidence is sufficient? Enough to be moderately convincing. When you write a research paper or report, you need to imagine a reader who is slightly hostile, who is *not* prepared to believe you. Thus you must present enough support for your argument to cause your hostile reader at least to say, "Well, you make a good case." You don't need absolute proof, just enough evidence to get your reader to take your view seriously.

If you don't have the evidence to do this, then you will have to be a lot more humble about sharing your views. Admit that evidence is scarce and that, therefore, any position you are taking on the matter is tentative.

Sometimes, the evidence is not available at all. If that's the case, admit it. Write something like, "There continues to be much debate over this issue, and no consensus seems possible until more evidence is found." (Don't suicidally write: "I can't understand this issue, so I haven't made up my mind.")

11.2.9 Know when to quote and when not to quote

You should quote:

- ❖ When you want to back up your view with that of a prominent scholar who agrees with you.
- ❖ When something someone has written is catchy or memorable in its wording. For example, Bruno S. Frey, in his book, *Dealing with Terrorism: Stick or Carrot,* gives the following clear analysis of the difference between deterrence and brute force:

> "Deterrence is not necessarily the same as using brute force. Deterrence involves the *threat* of damage to an adversary. It would be most successful if it were possible not to actually carry it out." (p. 28)

In a few short sentences, he explains a crucial distinction in such a way that little more needs to be said.

You should not, however, quote:

- ❖ When you can say it just as well in your own words.

❖ When the material you want to quote is over 5 or 6 lines long (unless it is absolutely crucial in its original wording and is necessary for the central theme of your paper).

❖ When you already have a quotation every page or two in your essay. You don't want to fill your paper with quotations. Your reader primarily wants your wisdom, not the words of everyone else.

❖ When the conventions of your discipline frown on quotation (sciences and often the social sciences). Check with your professor on this.

11.2.10 Know some basic principles for quotations.

If you are quoting, make it a habit to present your own material first, and then *back it up* with a quotation. Quotations should not normally be used to present new data. Here the issue is one of authority. Every time you present new data with a quotation, you are deferring to the authority of your source. That knocks the wind out of your own authority as an author. Let's put it this way: *Whose paper is it?* It's yours. Stand on your own two feet and make your own statements. Quotations are for backup and support.

Thus the pattern you should use is something like this: Present, in your own words, some data or a viewpoint, and then follow up with something like "As Joseph Schwartz has argued...", then quote from Schwartz in support of your data or viewpoint. Even if you are just presenting the views of someone (e.g., B.F. Skinner), present those views in your own words first, then if you need to, follow up with a quotation from Skinner that summarizes his position well.

Never, never, never, ever write a paper that strings together long quotations interspersed with only a few lines of commentary by you. Such papers are doomed, since your professor knows that her ten-year-old son could paste together the same quotations just as well. A research paper should state your case primarily **in your own words**, showing that you can present data clearly and use that data analytically to answer an important question. Use quotations sparingly, merely as support for what you are saying.

If you have a book or article that quotes another source, and you want to use that quotation, the rule is to *find the original source* that the quotation came from and quote that source directly. Until you go back to the original source, you can't know for sure whether the quotation was accurate or was quoted in its proper context. Only if you can't find the original source should you use the book or article in which you found the quotation. Even then, you need to indicate what you are doing, e.g.:

[3] Raymond Sludge, *The Red Rose,* 47, as quoted in Horace Roebuck, "Roses are Forever," *Flower Journal* 42 (May 2000): 76.

But think twice before you use this option. Some professors will punish you for doing so (and, of course, professors are the ones with all the power).

11.2.11 Know the uses of footnotes/endnotes/citations.

These days, most students are using short forms of citations (e.g., Jones, 241) instead of the more traditional footnotes and endnotes. But if you are using footnotes/endnotes, the following are options for you:

❖ Cite works you have quoted or borrowed ideas from. Most students are aware that direct quotations need to be noted/cited. But you need also to cite or note borrowed *ideas* if they are relatively unique. Here's a (perhaps simplistic but helpful) rule of thumb: If you use an idea that you can only find in one or two of your sources, it's better to cite the source(s). If the material is found in three or more sources and you can't see that these are borrowing their idea from a single source in the past, don't bother with a note/citation. An exception might be a view held by three or four people, yet the view is controversial and you may want to indicate to the reader where you got it from.

- ❖ State further bibliography for the reader who may be interested in pursuing the matter. This procedure, which might look a bit tedious, shows the extent of your research and could earn you appreciation from the reader (and a higher grade if the reader is a professor). Even if you are using a short citation format in the body of your paper, you can still add further bibliography as a footnote or endnote.

- ❖ Cite sources that agree with your position. This is especially useful if you know you've gone out on a limb and you suspect your professor is ready to cut it off at the trunk. The support of five other scholars who agree with you may not prove your case, but at least it shows that you are not a flake. Begin this type of footnote/endnote with something like: "So too Steven Johnson, [etc.]" or "This position is also held by..."

- ❖ Defend a certain position against possible objections. Here you are not sure someone will object to what you are saying, but you see a potential flaw in your argument. It's better for you to point out the problem yourself and respond to it before your reader can raise it as an issue. A format for this could begin, "It might be objected that...but [then give your response to the possible objection]." This type of note shows your reader that you are not trying to present a whitewash with only your side represented. If, however, you find that the argument you are presenting is important for the whole thrust of your paper, include it in the actual text of your paper. Notes are for additional or less relevant material.

- ❖ Deal with a related side issue that might spoil the flow of the essay itself if it were to appear in the text. This use is rare, but you may want to add to the depth of your paper in this way. Be careful, though, that you don't make the multiplying of notes a habit. I once spoke with a world famous scholar who admitted to me that he had a problem with his use of notes. I refrained from chuckling only because I'm a polite librarian.

One of this scholar's most celebrated works was published as two equal length volumes. The first volume was the text of his book and the second was his endnotes. I'd say he had a serious problem (though his notes were often fascinating). Avoid having the same difficulty yourself.

Clearing the Fog: Becoming a better academic writer

Very commonly in my experience, students struggle with how to present their research in such a way that it looks intelligent and mature. How do you become a better academic writer? I could simply throw that old adage at you - "Practice, Practice, Practice" - but we all know that practice can simply mean repeating the same mistakes. There's no progress in that.

Let me suggest a couple of approaches to help you improve your work. First, pay attention to the comments of your professors on previously submitted research projects. Most of us hate reading the comments. Why open yourself up to esteem-destroying criticism? But good comments can do a great job of awakening you to mistakes you are making and ways you can correct them.

Second, read *published essays/articles* on the topics you are writing about. Yes, actually read them, and do so very analytically, asking as you go:

- ❖ How does the author introduce the paper?
- ❖ How much basic information does the author provide at the beginning?
- ❖ How is the paper structured? Can you follow the line of argument?
- ❖ What kind of transitional language is used to guide you through the paper?

- ❖ How and under what circumstances does the author use citations?
- ❖ How does the author use persuasion?
- ❖ How does the author deal with opposing viewpoints?
- ❖ What is the nature of the conclusion the author makes?

These are just a few of the questions you can ask. The more you practice analytical reading of published academic work, the better you will be able to model such mature writing in your own work.

11.2.12 Watch your conclusions.

A good conclusion briefly summarizes the main focus of your paper and makes your final position clear. Avoid flowery, sentimental, or overly long conclusions. Say what you need to say and end it mercifully. In general, half a page at the end of a fifteen page paper is more than enough.

11.2.13 Give your final paper a professional look.

Your final project should avoid typographical or spelling errors (use your spell-checker). Find out what style manual your institution is using, and follow it rigorously for title page, outline page, page format, bibliography, etc. With bibliographies, make sure you follow the formatting rules you've been given. If you haven't been provided any, then choose a single style (APA, MLA, etc.) and follow it (See the APPENDIX for more on style).

You may be using a bibliographic manager (like EndNote, RefWorks, Zotero, or Mendeley) that has a bibliography generating function. While this is a big help, remember that no bibliography generator is foolproof. You will have to troubleshoot everything in the resulting bibliography. The best way to do this is to have a crib sheet for your style (a list of the most common examples of form:

books, articles, web pages, etc.) and compare it with the bibliography that you've generated, fixing things as needed. For links to crib sheets on the Net see the APPENDIX, section A.6.2 below

Word to the wise: Professors tend to assume that a sloppy product is evidence of a sloppy mind, so get your style in order.

Here's the final pep talk: Research can be exciting, even fun, so enjoy.

FUN??? Yes, as long as you see the path of discovery as an adventure. Research can be done well by virtually anyone, no matter what your initial ability may have been. I trust that I have introduced you to sufficient strategies that you can develop your skills and do first class work. The rest is up to you.

11.3 For further study

Study guide

1. What are the three steps to take in first establishing an outline?
2. In a research paper or report, what should you cover first?
3. Explain the longitudinal and cross-sectional approaches to outlining discussion of more than one view on an issue. Try each method with the following outline elements:
   Topic: Physician Assisted Suicide
   The points of view: Seeing it as a beneficial aid to sufferers vs. seeing it as wrong morally.
   The subsections under each view: The problem of unbearable suffering, the wishes of the patient, the risk that we are playing God.
4. What are the two purposes of introductions?
5. Why describe before you analyze?
6. What are some things to remember if you want your paper/ report to flow logically so that your reader can follow it?

7. What's a "bulge" in a research paper or report?

8. What is the mark of an educated person?

9. Explain types of flawed argumentation.

10. When should you not use quotations? Do you agree with William Badke's position that your quotations should be few? Why or why not?

11. Why would you use "notes" or "citations" in your research paper/report?

12. What should you avoid in a conclusion?

Practice/Assignment

Take a research project you have recently done and run it by the suggestions in this chapter. What would you change in the way it's been written?

Appendix

A research paper clinic: More tips and troubleshooting for development of great research papers

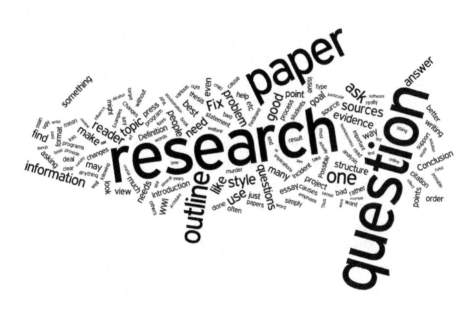

[The following material was created for a seminar on research paper writing. It supplements the book *Research Strategies*, but in some cases overlaps with it. If you experience a measure of déjà vu while reading the APPENDIX, be thankful for the enhanced examples of research question development, as well as essay preparation hints more detailed than those discussed in the body of this book. Or use it on its own as the basis for a mini–workshop.]

A.1 Research questions

A.1.1 Why many research projects miss the target

You have likely been trained to see a research project as a way to force you to read a lot of material from many sources, then report on what you have read, covering whatever topic you have been given, using as much depth as space will allow.

Thus, a paper on the causes of World War I would begin with a brief history of the events leading to this war, then would list several causes, and would perhaps conclude with a statement that war is bad and we should watch for warning signs so we can prevent war in the future. What would you say your research paper is about? "It's about the causes of World War I," you reply, looking at me strangely. You've read all about those causes in various books and magazines. You've put that material together (that is, you've synthesized it), and you've written a paper explaining the causes.

But your paper has failed as a research project. This is because a research project is not supposed to be *about* anything. Please understand this: If you were writing a genuine research paper, and I asked you, "What is your paper about?" you should be able to answer, "It's about nothing." That response, of course, would result in some questions: *"What do you mean, 'It's about nothing?' Does this mean there's no a topic? Are we in an episode of Seinfeld?"*

Certainly, you have a topic. The problem is that my question, "What is your paper about?" is wrongheaded. It assumes that a research paper is intended to explain a certain topic, using resources that you have studied. That's a false assumption. Studying up on a topic and compiling data about it is not research at all.

What, then, is the point of a research paper?

A research paper seeks to use data from various resources to answer a question or to solve a problem.

Data in this case is not an end in itself but a *means*, a *tool*. The goal of research is not merely to explain a topic. Research is a problem-solving exercise that takes data from various sources and analyzes it to help you answer a burning question.

A.1.2 Getting focused by asking the right question

If you are merely reporting on what you have read, then you don't have to worry about the purpose of your paper. Your purpose is to explain to your reader everything you know about your topic.

But if you are in search of an answer to a question, you're not really interested in knowing everything about a topic, only what is relevant. Sure, you will provide some broader background information to make sure the reader understands the issues involved. But the data you find and use will be selective, because what you really need to know is *only that portion of the data that can help you answer the question.*

EXAMPLE:

Instead of describing the causes of World War I, find a controversy that can become a research question. For example, it is often argued that the murder of Archduke Ferdinand was the chief cause of World War I. Your research very early tells you that this is an overly simple explanation. True, this particular assassination did lead to a series of events that began the War, but lots of important people are murdered every year without events turning into a worldwide conflagration. Thus you become interested in answering a question like this one: *Why did the murder of Archduke Ferdinand become the flashpoint that led to WWI?*

There are several assumptions here to test out:

❖ This was no ordinary murder.
❖ The murder must have meant something more to the various sides than is apparent.
❖ There must have been a background to this particular murder so that the sides that created a war out of it knew immediately what the murder meant.

When I teach research skills to students, the word I use more often than any other is "Focus." Most people approaching the research task are facing a crisis of lack of proper focus. This is what causes the anxiety, the belief that research is tedious, the shabby research papers, and the punishment from the professors who have to read them. Focus, focus, focus. The more your project forms a clear, narrow and single-minded image in your head, the better off you are.

This is where the research question comes in (or thesis statement if you want to go that route). It identifies the research problem and gives you the direction your research needs to take to solve it. The research question, along with a preliminary outline, provides you with a roadmap to success for any project. But a poorly constructed question will mess you up every time.

Back in Chapter Two we looked at bad and ugly questions. Let's pick up examples of those, see what they look like, and learn how to fix them.

A.1.3 The question that isn't there

Questions that aren't there are not necessarily projects without questions. It's just that the questions used don't lead to real research. These are the projects that simply compile information on a topic, then report on it. As such, gathering information is an end in itself, so there is no problem to solve.

Rubric:

Definition of good: The project not only has a question, but that question promotes a problem-solving exercise in which information is a tool, not an end in itself.

Definition of bad: The project has a fairly narrow topic but the question is merely informational in its goal. It simply asks you to look things up and report an answer.

Definition of ugly: The project not only just gathers information, but is itself a survey of a broad subject area without any question to answer.

Examples of bad and their fixes:

- *"What were the events of August 1914 that led to the start of the First World War?"* (You can look it up to find the answer.)
- ✓ Fix it by asking: *"Was the assassination of Archduke Ferdinand really as significant a cause of WWI as many scholars assume?"*
- *"What foods are good sources of low fat protein?"* (You can look it up.)
- ✓ Fix it by asking: *"Is tofu a viable option for the primary source of low fat protein in our diets, considering the problem we have with making it palatable?"* (or, *"...considering the problem we have with tofu allergies in the population?"*)
- *"Who are the Taliban?"* (You can look it up.)
- ✓ Fix it by asking: *"Is the military suppression approach to dealing with the Taliban of Afghanistan and Pakistan the best way to address the problem?"*

Examples of ugly and their fixes:

- *A survey of terrorism today*
- ✓ Fix it first by narrowing to at least one arena of terrorism, then formulating a question: *"Have the use of drone attacks proven ultimately helpful or harmful to the suppression of terrorism?"*
- *A description of Samsung's latest innovations.*
- ✓ Fix it first by narrowing to one area of operation, then formulate a question: *"Why did Samsung succeed so well in its battle for market share with Apple in the mobile device arena?"*

A.1.4 The fuzzy question

The fuzzy question is either unclear or ambiguous. It carries no certainty that there is a single, well-defined goal. When you ask it, your reader says, "Huh?"

Rubric:

Definition of good: The question is focused clearly. Not only does your reader have a solid understanding of your goal, but so do you.

Definition of bad: The project has a fairly narrow topic but the question does not provide a clear mental image of your goal.

Definition of ugly: Neither the topic nor its goal are defined clearly enough to be understood.

Examples of bad and their fixes:

- *"Was it good that the once secret documents from the history of the CIA were made public?"*
- ✓ Fix it by pondering: Good for whom? What do you mean by "good?" Who determines what is "good" and what is not "good?" Then ask, *"Did it improve public confidence in the current CIA that the secret documents from its early days were released?"*
- *"What should we make of all the recent speculation about the nature and life of the historical Jesus?"*
- ✓ Fix it by determining what you mean by the ambiguous "what should we make of," then ask, *"To what extent can we say that the speculation about Jesus in the book/movie* The Da Vinci Code *actually has sound evidence to support it?"*
- ✓ *"How can we make sense of the harm reduction policies put forward by some experts who deal with users of illegal drugs?"*
- ✓ Fix it by deciding what sort of sense you want to make, then ask: *"If the harm reduction procedures for illegal drug users in Europe and Canada have been shown to reduce drug use, why are they not being implemented everywhere?"*

Examples of ugly and their fixes:

- *"Is Globalization a good thing?"*
- ✓ Fix it first by defining the main term in your topic. "Globalization" can be economic, political, religious, etc.

Also decide what you mean by "good thing" and who determines what is and is not "good." Then ask, *"What evidence is there that the development of global free trade actually improves the economic life of the poorest producers of goods?"*

- *"Why are people so paranoid these days?"*
- ✓ Fix it by setting a definition for "paranoid." Are you speaking of a psychological condition or a mood of distrust? Next determine which people you are describing and make clear the nature of their paranoia. (Right now you have a generalization that can't be supported, in that only a small portion of the population is likely to be "paranoid" by whatever definition you give to the word.) Then ask, *"If serious crime rates are going down, why do so many people continue to believe that there is more crime in their neighborhoods than there once was?"*

- *"What's the best solution for the problem of street people?"*
- ✓ Fix it first by defining what you mean by "street people" Do you mean homeless people? People who drink too much and hang around in public places? Street sex workers? Second, determine what the problem is and who is supposed to do something about it. Third, ask, *"To what extent are volunteer organizations which deal with people without permanent homes in_____ (an inner city) making more progress toward housing these people than are government sponsored programs?"*

A.1.5 The multi-part question

One research question per project is the rule. You don't want multiple goals, which divide your paper up into mini-projects and destroy unity.

Rubric:

Definition of good: The question is absolutely singular: one goal expressed as one simple question.

Definition of bad: There are two or more related questions on the same topic so that it is unclear which question is the primary goal.

Definition of ugly: There are two or more questions really dealing with different aspects of the topic, so that no attempt to unify them into one question is going to succeed.

Examples of bad and their fixes:

- *"I want to look at the causes of WWI and discuss why war is a great evil and show how WWI could have been avoided."*
- ✓ Note that this is more of an agenda than a question, and it is multi–part. Fix it by determining what your main goal is and eliminating any other goals or making them subordinate to the main goal: *In examining the causes of WWI, how could this war have been avoided?*
- *"What are the difficulties facing homeless children and how can we help further their education?"*
- ✓ Fix it by asking: *"Given the challenges facing urban homeless children, what is the best way to ensure that they get a good education?"*
- *"What are we doing about the use of illegal guns and how can we prevent so many young people dying in our cities?"*
- ✓ Fix it by asking: *What is the best way to decrease the number of shooting deaths among urban youth?*

Examples of ugly and their fixes:

- *"Will drug companies ever drop their prices for rare disease medications, and how can we fund people who really need such drugs, and should the government punish drug companies for price gouging?*
- ✓ Fix it by determining what is the most important issue, then ask: *"What is the best way for government and drug companies to work together to ensure that people with rare diseases are able to afford appropriate medication?"*

- *"Did Shakespeare actually write the plays attributed to him, and what are the basic features of his tragedies, and in what way could Twelfth Night be viewed as a tragedy rather than a comedy?"*
- ✓ Fix it by choosing one, dropping the others, then asking: *"How valid is it to view Twelfth Night as a tragedy rather than a comedy?"*
- *"What causes Fetal Alcohol Spectrum Disorder and how can we help women not to drink during pregnancy and how could the legal system do a better job of keeping Fetal Alcohol youth and adults out of jail?"*
- ✓ Fix it by choosing one, dropping the others, then asking: *"How could the legal system do a better job of keeping Fetal Alcohol youth and adults out of jail?"*

A.1.6 The open-ended question

Open ended questions are like fishing expeditions. They are capable of having many possible answers. Often they begin with something like, "What were the results of..." or "What are the implications of..." or "What are the reasons for..."

Rubric:

Definition of good: The question sets its boundaries clearly so that there is no risk that the answers will go off in several different directions at once.

Definition of bad: The question is fairly narrow, but it is capable of being answered in a variety of ways.

Definition of ugly: The question is quite broad and is capable of being answered in a variety of ways.

Examples of bad and their fixes:

- *"What were the results of the end of WWII for French industry?"*
- ✓ Fix it by narrowing to one type of industry and determining what sorts of results you are considering. Then turn the

fact-finding mission into an analytic quest: *"What was the primary reason why French automobile manufacturing rebounded after WWII?"*

- *"What are the implications of the Crusades for modern Arabs?"*
- ✓ Fix it by defining "implications" more narrowly and clearly, then ask, *"What is the best way for the West to overcome the perception of some Muslims, brought on by reference to the Crusades, that the West wants to destroy Islam?"*
- "If we were to legalize all currently illegal drugs, what would that mean for our country?"
- ✓ Fix it by defining "mean for," then ask, *"How valid is the argument that legalizing all currently illegal drugs would cut crime and stabilize or diminish drug use?"*

Examples of ugly and their fixes:

- *"What trends should we be looking for in the world of technology over the next decade?"*
- ✓ Fix it by asking narrowing dramatically, then asking: *"With many smartphones now being big enough to do most mobile functions, what is the future of the tablet?"*
- *"What were the results of the housing crisis of 2008 and following?"*
- ✓ Fix by narrowing dramatically, then asking: *"Have US mortgage regulations changed sufficiently to avoid another major crisis similar to the one the housing market experienced in 2008 and following?"*
- *What does the rise of the Internet mean for information today?*
- ✓ Fix by narrowing dramatically, then asking: *"How did the user created reference resource, Wikipedia, succeed in providing mainly reliable information despite its lack of traditional editors?"*

A.1.7 The question that will not fly

This type of question is formulated by a creative person who wants to venture into the unknowable. Often such questions have been asked before (with no answer found), they may be seeking solutions that can't be tested or measured, or they are looking into a mysterious future. The cure for this kind of question is to resist ever writing a research project using one of them.

- *When will the next major earthquake hit San Francisco?*
- *How many angels can dance on the head of a pin?*
- *What is the nature of life on other planets?*

There is no cure for questions that simply cannot be answered given our current state of knowledge. Questions that have no clear answers are doomed. Abandon them or foolishly devote your life to searching for solutions to things that can't be solved. If you choose the latter, you'll end up as a delightful eccentric, but your efforts won't even raise a blip on the importance scale.

A.1.8 Thesis statements

Some professors prefer you to use thesis statements. Put quite simply, a thesis statement is a proposed answer to a research question. It's not a conclusion as such (which demands that you've gone through all the evidence) but a proposal, like a hypothesis in a scientific experiment, that needs to be demonstrated.

For example, you might ask: *"Are government sponsored programs or nonprofit charitable programs better able to address the needs of homeless people in city cores?"* The corresponding thesis statement might be: *"Nonprofit charitable programs are better able than government sponsored programs to address the needs of homeless people in city cores."* This is not a dogmatic statement but a position you want to try to defend with evidence.

If you're not yet comfortable with doing research papers, the research question approach is best, because with a thesis statement there is always a tendency for you to be biased in favor of the evidence that supports your thesis, thus ignoring or misusing the evidence that doesn't.

If you do take the thesis method, e.g., "The following paper will argue that..." you need to be very careful to look at the counter-arguments as well. You might in the end discover that you're wrong.

A.2 Practice with research questions

A.2.1 The questions:

Determine whether or not each of the following the research questions is a good one. Then check the key below to see what I thought of the question:

1. *Did Martin Luther, the German reformer, write anything criticizing the Jews?*
2. *What effect does homelessness have on the price of beds in Canada?*
3. *What's happening with Bill Gates now that he's donated so much money to educational technology?*
4. *Is there evidence that changes in emphasis in the _____ child welfare program in the past 5 years are the result of pressure from the press?*
5. *What happened in Iraq in 2003?*
6. *How could the looting of the museums in Iraq in 2003 have been avoided?*
7. *What are the main features of Fetal Alcohol Spectrum Disorder and what can be done both to treat and prevent this condition? Should all alcohol containers carry a warning?*
8. *What are the ethical implications of human cloning?*

A.2.2 Suggested key for the questions:

1. *Did Martin Luther, the German reformer, write anything criticizing the Jews?*
   Bad question: Anyone with the works of Luther available (or access to Wikipedia) can find the answer quickly (the answer is "yes," though you may want to ask, instead, why he took the stance he did toward the Jews). A research question is more than discovery of a fact. It has to deal with an issue that can be analyzed in depth.
2. *What effect does homelessness have on the price of beds in Canada?*

Bad question: This question is the never-will-fly variety. It's based on supply and demand: Fewer homeless people means more demand for beds (and less demand for large cardboard boxes and shopping carts?) Yet, if there is some connection between homelessness and the price of beds, there is no conceivable way for you to find out the nature and extent of the connection. Sometimes two ideas simply have no obvious relationship or the relationship is such that no amount of searching will help you find out what it is. A similar sort of question might be one like this: *What has been the influence of the rise of the automobile on morality in the United States?* There may be an influence, but I can think of no survey or statistical tool that would give you an answer. The key to avoiding these kinds of questions is to ask yourself: Is there a reasonable hope that I can gather evidence that will lead to an answer? If there seems to be no hope, drop the question.

3. *What's happening with Bill Gates now that he's donated so much money to educational technology?*

    Bad question: The point is fuzzy, not focused at all. What are you trying to discover? What Bill Gates does with his day? Whether he's enjoying his remaining money? Whether his financial give-away plan is the best use of his money? As long as your question doesn't indicate a point or a direction, you have no idea how to develop your paper. Besides, all aspects of Bill Gates' life are tracked so publicly that even a fuzzy question like the one above would likely be easily answered without much thought (though it could be answered in several possible ways). Here's a good focused research question to replace it: *Is Bill Gates' extensive plan to fund technology in education leading to an undue influence over educational methods in K-12?*

4. *Is there evidence that changes in emphasis in the _____ child welfare program in the past 5 years are the result of pressure from the press?*

Good question: Why? It demands research and analysis and there is evidence available to support that research. You would need to discover when various complaints about the child welfare were prominent in the press, and then see whether or not changes in procedure consistently followed such periods of complaint.

5. *What happened in Iraq in 2003?*

   Bad question: This question likely wants the writer to recount the story of the Iraq War (which would only be a descriptive paper), but it's not clear from the question what the author is seeking. Many things happened in Iraq in 2003.

6. *How could the looting of the museums in Iraq in 2003 have been avoided?*

   Good question: In hindsight, it should be possible to look at what happened and show what protection measures could have been in place to prevent the looting. Considerable writing has been done on the issue, so there should be lots of information.

7. *What are the main features of Fetal Alcohol Spectrum Disorder and what can be done both to treat and prevent this condition? Should all alcohol containers carry a warning?*

   Bad question: This is your classic multi-pointer. With this many questions to answer, you will find that your project is cut up into a number of smaller projects and has no overall unity. Follow this rule—every research project must deal with only one issue expressed by one question. So choose one of the questions above (except for the first one, which is only information-gathering), and dump the rest.

8. *What are the ethical implications of human cloning?*

   Somewhat good question: There's a lot to research and analyze but you may well find that the question is too open-ended, so that you run into far too many ethical implications to deal with. To solve this, limit your scope. For example, ask something like this: *With the high risk of early death of clones, is experimenting with human cloning ethical?*

A.3 Types of research papers

Here are some common research paper types:

A.3.1 Descriptive paper

This type of essay aims at merely discovering and sharing information about something. It is not a true research paper but just a report on what you've read. Avoid this approach unless your professor explicitly asks for summary of reading or an overview without evaluation.

A.3.2 Analytical or investigative paper

This type of essay seeks to find out the truth about something. It often focuses on questions like Who? What? When? Where? Why? or How? For example:

- ❖ *Why is the United Nations Organization so slow in responding to situations of genocide in the world?*
- ❖ *When did the Protestant Reformation actually begin?*
- ❖ *What is the truth behind the legend of Robin Hood?*
- ❖ *How were the pyramids of Egypt constructed in a time when machinery was so simple?*
- ❖ *What would be a better method to respond quickly to large international disasters before hunger, thirst and disease overtake the survivors?*

If you are writing this type of paper, you need to be sure that what you are investigating does not have an obvious answer but requires a lot of digging, study and analysis.

A.3.3 Persuasive paper

This type of essay takes a position on a particular issue, seeking to persuade the reader of the truth of something and is generally expressed through a thesis statement rather than a research question. There are two major types:

❖ Cause and effect: This type has the goal of persuading you that something or someone was the cause of some event or situation. For example, consider these possible thesis statements:

Support for assisted suicide creates a slippery slope in which society loses its respect for life, thus putting at risk the elderly and disabled.

The reason why terrorism flourishes is that we have not paid sufficient attention to the problems of injustice in the world.

Note that cause and effect is notoriously difficult to demonstrate, because two events are often related only by coincidence or because an effect may have several causes rather than just one. To show cause and effect, you have to demonstrate that the effect was caused by one factor out of all other possible factors. That's not easy to do.

❖ Evaluation: This type of paper seeks to persuade you that one view on a certain topic is better than another. For example:

The problem of homelessness is best solved by local non-governmental initiatives rather than federal programs.

Early intervention programs are a better way to deal with juvenile crime than punishment after the fact.

With persuasive papers, always be sure to include all relevant viewpoints in your discussion. Persuasion brings with it a temptation to ignore opposing arguments. Don't do it.

A.3.4 Literature review

A literature review is usually just the first portion of a paper that plans to report a study or experiment done in a social scientific or scientific setting. Occasionally the literature review will stand on its own as a full article. A lot of students are confused about the nature of such reviews. The goal of a literature review is essentially to explain what has been done within a certain subject area, including the types of studies published, the key players in this field, and a sense of what still needs to be done. I like to think of a literature review as a narrative, starting with earlier research and coming down to the most recent.

But reviews must never be simply lists of studies (books, articles) with a bit of commentary. Instead, they need to revolve around themes or emphases. You might indicate what people were thinking about the subject at the beginning, then how the emphasis changed. You might spell out various schools of thought that developed around the topic and explain significant examples of the writings or experiments of the major scholars supporting those schools of thought.

Overall you want to group the various movements and stages in the topic's history so the reader will have a strong sense of the best work that has been done on it. Then, near the end of the review, you need to point to something that still needs to be done. This could be a gap that remains in our knowledge or some flaw in the research to date that needs to be corrected. That gap or flaw then becomes a launch pad for further research.

Is a literature review the same as a research paper? Not usually, but to the extent that it has a clear goal and clear question (to determine what is lacking in this subject area) it can either stand alone as a research paper or form a useful introduction to one.

A.4 The outline as a research paper guidance system

Most struggling research papers have one of two problems: Lack of a good, well-focused research question or lack of a proper structure that can take you from question to conclusion clearly and faithfully. In a research paper, a lack of structure is solved with the outline.

A.4.1 Why worry about an outline early in the research process?

Many paper writers leave the outline to the end of the process. Some people even write the paper, and then discern an outline so that it can be included on a contents page. The real point at which outline construction needs to begin is *as soon as you have a research question.*

- ❖ The points of your outline tell you what you need to cover, and thus the outline serves as a blueprint for your research. It also keeps you from missing anything.
- ❖ The outline gives body to your research question, showing the direction you have to take to reach your target. As you are doing your research, the outline will help you begin visualizing the completed product, thus giving your paper more depth and substance.
- ❖ It takes time for a paper to germinate in your thinking. The outline provides a structure to allow that germination to develop properly.
- ❖ The very structure of a research paper is crucial to making the paper work. If you get things out of order, or if the order is not clear, it won't matter how much good information is there. The reader will see the paper as a failure. Thus, if you start thinking about structure and order early in the process, you are more likely to have the order right when you're done.

A.4.2 Steps to a good outline

Use your research question to identify key terminology

Your research question expresses the goal of your essay. Embodied in it is the basic embryo of your outline. Suppose your research question was as follows:

Was the assassination of the Archduke Ferdinand as crucial a cause of WWI as is often asserted?

First, identify the key words in your question:

Assassination of Archduke Ferdinand, Cause of WWI, Crucial cause

Think through your goal

Now have a good look at your question and ask yourself, "What am I trying to accomplish?" In a few sentences, analyze your purpose, fleshing out your research question.

You could expand on it like this: Commonly the assassination of the Archduke is seen as the flashpoint that led to WWI. Yet one has to wonder how a single murder could have led to worldwide conflict. This murder must have meant something more than other murders did. If so, maybe the background or context to the assassination had more to say about the cause of WWI than did this single event.

Determine the scope of your paper

With your analysis of your research question before you, ask yourself: *What do I need to include in order to answer my question?* From your question, keywords and goal analysis above, you will need to:

❖ Present the common view that the assassination was a *crucial cause* of WWI
❖ Explain the historical and political context of the *assassination of Archduke Ferdinand.*
❖ Consider all the evidence with regard to the role of Ferdinand's murder in the events leading to WWI and determine whether or not it was *as crucial a cause of WWI as is often asserted*

You now have the elements of an outline. It may not be in the right order, and you may have to revise it, even add or subtract elements, but the basics are there. It might look like this:

Introduction: The Common Interpretation of the Assassination as a Crucial Cause of WWI
The Historical and Political Context of the Assassination of Ferdinand
As Crucial a Cause as is Often Asserted?
Conclusion

Begin thinking about order

You don't need to make any final decisions about the order of your outline headings yet, but here are some tips:

❖ You will need an introduction that serves two purposes: to provide your reader with enough background information to be able to understand your topic, and to declare your research question. Alternatively, you may want to formulate a thesis statement, which is a proposed answer to your question, along the lines of, "The following paper will argue that..."

❖ If there is any further development of background material that's more complex, it will have to go next as a separate section.

❖ You well may find that you are dealing with more than one point of view. Once you determine which point of view you are going to support, cover the view(s) you do not support first, then cover the view you do support. Never reverse this order.

❖ Think about your reader. What needs to be covered before something else makes sense?

❖ Avoid stringing out your outline into 6, 7 or more points. A structure of 3 to 5 points works far better for the reader, unless you are working on a thesis or a book, where 6 to 10 main sections may be needed. Group things together so that you use fewer main points, even if it means that each main point has two or more sub-points.

Germinate

Memorize the outline you've created, even if it's still quite basic, and develop the habit of *germination*. What's "germination?" This is a hard thing to describe, but it's something like letting a seed of your research project grow inside of you. Take time through your day to think about your outline: *Would this order work better than that order? Have I left anything out? Have I included anything that isn't really relevant to my research question?*

Then, as you gather your books, articles, and so on, and start to read them, begin to write your paper in your head, thinking constantly about your reader: *At what points might my reader become confused? What would I change to make those points clearer? Am I being fair and complete by including all sides of an issue? Is my research question itself in need of some revision, and, if so, how will that change my outline?*

By the time you write your paper, your outline should be working well for you, and your paper should be already pretty much written in your head.

Why do you need germination? Because depth and maturity in a research paper comes through working on it over time. Without this process, you simply have another one of those half-grown products that is dashed off at the last minute. It will be superficial and lacking in substance. Truly great writing needs germination. Your paper has to live and grow in you, or it will never have the power it should have for a reader. The best way to encourage it to grow is to take the time to shape it around your ever-maturing outline.

Structure your final outline

Ultimately, just when you are beginning to enjoy framing your arguments in your head, your germination process needs to come to an end. This happens somewhere either just before the writing process begins, or during the writing. But one thing must be virtually complete before you start writing: your final outline, which forms the roadmap for the final composition of your research paper, telling you at each point what you need to cover to develop your paper from introduction to conclusion. A paper written without an outline firmly before you or in your mind is a paper destined to confuse your reader and resist your hopes to communicate what you have discovered.

I cannot stress this strongly enough—your outline is the crucial element in hitting the target your well-formulated question is aiming at.

So how do you go about structuring your final outline? If you have any uncertainty about your skills, follow a simple formula: Introduction, 3 or 4 points, Conclusion.

KEEP IT SIMPLE. If you find there is need for some complex discussion in point 2, then use sub points, like this:

I. Introduction: The Common Interpretation of the Assassination of Ferdinand as a Cause of WWI
II. The Historical and Political Context
  A. Prior to August 1914
  B. August 1914 and Beyond
III. Evaluation of the Significance of the Assassination
IV. Conclusion

A.4.3 Practice with outlines

For the following questions, create a 3 or 4 point outline, then compare your outline with mine in the suggested key (remember that outlines may vary and yours might be better than mine):

1. *To what can we attribute the fact that Martin Luther's attitude toward Jews grew more and more negative through his lifetime?*
2. *What is the best approach to reducing homelessness in an urban setting?*
3. *Is the growing influence of Google in online search really as bad for the world as many critics say it is?*
4. *Is there evidence that changes in emphasis in the _____ child welfare program in the past 5 years are the result of pressure from the press?*

5. *How could the looting of the museums in Iraq in 2003 have been avoided?*

6. *What is the best way for the legal system to deal with non-violent teens in trouble with the law but afflicted with Fetal Alcohol Spectrum Disorder (FASD)?*

7. *What are the implications of human cloning for our definition of a "person?"*

8. *Was the religious "conversion" of Roman Emperor Constantine genuine or a fraud carried out for political reasons?*

A.4.4 Suggested key for practice with outlines

1. *To what can we attribute the fact that Martin Luther's attitude toward Jews grew more and more negative through his lifetime?*

Possible outline:

Introduction [Explain who Luther was, and ask the research question]

I.   Evidence of Luther's Growing Anti-Semitism

II. Possible Explanations

      A.

      B.

      C. etc.

Conclusion

2. *What is the best approach to reducing homelessness in an urban setting?*

Possible outline:

Introduction [Explain the problem of urban homelessness and ask the research question]

I.   Current Approaches to Reducing Urban Homelessness.

      A.

      B.

      C. etc.

II. Critique of Such Approaches

   A.

   B.

   C.

III. A Proposed Best Approach

Conclusion

3. *Is the growing influence of Google in online search really as bad for the world as many critics say it is?*

Possible outline:

Introduction [Introduce the growing influence issue and ask research question]

I.   Arguments that the Influence is Bad for the World

II. Arguments that the Influence is Good for the World

Conclusion

4. *Is there evidence that changes in emphasis in the _____ child welfare program in the past 5 years are the result of pressure from the press?*

Possible outline:

Introduction [Introduce the issue and ask the research question]

I.   The Nature of Changes in the Program over the Past 5 Years.

II. Instances of Coordination between Press Pressure and Changes

   A. Incident One

   B. Incident Two

   C. Incident Three, etc.

III. Role of the Press in bringing about Changes in the Program

Conclusion

5. *How could the looting of the museums in Iraq in 2003 have been avoided?*

Possible outline:

Introduction [Explain the problem and ask the research question]

I.   An Account of the Looting and the Failure to Prevent it

II. Possible Alternate Security Measures that Could Have Been Introduced

    A.

    B.

    C. etc.

Conclusion [Analyze possible alternate measures and state an overall plan that might have worked]

6. *What is the best way for the legal system to deal with non-violent teens in trouble with the law but afflicted with Fetal Alcohol Spectrum Disorder (FASD)?*

Possible outline:

Introduction [Explain problem of non-violent FASD offenders and ask research question]

I.   Common Current Approaches to the Problem

II. A Critique of Such Approaches

III. A Suggested Better Approach

Conclusion

7. *What are the implications of human cloning for our definition of a "person?"*

Possible outline:

Note that this is still quite an open-ended question allowing for many possibilities. Thus a variety of outlines are possible. Here's one.

Introduction [State the problem and ask the research question]

I.   Traditional Definitions of a Person

II. Elements of Cloning that Redefine "Person."

III. A New Definition of Personhood.

Conclusion

8. *Was the religious "conversion" of Roman Emperor Constantine genuine or a fraud carried out for political reasons?*

Possible outline:

Introduction [Introduce Constantine and his conversion; ask research question]

I. Evidence that the conversion was genuine.

II. Evidence that the conversion was a fraud with political motives

Conclusion

A.5 Building the substance of the essay

In this section we will look at the main body of this thing called a research essay. We will consider how it is put together and study the crucial elements that make a mature, thoughtful paper.

A.5.1 Intent and direction

The best research papers are characterized by strong goal-orientation. This means that they have a purpose, defined by the research question, and a sense of movement from problem to solution.

A research essay is like the flight of an arrow from bow to target. When you aim the arrow, you see a target, a specific destination. You know that to hit the target you will have a launch, a period of travel through the air, and a conclusion when the arrow hits its mark.

But an arrow in flight is also subject to things like wind speed and wind direction. Similarly, a research essay cannot ignore the influencing factors: context of the issue and the various options that could be answers to the question. There needs to be opportunity for recognition and analysis of other points of view, even opposing ones, as long as you make sure you stay on target with your main intention—to answer the research question. Remember that scholarship is a conversation.

Here's an insight: *Every part of your paper needs to contribute ultimately to answering your research question. There is no room for irrelevant details, even if they are interesting.*

Keep your paper goal-orientated. Don't allow it to wander or lose its sense of purpose.

A.5.2 Building the paper

There are simple procedures that make the difference between a well-constructed paper and a mess. Here are some of them:

Use your outline like a blueprint.

Careful structure will contribute more to the success of your paper than anything else. *Follow the plan.*

You may be the sort of person who resists structure and organization in your writing, believing that structure limits your freedom of expression. But remember this: Structure is not just for your benefit, but also for the benefit of your reader. The reader has a distinct disadvantage: He or she doesn't know where you're going in your paper. Without structure, much of what you have to say will remain foggy to the reader. With structure, your reader is never lost.

Beyond wanting to help your reader, you want to avoid leaving out anything that is important or including anything that is not important.

Carefully adhering to your outline as you write ensures that everything that needs to be in your paper is there. Write or print out your outline and keep it (along with your research question) ever before you as you produce your paper.

Build your paper from the paragraph up.

While sentences are the basic building blocks of communication, paragraphs are the basic building blocks of an essay. Each paragraph advances your argument, like steps in a staircase. Think of your paragraphs as the smallest sub points of each point in your outline. Each has a topic and a unity that advances whatever you are covering in that particular element of your outline.

A.5.3 Using sources well

A research paper has some very definite features that make it different from an opinion piece or a speech. First, it is an investigation of a problem, leading to a solution. This means that there is room for actual application of your solution only in the conclusion section itself, and even then the application should be brief.

Second, if a research paper is an investigation leading to a solution, it is a journey that requires the help of others, that is, the help of the books, articles, etc. that you gather during the research process. While you could simply follow a logical process of argumentation, leading to a conclusion, you need to recognize that no topic is truly original, even if your solution may be. Others have also dealt with the issue and have put forward points of view and evidence for their own interpretations (scholarship is a conversation).

In fact, finding a solution to a research question most often involves weighing the conflicting interpretations of others and finding your answer as a result of your evaluation. Spend a lot of effort on listening to and evaluating the publications of others.

Using sources can be tricky. At one extreme, your paper could be primarily a set of quotations from books and articles, with brief commentary from you. At the other extreme, you could virtually ignore your sources and do most of the analysis yourself. The ideal is somewhere in between, where you use your sources extensively but you still keep in control of the analysis.

How do you achieve the ideal use of sources?

Group your sources by the particular issues they address, and especially by the particular viewpoints they support. Thus you should have a group of sources that deal with or support view A., a group that deal with or support view B., and so on.

Keep your quotations to a minimum, usually only one quotation for every page or two. For social science and science projects, quotations are generally not needed unless you have to present key information "from the horse's mouth." If you are using quotations, keep them under 5 lines for the most part. Instead of quoting, refer. Use language like: *Smith has argued that Constantine embraced Christianity solely because he saw its power as a political force in the Roman Empire.* You are not quoting. You are referring to or describing a viewpoint in your own words. You'll still need to provide a citation [either in the text (Smith, 234) or as a footnote or endnote], but you'll avoid having your sources do all your speaking for you.

Recognize that the research paper is not supposed to be simply an account of what the world already knows but an analytical investigation of a problem while you are in dialogue with others who are also addressing the problem. Thus, your own analysis, indeed your own presence, has to be seen in the paper. This means that you control your sources. They do not control you. It is you who must lay out the information that your sources provide, e.g., *Smith (2013) has argued that...Jones (2015) provides a contrary view...Green (2016) has added a new voice to the issue by asserting that* [and so on]. You are using your sources to be sure, but you are controlling the process.

Almost never provide new information with a quotation. Use quotations to support a statement you have made first or to present a striking way in which an author has made a point.

Use sources that you agree with as well as sources you disagree with. A research paper needs to show evidence that you've investigated all relevant points of view and have treated your sources fairly. In general, even for writers with whom you disagree, explain what the source is saying before criticizing it. Let your source be heard fairly before you evaluate it. When you do criticize, avoid the language of ridicule. Make your criticisms logical and fair.

A.5.4 Avoiding theft of other people's work

Plagiarism is passing on the thoughts or words of someone else as if they were your own. It ranges from quoting others without acknowledging them to using other people's unique ideas as if they were your unique ideas.

It's relatively easy to make sure, when you quoting a source, that you include the required quotation marks and a bibliographical note. It's a little trickier, however, to determine if you've stolen someone's ideas. A general rule of thumb is that, if an idea is found in two or three other sources which are not all dependent on one earlier source, you can generally use it without acknowledging its source. To be on the safe side, make a bibliographical note if a source is stating a point of view with which you aren't familiar.

There is another type of theft that is often not recognized—the use of paraphrases by which you take your source, sentence by sentence and simply rewrite each sentence using different words. In this case, you are not interpreting and explaining your source, but using your source's paragraph structure and thoughts in something that is very close to quoting. This too can easily become plagiarism.

Here's an excerpt from an article that I published on the Internet on the challenges regular users of university websites face in trying to navigate to needed information. The original paragraph is:

> **Many higher educational institution websites have been designed to attract new students and impress the constituency rather than to inform current students. A user's sheer frustration in trying to find a particular department, a faculty member's e-mail address, or a how-to for some obscure academic procedure, points to a website that is a barrier rather than a support** (William Badke. "The key word is access." **http://www.evolllution.com/opinions/ the-key-word-is-access/**).

A paraphrase, which would *not* be acceptable, might read:

A lot of websites of universities are set up to draw new students and impress supporters rather than give information to registered students. Students are frustrated trying to find departments, e-mail addresses for professors, and ways to carry out procedures. This makes the website an obstacle rather than a support.

Notice that I've borrowed sentence structure and even words from the original without really interpreting it. Now let me express the material in my own words:

Badke argues that university websites, created for recruitment and flying the flag of the institution, can prevent current students from finding the information they need. Such websites fail to provide access to a large user group: students.

What I have done is to *interpret* what I've read and to express it mostly in different words (though it's all right to use a few words from your source, maybe 5% or less). Remember that the point of a research essay is not simply to quote or interpret others, but to evaluate their work and provide your own arguments. Your own analysis is extremely important.

A.5.5 Practice with essay structure

Let's walk through the development of a research paper around the following question:

Is there evidence that changes in emphasis in the _____ child welfare program in the past 5 years are the result of pressure from the press?

Introduction [Introduce the issue and ask the research question]
I.   The Nature of Changes in the Program over the Past 5 Years.
II. Instances of Coordination between Press Pressure and Changes
       A. A. Incident One
       B. B. Incident Two
       C. C. Incident Three, etc.
III. Possible Alternate Explanations for Timing of Changes
Conclusion

Here's a way we could develop our ideas:

Introduction

It is common for government departments to take press criticism seriously, even to revise programs rather than have the press go on influencing public opinion in a negative way. There have been changes in the _____ child welfare program over the past number of years, many of them appearing to be reactions to press criticism. Is there evidence that changes in emphasis in the _____ child welfare program in the past 5 years are the result of pressure from the press?

I.   **The Nature of Changes in the Program over the Past 5 Years**

Survey, with documentation, the major changes that have occurred, using chronological order as your organizing principle. By doing this, you are showing evidence that significant and frequent changes have been made.

II. **Instances of Coordination between Press Pressure and Changes**
       A. **Incident One**
       B. **Incident Two**
       C. **Incident Three, etc.**

Now take each instance of change and follow this kind of structure: Incident One: Prior press reaction, timing of change, determination of whether or not the change is a correction of the problem raised by the press. Incident Two: Follow the same process as One, and so on.

III. **Role of the Press in bringing about Changes in the Program**

You have shown a correlation between press criticism and changes, but you have to show that there is actually evidence of a pattern in the data you presented in II.

Conclusion

Summarize briefly what you have covered, and make a final statement either supporting or rejecting the implication of your research question.

A.6 Bibliographic style

Many faculty members place an emphasis on papers being presented in a certain style (MLA, APA, Chicago/Turabian, etc.) which determines what the notes and citations to various sources of information will look like. This has long been a challenge for students, both because perfect style is so hard to achieve, and because it doesn't make much sense to give so much effort to something that really doesn't seem crucial to the construction of a research paper. Good style is important, however, for several reasons:

- ❖ The reader has fewer distractions away from content when the style (even proper title pages and tables of contents) is consistent and clear.
- ❖ The reader is better able to navigate a properly formatted paper.
- ❖ Adhering to style helps to guarantee that nothing important in your citations will be left out. This is particularly true in notes and bibliographies, where sloppy style can result in dates, volume numbers, pages, and publisher information being omitted.

❖ Your professor wants proper bibliographic style, and that makes style important in its own right (if, indeed, you're at all interested in getting good grades).

A.6.1 Style software

Personally, I think students are often made to devote too much effort to getting the right punctuation in the right place in a bibliography. Most of your essay-writing effort should be focused on actually writing and revising the essay. But style is important, so what are you to do? The use of bibliographic managers like EndNote, RefWorks, Zotero, or Mendeley (see Chapter 8) has made formatting notes and bibliography a much less painful experience than it used to be. So have online and commercial style formatters.

My recommendation is to use the electronic style resources available to you to get the grunt work done. Then, armed with a crib sheet of style examples, clean up what the software could not.

There are several types of electronic style resource available to you:

Style formatters in most recent word processing programs: Check these out by looking for a tab that says "references" or something similar. You can set your format and create citations using fill in the blank forms. The program will generate a bibliography for you when you have finished typing the paper. But be careful: Depending on the age of your word processing program, you may or may not be working with the most recent version of your style format.

Bibliographic managers: See 8.5 above. Most of these do not actually format your paper (title page, section titles, etc.) for you, just the notes and bibliographies (though EndNote has downloadable Word templates at **http://www.endnote.com/support/ entemplates.asp**).

Style generators embedded in databases: Some journal database vendors (such as EBSCO and InfoTrac) have provided the ability to save or e-mail journal records in a variety of formats. The multi-catalog search tool WorldCat (**http://www.worldcat.org**) enables you to cite any book you find in a variety of formats (open a book record and click on Cite/Export icon). Google Scholar has a citation style feature (click on "More" or "Cite" under each citation). Note that most of these style generators have glitches. Be sure to check your formatted citations to make sure nothing is left out and the format is correct.

Commercial style software: Commercial style software is available for a price. It enables you to format the whole research paper, not just notes and bibliography. Let's look at what a few of these products can do, with the disclaimer that I have received no promotional fee from the makers of these products, nor was I asked to promote them.

> *EazyPaper* (**http://www.eazypaper.com/index. cfm**) is a truly amazing research paper formatting program for APA, MLA and Turabian, written by a former student of mine, Michael Hu, a tech genius in his own right. Not only does it enable you to format papers, notes and bibliographies, but the formatting can be configured according to your professor's specifications. It will let you input references into a database, ready to be cited in your paper (though you can't direct download or import citations from journal databases). But what about all those references you stored in RefWorks or EndNote? How would you get them into EazyPaper? Easily. Just generate a bibliography of them, copy citations and paste them into the EazyPaper database. It also inserts Zotero references directly into a research paper. It will recognize the difference between an author and a title, etc. and generate records that you can then use

for citations. In its Pro version, EazyPaper even allows you to search and download book records from a wide variety of libraries. Nice work, Michael.

EasyBib (**http://www.easybib.com**) is an online tool that creates citations in the main three formats, through basic input from you, and then generates bibliographies. You generally only need to specify what type of resource it is (book, article) and enter an author name and title keyword. EasyBib will find the information online to enable you to generate a citation. It comes in a free and more advanced subscription format.

Noodle Tools (**http://www.noodletools.com/**) is an online resource that provides "integrated tools for note-taking, outlining, citation, document archiving/ annotation, and collaborative research and writing." Thus it is more than a citation generator and is well worth checking out.

Free internet-based citation format tools

If you lack access to a bibliographic manager and don't want to spring for style software, there are online tools that can help you. By searching on the WWW for a style type with the word "template" (e.g., Turabian template, APA template), you can often find word processor templates that will help you format title pages, proper spacing, and so on. But be careful: Some of these are generated by professors who have their own idiosyncratic rules for research paper structure. Professors, being the truly special bunch that they are, may have you doing some very non-traditional things. Or, if you're skillful, you can create your own template.

There are a number of good citation generators online. Check out EasyBib in its basic, non-subscription, form (**http://www.easybib.**

com), Citation Machine (**http://www.citationmachine.net/**), ETurabian (**http://www.eturabian.com/turabian/index.html**) and Cite This For Me (**http://www.citethisforme.com/**: very cool tool, but citations generated have to be saved to a document or they disappear after a time; a premium account is available). Each of these asks you to choose format and type of source. Then you to enter citation information and generate an accurate citation.

A.6.2 Crib sheets

All of the major bibliographic styles have their own detailed books for sale which detail most aspects of formatting. If you are doing serious research, buy the book. You can often get a copy at a reduced price as an e-book (Kindle, iPad, etc.).

There are, however, a number of WWW-based crib sheets that give you examples of the most common formats. These can be very useful in conjunction with bibliographic managers or style software, just to check your results (especially important when you are using bibliographic software).

Here are some web addresses, but recognize that URLs go out of date almost as quickly as yesterday's hip-hop stars:

APA (6th ed., 2009)

http://library.nmu.edu/guides/userguides/style_apa.htm

http://www.wisc.edu/writing/Handbook/DocAPA.html

http://nova.campusguides.com/apa

A word about the DOI in APA 6. A DOI (digital object identifier) is a unique code assigned to each journal article published by many of the newer journals (it's like a barcode on a corn flakes box). Since each DOI identifies a specific article, APA 6 has determined that the DOI should be supplied as the last element in a journal article citation that you have retrieved in electronic format. Thus:

Badke, W. B. (2005). Can't get no respect: Helping faculty to understand the educational power of information literacy. *Reference Librarian, 43*(89), 63–80. doi: 10.1300/J120v43n8905

But, *if the electronic format journal does not yet use the DOI system*, you must do a search on the Net for the journal's home page and use the URL for that home page instead:

Badke, W. B. (2000). Questia.com: Implications of the new McLibrary. *Internet Reference Services Quarterly, 5(3)*, 61–71. Retrieved from http://www.tandfonline.com/loi/wirs20

MLA (8ᵗʰ ed., 2016)

http://www.easybib.com/guides/citation-guides/mla-8/

http://www.lib.sfu.ca/help/cite-write/citation-style-guides/mla

https://owl.english.purdue.edu/owl/resource/747/01/

Turabian (8ᵗʰ ed., 2013) / Chicago (16ᵗʰ ed., 2009)

http://www.press.uchicago.edu/books/turabian/turabian_citationguide.html (official Turabian site, quick guide)

http://writing.wisc.edu/Handbook/DocChicago.html

http://libguides.msubillings.edu/turabian

Sample Papers:

APA (6ᵗʰ ed.) Sample Paper:

http://supp.apa.org/style/PM6E-Corrected-Sample-Papers.pdf

MLA (8th ed.) Sample Paper:

https://owl.english.purdue.edu/owl/resource/747/13/

Turabian (8th ed.) Sample Paper: http://www.liberty.edu/media/2030/Turabian_8th_Edition_Sample_Paper_Spring_2015.pdf

A.7 Conclusion

Research papers do not have to be the painful experience many people make them. It is possible to develop significant skills in order to make the writing process much easier than you thought. We've seen a detailed explanation of them above, but let me summarize:

- ❖ Develop a well-focused analytical research question.
- ❖ Structure your paper with a solid outline that answers the question.
- ❖ Write intentionally, filling in the blanks in your outline with paragraphs that focus on your single goal, which is dealing with the research question.
- ❖ Use your sources skillfully and ethically at all times.
- ❖ Let the tools available for formatting help you produce papers that professors will find a pleasure just to look at.

Happy Researching!

Index

Topic	Section

CPSIA information can be obtained
at www.ICGtesting.com
Printed in the USA
BVOW06s0751020917

493850BV00014B/468/P